# ROUTLEDGE LIBRARY EDITIONS: PUBLIC ENTERPRISE AND PRIVATIZATION

Volume 1

# BRITISH PUBLIC UTILITIES AND NATIONAL DEVELOPMENT

# BRITISH PUBLIC UTILITIES AND NATIONAL DEVELOPMENT

MARSHALL E. DIMOCK

Routledge
Taylor & Francis Group

LONDON AND NEW YORK

First published in 1933 by George Allen & Unwin

This edition first published in 2019
by Routledge
2 Park Square, Milton Park, Abingdon, Oxon OX14 4RN

and by Routledge
52 Vanderbilt Avenue, New York, NY 10017

*Routledge is an imprint of the Taylor & Francis Group, an informa business*

© 1933 Marshall E. Dimock

*British Library Cataloguing in Publication Data*
A catalogue record for this book is available from the British Library

ISBN: 978-0-367-14233-9 (Set)
ISBN: 978-0-429-25929-6 (Set) (ebk)
ISBN: 978-0-367-14841-6 (Volume 1) (hbk)
ISBN: 978-0-429-05449-5 (Volume 1) (ebk)

**Publisher's Note**
The publisher has gone to great lengths to ensure the quality of this reprint but points out that some imperfections in the original copies may be apparent.

**Disclaimer**
The publisher has made every effort to trace copyright holders and would welcome correspondence from those they have been unable to trace.

# British Public Utilities
and
# National Development

Marshall E. Dimock, Ph.D.

*Associate Professor of Political Science
in the University of Chicago*

LONDON
George Allen & Unwin Ltd
MUSEUM STREET

FIRST PUBLISHED IN 1933

TO

# MY MOTHER

AND

# FATHER

"The development of public utilities is, particularly at this present stage of our economic life, the development of the nation."

Franklin D. Roosevelt in *Looking Forward*


"In the years to come activities which have hitherto been left to other agencies must be brought within the public utility field. . . . Right decisions on these problems will be of the first importance."

*The Listener* (London), 1931

# PREFACE

One of the most important trends in post-war Britain has been the extension of the number and variety of public service undertakings. Unlike the development in the earlier stages, these services have been primarily national in character and have dealt with the most significant aspects of national progress, such as industrial power, transport, electrical communication, and broadcasting. All of this is indicative of the fact that British leaders of many shades of political opinion, empirically and sometimes grudgingly, have begun to regard the State in a new light—as the means of stimulating and controlling the economic development of the entire country. The new attitude toward government is so recent that in many cases it is intuitively felt rather than logically reasoned. However, one common conviction is found in the minds of leaders of wide differences of opinion—the belief that a rather rapid extension of national public service monopolies, under one or another type of control, is a certain development irrespective of political fortunes. This study assumes greater importance in view of what seems to be in store, therefore, than from the national public utilities already in existence.

The empirical nature and the recent importance of British public utility development are indicated by the fact that this is the first study which has appeared dealing in a comprehensive manner with British public service undertakings. In order to give completeness to the book and also to provide a suitable background, the local utility services water, gas, transport, docks, and harbors have been considered. The primary emphasis has been placed upon national utilities, including the railways, road transport, telegraphs and telephones, national electricity planning, and broadcasting. These services have been considered from the viewpoint of their rôle in national development, involving a consideration of policy, organization, management, control, and constructive criticism. In the concluding chapter the tendencies appearing in existing services have been weighed and I have tried to suggest possible lines of future policy. The criticisms and suggestions are in no way attributable to any outside person or interest group, or to any political party. Impartiality and objectivity have been the writer's ambition. However, an effort to postulate a philosophy of public service management has seemed desirable, because differences of opinion and discussion should be provoked if the future progress of national utilities is to be intelligently guided.

The trends of recent years make a rediscovery of political economy imperative and urgent. This study is an effort to reunite economics, public administration, law, and philosophy in the consideration of British public utilities. The State is conceived as a creative force, capable of stimulating and undertaking national economic development. Although there are several important elements to be considered, the exercise of public control occupies the central position. Many of our past mistakes have been due to the fact that we have failed to recognize the inescapable necessity of government control over economic development. The admitted necessity of exercising control over currency and credit is at present the most outstanding illustration of the positive obligations devolving upon the State in the machine age. In a few years the question of public control over utility services may be just as acute. The creation of a philosophy and a technique of popular control is a task deserving a great deal of attention.

The three main methods of securing public control are: (a) regulation by the establishment of legislative standards and by the creation of supervisory bodies, such as the Railway Rates Tribunal; (b) operation by a government department, such as the Post Office, or by some other governmental authority; (c) operation by a public utility trust, such as the Central Electricity Board. A comparison of the relative merits of these three forms of control and administration has been one of my chief objectives. In addition, the possibilities of the "mixed enterprise," as illustrated by the Manchester Ship Canal Company, have been given incidental consideration.

The management of public service enterprises has also been emphasized. Control and management cannot be completely separated; each conditions the other. Public administration comprehends the entire field of the present study, because it is concerned with powers, management, and control. However, the administration of public commercial undertakings presents distinct problems for the student of public administration, and this study is an effort to point out some of the middle ground that lies between business and government administration.

I have attempted to analyse and describe British public service undertakings in an intimate and non-technical manner. An effort has been made to view the subject through the eyes of the intelligent citizen who is interested in public affairs, but the special interests of the public utility official, the labor leader, the person in public office, and the university student have also been borne in mind.

This investigation was supported by the Social Science Research Council of New York City and also by a faculty research grant from the University of California. The book has been written during a nine months' residence in Great Britain, and is based upon extensive observations and interviews in most of the services considered.

Mr. Henry Hartley (B.Sc.(Econ.) London) has acted in the capacity of my research assistant, and has participated in every phase of the work except the interviewing and the actual writing. His devotion and helpful criticisms deserve more appreciation than I am able to express.

Sir Henry Bunbury, Accountant-General and Comptroller of the Post Office, has been my chief benefactor. He has arranged many interviews and has criticized a large part of the manuscript. His helpfulness and cordiality have been enjoyed by a large number of American scholars, who regard association with him as one of the chief inducements to return frequently to London.

Due to the comprehensive nature of the subject and the many contacts involved, it is impossible to acknowledge more than a portion of the assistance received from persons who were everywhere courteous and generous in the facilities offered. I do wish to express special thanks for the cooperation of the following: to Sir Josiah Stamp, President of the Executive of the L.M.S. Railway; to Sir Evelyn Murray, Secretary to the Post Office, and to Mr. L. Simon, Director of Telegraphs and Telephones; to Mr. Hugh Quigley, statistician and publicity director of the Central Electricity Board, who read parts of the manuscript; to Mr. R. T. G. French, Secretary to the Electricity Commission; to Sir John Reith, Director-General of the British Broadcasting Corporation, who also criticized part of the manuscript. In addition, I should like to acknowledge the aid of Sir Cyril Hurcomb, Secretary to the Ministry of Transport; Mr. J. W. Bowen, Secretary of the Union of Post Office Workers; Mr. Cole Deacon, Secretary of the Railway Companies' Association; Mr. C. E. R. Sherrington, Secretary of the Railway Research Service; Major C. S. Atkinson, Director of the Foreign and Overseas Division, B.B.C.; Sir Stafford Cripps, K.C., M.P.; Mr. Guy Buckeridge, of the London Telephone Service; Major C. R. Attlee, M.P.; Sir William Beveridge, Mr. William A. Robson, and Mr. H. B. Lees-Smith, all of the London School of Economics and Political Science; Mr. N. F. Hall, University College (London); Mr. C. S. Steadman, Assistant Secretary, Ministry of Transport; and the officials of the Institute of Public Administration, who arranged a large number of interviews. No acknowledgement would be half complete without reference to the active cooperation and endless patience of my wife.

MARSHALL E. DIMOCK

LONDON,

*June* 1933

# CONTENTS

B

# BRITISH PUBLIC UTILITIES AND NATIONAL DEVELOPMENT

## CHAPTER I

## THE SETTING

NATIONAL PUBLIC UTILITIES AND POST-WAR
REORGANIZATION

One of the most significant developments of the last decade
in Great Britain has been the creation of monopolies to
deal with vital fields of national expansion, such as broadcasting and electrical power. The public utility idea has
been widely discussed, and some are now beginning to talk
about "the public utility principle in industry" as a means
of economic recovery. Parliament has spent many days dis-
cussing various forms of public utility control. Conservatives,
Liberals, and Socialists have been able to agree that Parliament should bestow special privileges and obligations
upon certain essential enterprises, and that they should be
dealt with as national problems. Railway transport and the
Post Office communication services have been given serious
reconsideration since the war, while electricity development,
broadcasting, national road transportation, and London
passenger traffic have been brought within the ambit of
public service undertakings which are of nation-wide importance. The further extension of public control over
economic services seems to be a foregone conclusion.

The rapid extension of national public services marks a
revolution in British thought and life. Traditionally, Parliament has assumed as little responsibility as possible for
the development of the country's industry and commerce.
With the relative decline of Britain's position in world
trade during the post-war years, the home market has

increased in importance. Attention has therefore been focussed upon the necessity of utilizing the country's resources to the best advantage. At the same time the constructive proposals of economists like Henry Clay and G. D. H. Cole have had a pervasive influence upon the leaders of British thought. National planning of basic industries is favored by many of the leading economists. The engineering profession has also played an important part in emphasizing the necessity of large-scale organization and scientific technique as a remedy for the policy of "drift." A well-known engineer stated recently that the reorganization of industry on the basis of the public utility concept might be said to have begun about 1924 and that "the final stages in that revolution may, in a short period of years, bring this country to a position in world development higher than that which it has enjoyed in its previous history."

The extension of public utilities has also been influenced indirectly by the policies of foreign countries. The development of cartels and mixed enterprises on the Continent, the merger movement in the United States, and the creation of State trusts in other countries have forced home upon the British the futility of attempting to maintain small competitive enterprises. Increased world competition and shrinking markets, combined with chronic unemployment, have caused British leaders to undertake an intensive and realistic analysis of industrial organization. The fruits have begun to appear.

The Conservatives and the Liberals regard public utilities as a convenient and necessary compromise between the *laissez-faire* of the old order and the program of national Socialism advocated by the Labor party. Being opposed to the direct management of economic services by the State, the two former hope to obtain the advantages of monopoly without relinquishing all of the prerogatives connected with private enterprise. Moreover, public service undertakings have been favored because they usually add to the number of gilt-edged investments available—the highest desideratum in recent troubled years. The Conservative party, age-old champion of non-interference by the State, now sponsors rationalization of monopoly services under private management but subject to nominal public restrictions. Some say this is individualism in a new guise. Conservatives are usually sceptical of large-scale planning but believe that each problem should be solved as it arises. The Liberal and the Labor parties have more faith in comprehensive long-term programs, and each party has outlined its respective industrial program in party publications.[1] Granting the necessity of rationalization, the Liberals propose more rigid regulation, the support of municipal public utilities, and the creation of public trusts for public utility undertakings. The Labor party goes further and advocates the nationalization and State management of the most vital financial and industrial undertakings affecting the life of the entire nation.

The Socialist sees in public utility development the creation of monopolies, the elimination of the speculation motive, and the curtailment of the dictatorial power of the employer. The conversion of public service enterprises into State trusts is not a long step. Already, as the Liberal party has pointed out, public utility services "must comprise at least two-thirds of what may be called the large-scale undertakings of the country," and they represent a capital in the neighborhood of £4,000,000,000.[2]

The common thread in all party programs is the acceptance of large-scale monopolies under public control as the necessary step in future reconstruction. The principal differences of opinion arise over the nature and degree of public control. A variety of public service enterprises have been created, but they may be divided generally into the

[1] The Liberal party's program is set forth in *Britain's Industrial Future* and the Labor party's plan may be found in *Labour and the Nation* and later conference proceedings.

[2] *Britain's Industrial Future*, 74, London, 1928.

statutory company under regulatory control, the Department of State as a public commercial undertaking, and the public utility trust—the latest form of public service organization.

Our task is to analyze the contribution to the national welfare of the existing public utilities. This will involve a study of the efficiency of each of the services and the relative merits of the three types of organization. The effectiveness of public control in passing on to the consumer the benefits of monopoly will naturally be one of the principal criteria. The advantages enjoyed by the employee in the several forms of public utility enterprise will be another consideration worthy of careful attention. Comparisons are difficult, hazardous, and in some cases impossible, but the effort is justifiable. British public service undertakings are in a formative stage. A variety of experiments have already been made and others are likely to be tried before the process of reorganization has been completed. A mariner always takes bearings. But before we go further on a partially charted sea we need to consider what is meant by public utilities in Great Britain.

### THE BRITISH PUBLIC UTILITY CONCEPT

The term "public utility" is just coming into common usage in Great Britain, but the concept is very old. Long before Sir Matthew Hale referred judicially to different types of business which he said were affected with a public interest, Parliament had recognized the necessity of treating certain undertakings as special cases requiring regulation.[1]

However, unlike the United States, until recently there had been little effort by British writers to develop a systematic theory regarding the circumstances under which State intervention might be expected, and the consequences

[1] W. H. Hamilton, "Affectation with public interest," (1930) 39 *Yale Law Journ.*, 1089; B. P. McAllister, "Lord Hale and business affected with a public interest," (1930) 43 *Harvard Law Rev.*, 759; and Herman Finer, "State activity before Adam Smith," (1932) 10 *Public Administration*, 157.

thereof.[1] The same observation applies, in lesser degree, to the question of the operation and control of public utilities. As A. L. Dakyns has stated, the law and practice relative to public utilities have been largely neglected by English universities. Outside of a few courses offered in the newer universities, public utility problems seldom receive serious independent examination. The literature relating to public utilities may be characterized as fragmentary.

The setting of British public utilities is markedly different from that in America. This, as we shall see, largely explains the difference in emphasis in the two countries. However, it does appear that British public utility regulation has not been a popular subject of university research because it has been a sort of "No Man's Land" between law, government, and economics. Recent emphasis upon the field has come principally from the Public Administration group, and in particular from the Institute of Public Administration.

The failure of the British to stress the public utility concept has not been without its advantages, if one considers social control of industry a desirable end. In America the public utility concept has had the effect of creating two fairly distinct categories of business: the private and the public. In England there has been no such clear-cut division. Governmental supervision has been merely a matter of degree. Practically every business is subject to public interference in certain respects. Furthermore, there is no judicial obstacle in the way of extending the degree of regulation whenever Parliament desires. The English view does not differ materially from the realistic concept of Justices Holmes and Brandeis, who have consistently insisted that specific

[1] The principal discusssions relative to the legal and theoretical side of public utilities are these: F. N. Keen, *The Law Relating to Public Service Undertakings*, London, 1925; Herbert Morrison, *Socialization and Transport*, London, 1933; A. C. Pigou, *The Economics of Welfare*, ch. xxi, London, 1929; F. C. Benham, "Economic significance of public utilities," (1931) 11 *Economica*, 426; the best single discussion will be found in a symposium of twelve papers entitled, "The administration of public utilities," (1926) 4 *Pub. Admin.*, 287–430.

industries do not become liable to control because of inherent, self-evident differences which set them apart from other enterprises, but rather because the legislatures establish more complete regulations over businesses which the voters fear will injure their interests if public regulation is not sufficiently exercised.

The principal reason that public utility doctrine has been emphasized more in the United States than in Great Britain is to be discovered in the American system of judicial supremacy as contrasted with the English regime of Parliamentary omnicompetence.[1] Categories of black and white are the handiwork of the American judiciary. Parliament has not needed to define a public utility because it is unnecessary to satisfy the courts that certain conditions must exist before public intervention in private business can take place. For example, the regulation of theatre ticket brokerage and private labor exchanges[2] would be clearly within Parliament's right. Parliament can establish any degree of control which seems best, and the question of satisfying the "business affected with a public interest" category could not arise later by judicial review.

To most readers all of this is already well understood. Comparison has been resorted to merely to elucidate the principal characteristics of the British constitutional setting, which may be postulated as follows: Any private enterprise becomes a public utility whenever Parliament chooses to designate it as such or when the degree of regulation has reached the point where public opinion, acting through Parliament, regards the undertaking as peculiarly a public service. The present legal position of road passenger transport undertakings illustrates this transition very clearly. The courts cannot, and do not, seek to set limits to

[1] Charles G. Haines, *The American Doctrine of Judicial Supremacy*, revised edition, Berkeley, 1932.

[2] The former regulation was held to violate the requirements of "due process of law" in Tyson *v.* Banton, (1927) 273 U.S. 418, and the latter law suffered the same fate in the case of Ribnik *v.* McBride, (1928) 277 U.S. 350.

what Parliament may do. Hence the term "public utility" is a concept of Parliamentary and common usage, and not a legal rule.

After this preliminary discussion, a certain number of definitions may be attempted, because these will further illustrate the various facets of the approach. "A. public utility," states R. G. Hawtrey, "may be defined as a service in which a tendency to a local monopoly necessitates the intervention of a public authority to defend the interests of the consumer." A former official of the Board of Trade defines a public utility as "any undertaking that meets the needs or convenience of a considerable section of the public, and that places the undertakers in a position justifying the imposition of control in return for monopolistic or other special privileges."[1] This may be called the "political" view. As recently as 1810 an English court, following the reasoning of Sir Matthew Hale in 1670, asserted the following rule: Where private property has been devoted to a public use its owner has no right to exploit its scarcity value to the detriment of those who use it. He may withdraw his property from the use of the public altogether; otherwise he must fix reasonable rates of charge for it or submit to be controlled to the extent of the interest which has been created in it.[2] This dictum may be called the "judicial view." An "economic" interpretation may also be distinguished. The economist's task, according to some writers, is to tell us the results which are likely to be produced if regulation is not forthcoming, but not when or how such undertakings should be controlled.

The orientation which best suits the writer's need may be called the "public" view. Sir Henry Bunbury, a recognized authority on public utilities, said to the members of the Institute of Public Administration, "I will not spend

[1] Garnham Roper, "The principles of regulation," (1926) 4 *Pub. Admin.*, 287. Roper's article and appendix provide a good background for British public utilities.

[2] Allnutt *v.* Ingles, (1810) 104 *Engl. Repts.*, 206.

any time in trying to define what is meant by a public utility service because the application of that term is no doubt familiar to all of you. But I propose as typical examples railways, tramways, supplies of electrical energy, postal services, telegraphs, and telephones."[1]

Americans may have some hesitance about classifying the Post Office as a public utility, but it appears entirely justifiable to be so regarded. British writers do so consistently. For example, Keen states, "The Post Office and the telegraphic, telephonic, and wireless systems must clearly be classed as public service undertakings." Any agency, either private or public, which operates the telegraph and telephone services of a country may properly be considered a public utility. To be sure, the Post Office presents a somewhat distinctive problem of control, but its fundamental problems of organization and management are comparable to those encountered by public service undertakings generally.

Some of the principal differences between the Post Office and other public utilities will appear in an analysis of the forms of public service enterprise and how they are created by governmental action.

### THE FORMS OF PUBLIC UTILITY ENTERPRISE

At the very outset of an effort to analyze the problems of administration and control of British public utilities, it is desirable to explain the several types of parties by whom utilities may be organized and conducted. This is not as simple as it might seem. As A. L. Dakyns concludes, "What is lacking is anything approaching a sytematic study of the different agencies of public control which . . . have emerged amid the welter of private business." Parliament has never aimed at consistency as between one type of service and another, nor have the law courts been called upon to attempt

[1] "The elements of rate-fixing for public utilities," (1925) 3 *Pub. Admin.*, 47.

it. This has been regarded by most British writers as a salutary factor. It probably is, because it may be said tentatively that different forms of business require different types of organization and control. However, Dakyns shows great discernment when he protests, "If the hall-mark of most British public utilities is the grant to the undertakers of a special privilege, a local monopoly or the right of 'eminent domain,' it would be rash to assert that such a grant is the *raison d'être* of parliamentary or governmental control. For public control has emerged slowly and late in the history of the privileged bodies. . . . It seems to have spread by a process of trial and error in which each case for control has had to be separately considered and separately fought for against the opposition of vested interests." These are significant words and they exactly explain the circumstances under which the several forms of public utility undertaking have evolved.

British public utilities may be divided conveniently into the following five classes, namely, the public authority (public ownership and operation); the private company operating under a limited monopoly; the public utility trust; "mixed" undertakings composed of private and public capital; and the private individual.

The mixed enterprise and the personal concession may be dismissed with brief reference, because the former development is in a very formative stage in Great Britain, while the latter type of public utility is no longer of much importance. Ferries are probably the only survival of the parliamentary concession granted to the individual person. On the other hand, mixed undertakings may some day assume a position of great importance, judging from Continental experience. A mixed enterprise is a public utility in which the invested capital and the actual management are jointly contributed by a private company and a governmental body. In Europe the most important public utilities, including electricity, water and gas supply, are frequently controlled by mixed undertakings. In Great Britain, however, the only examples of the mixed undertaking are the Southampton Harbor Board, the Manchester Ship Canal, and Sheffield local transport.[1] These developments were primarily the result of fortuitous circumstances, rather than the product of a definite theory such as is found in Europe.

The three forms of public utility organization which will receive attention, therefore, are the statutory company under regulatory control, the public authority undertaking, and the public utility trust. Before going into detail, it may be suggestive to point out how the services under consideration in this book fit into the suggested category. The Post Office is a public authority undertaking, the railway companies are limited companies, and the Central Electricity Board and the British Broadcasting Corporation are public utility trusts. Several other explanatory examples will be provided in the more detailed explanation which will follow.

The administration and control of the British Post Office with special reference to the telegraph and telephone services, forms the subject-matter of chapters iv and v. A generalization regarding the constitutional position of the department will suffice at this juncture. The Post Office is one of the ordinary Departments of State in the British central administration and as such it is subject to direct Ministerial responsibility to Parliament and to Treasury control. This relationship has raised an issue which has been brought very much to the fore in recent years; it is the theme which should be kept in mind throughout the discussion of the British postal services. Can a commercial service such as the Post Office be made to operate efficiently under parliamentary control; if not, what alternative is there? Again, can commercial efficiency be obtained

---

[1] Sir William Hart, "Mixed undertakings," (1932) 10 *Pub. Admin.*, 138–156; the author has discussed the European development in "Les entreprises mixtes," (1931) 20 *National Municipal Review*, 638.

under Civil Service regulations? The Post Office is only one example of the public authority type of utility organization. In the same category should be included the commercial undertakings of the municipalities, the most prominent among which are water, gas, transport, and electricity services.

The second group of public utilities, the limited companies, constitute by far the most numerous class of public service enterprises in Great Britain, because water, gas, tramway, and railroad companies are typical examples. It is important that we should see how these corporate bodies come into existence.

### THE CREATION OF PUBLIC SERVICE UNDERTAKINGS

All power to establish public utility undertakings belongs to Parliament. This is the cardinal theory, but in actual practice Parliament has delegated important duties to Ministers. The powers of British public utilities are derived from several forms of authorizing action, namely the Special Act of Parliament, General Acts, the Order in Council, Provisional Orders, and Special Orders. In the last two cases Parliament must later confirm the action of the government department.

The Special Act of Parliament is frequently referred to as Private Bill procedure. Briefly, it consists of hearings before a select committee of the Houses of Parliament. The procedure is in the manner and the spirit of a law court. If the application and specifications of the entrepreneurs are reported favorably, the confirming of the Order by Parliament is ordinarily just a formality. Private bill legislation performs the double function of conferring a franchise and of laying down regulatory standards. This is the principal method of creating a public utility.

There are certain cases in which the general law authorizes the carrying on of public service undertakings without the necessity of special sanction: this is made possible by General Acts. An instance of the General Act is the power given to municipalities by the Public Health Act, 1875, to establish water and gas undertakings for the supply of their own districts where there is no company or other body empowered and willing to give the same service. The London Transport Board, the Central Electricity Board, and the Port of London Authority were created by the application of General Acts to the particular case. Clauses Acts have also played an important part in the creation of public utility enterprises. Clauses Acts are merely General Acts in a particular form. By means of them, large groups of sections, which used to be repeated in much the same form in Act after Act, can now be adopted and applied *en bloc*, subject to any variations necessary to meet particular cases.

The Order in Council is, *inter alia*, a procedure whereby companies are formed by Royal Charter. It is an exercise of the Royal Prerogative. The Privy Council authorizes the incorporation, on the advice of the Minister and after the Cabinet has approved the principles. Until the creation of the British Broadcasting Corporation in 1927 this means of forming public utilities had not been utilized for many years.

The Provisional Order is an increasingly popular means of securing public utility privileges. It has become, to a considerable extent, a substitute for Private Bill procedure. The company or the public authority will go to the appropriate central government department, usually the Ministry of Transport, the Ministry of Health, or the Board of Trade, where after hearings, evidence, and investigation, the powers are either granted or refused. The proceedings are usually held in the field rather than at Whitehall. The responsible Minister's action is later confirmed by an Act of Parliament, but this has become in practice simply a matter of course. The administrative control of Whitehall is unquestionably the most effective form of regulation over the older utilities such as water and tramway undertakings.

The remaining avenue of utility development is known as the Special Orders procedure. It is similar to the Provisional Order, except that it is a special administrative procedure employed primarily by gas and electricity companies. In the case of electricity Parliament provided that Special Orders should be made by the Electricity Commissioners and confirmed by the Ministry of Transport in all cases which, prior to the Electricity (Supply) Act of 1919, would have been considered by Provisional Order procedure or by action of Parliament. Parliament retained the right to reconsider these Special Orders, but in fact it never does so.

In the matter of regulating public utilities, as well as in other important respects, Parliament has been forced to delegate broad powers of control to the Administration.[1] Parliament does not have the time or the competence to do otherwise. The private Bill procedure is still extremely important, but even in that case the higher administrative officials are almost invariably called upon to undertake an independent investigation of the case, to make recommendations, and to give evidence. It is not an exaggeration to say that the applicants have little chance of success before a Private Bill committee if the departmental report has been unfavorable.

The central government virtually monopolizes the field so far as the creation and regulation of public service companies is concerned, leaving British municipalities less control over local utilities than they have over most other matters. This circumscription of local freedom applies to the municipality's desire to undertake new forms of

---

[1] One of the best treatments of the subject will be found in an article by W. Ivor Jennings, "The report on Ministers' powers," (1932) 10 *Pub. Admin.*, 333. The article contains a detailed bibliography. See also William A. Robson, *Justice and Administrative Law*, chaps. iii, vi, London, 1928.

commercial service itself, as well as to regulative powers over private companies. Local authorities are on the same footing as private undertakers so far as parliamentary requirements relating to new enterprises and additional powers are concerned. The central government's control of the trading functions of local authorities appears to be growing increasingly unpopular, especially in communities where the Labor party holds power. Professor Hormell accurately describes the situation when he says that "on the whole municipal ownership and operation have proved successful. . . . Many of the leading Conservatives who oppose national socialism consider municipal socialism to be merely good business."

Having considered the creation and empowering of public utility companies, we may return to some typical examples of the earliest and most numerous type of public service undertaking, namely, the limited company operating under a limited monopoly. The best examples of these, aside from the railways, are the water, tramway, and gas companies. Reference to these at this point will help to make our consideration of the principal public utility services more complete.

## THE REGULATION OF PUBLIC SERVICE UNDERTAKINGS

### Water Supply

The most important means of empowering and regulating water companies consists of detailed Acts of Parliament, both general and special, which have been passed since 1847.[1] Due to the clarity of the law, the long experience

[1] The more important of these provisions are included in the Waterworks Clauses Acts, 1847 and 1863, the Water Companies (Regulation of Powers) Act, 1887, the Gas and Water Works Facilities Acts, 1870 and 1873, and the Public Health Acts of 1875 and later dates. Keen analyses all of the Acts prior to 1925 in chapter ix of his book. The most important legislation of recent years consists of the Water Undertakings (Modification of Charges) Act, 1921, and the Reservoirs (Safety Provisions) Act, 1930.

with problems of water supply and the relatively moderate returns to be expected from the business, the problems of administration are not particularly difficult. Furthermore, as in America, a large percentage of water systems are publicly owned.

The Public Health Act, 1875 (Sect. 51), empowers any urban authority to provide its district or any part thereof, and any rural authority to provide its district or any contributory place therein, with a supply of water for public and private purposes. As a result of this and supplementary provisions the water supply is publicly owned in virtually all of the boroughs, in roughly two-thirds of the county boroughs, and in about half of the urban districts. The Liberal Industrial Inquiry reported in 1928 that 977 out of 1,236 water systems in England and Wales were owned by public authorities. In 1902 the water supply of metropolitan London was transferred from private companies to the Metropolitan Water Board, a public utility trust form of organization. The number of such boards is not less than fourteen, representing an aggregate capital of £69,730,000. The Act of 1875 further provided for the compulsory taking of land and the acquisition of existing private companies, subject either to arbitration or to a provisional order confirmed by Act of Parliament. The majority of cases have been settled by agreement. The national policy relative to water supply has been made clear, because "it has been for many years the settled policy of Parliament not to withhold its sanction to applications from urban authorities seeking control of the water supply in their districts."[1]

So far as existing private companies are concerned, the enforcement of the provisions of law is entrusted to the Ministry of Health. The authority for making Provisional Orders was originally the Board of Trade's, but it was transferred to the Minister of Health by an Order in Council made in November 1920. As regards water supply, the

[1] (1932) *Municipal Year Book*, 1027.

purposes for which a Provisional Order may be made are defined as follows:

"To construct or to maintain and continue waterworks and works connected therewith, or to supply water in any district within which there is not an existing company, corporation, body of commissioners, or person empowered by Act of Parliament to construct such works and to supply water;

"To raise additional capital necessary for any of the purposes aforesaid;

"To enable two or more companies or persons duly authorized to supply water in any district or in adjoining districts to enter into agreements jointly to furnish such supply, or to amalgamate their undertakings;

"To authorize two or more companies or persons supplying water in any district or in adjoining districts to supply water, and to enter into agreements jointly to furnish such supply, and to amalgamate their undertakings."

The municipality exercises certain limited forms of control over statutory companies, these being applicable to gas and tramway companies as well. In case of a new private enterprise the consent of the local authority must be obtained (subject to the Minister's authority to dispense with it). In times past the local corporations have been able to limit or to prevent entirely the private company's use of eminent domain, notably in the case of the National Telephone Company. Finally, permission must be obtained to tear up streets and lay mains.[1]

In recent years there has been a marked tendency for Parliament to put the water supply into the hands of ad hoc bodies representing large areas, the members of said boards being elected indirectly by the constituent local authorities. In 1932 there were thirty-three Joint Water Boards in existence. The proposed establishment of regional committees points in the same direction. In order to bring about the most advantageous exploitation of the nation's water resources, a permanent advisory body has been created,

[1] Michael and Will, *The Law Relating to Gas and Water Companies*, 2 vols., London, 1924-25, particularly chapter v, vol. ii, which deals with powers of local authorities with reference to water supply.

entitled the Ministry of Health Advisory Committee on Water Supply.

## Water Companies: Rate Determination

As a rule, questions regarding water rates are decided by reference to very specific provisions contained in general or special Acts of Parliament. The basis of later special Acts has been Section 68 of the Waterworks Clauses Act of 1847 which provides that water rates shall be payable according to the annual value of the tenement supplied with water. If any dispute arises as to such value, the Act continues, it is to be determined by two justices. When the provision regarding "annual value" became incorporated in special Acts a good deal of litigation arose as to the meaning of the term. In the leading case of Dobbs *v.* Grand Junction Waterworks Company,[1] the House of Lords (reversing the Court of Appeal) held that "annual value" means "rateable" (local taxation) value. By the Water Rate Definition Act of 1885 it was provided that the "annual value" should be the rateable value as settled from time to time by the local authority. "Now, under the Acts of the Metropolitan Water Board, rateable value has been made the basis for the charging of the rate for domestic purposes throughout the whole area of jurisdiction of the Board."[2] The usual practice now followed in special Acts is to avoid ambiguity by describing the assessment on which the maximum percentages are to be calculated either as "rateable value" or as "gross estimated rental."

The Waterworks Clauses Act (Sects. 75-83) deals with the profit to be derived by water companies. Briefly, it is provided that profits to be divided in any one year are not to exceed 10 per cent on the paid-up capital of the undertaking, but this may be exceeded when a past dividend has fallen short of the allowable return. Excess profits may be invested in government securities until such time as the re-

[1] (1883) 9 *App. Cas.*, 49.      [2] Keen, op. cit., 155.

serve fund amounts to one-tenth of the capital. The reserve fund may be used for only two purposes: either to meet a deficiency which occurs at any time in the amount of dividable profits or to meet any extraordinary claim or demand which may arise. The propriety of such claim must be certified by two justices. If in any year it is alleged by two or more water ratepayers that profits have been earned in excess of the aforesaid provisions, the Court of Quarter Sessions is given power to hear the complaint. The court may order any such rate reduction as seems reasonable.

This procedure brings out the traditional British method of rate regulation, with suggestions which may be of possible interest to American readers. However, the situation just described has been modified somewhat by later special Acts. The modern practice is to insert a clause defining the maximum charges the company may make for domestic supply, and commonly also a maximum price per thousand gallons for meter supplies. In practice the rate of return has not usually reached the 10 per cent allowed by law. As a general rule the maximum of 10 per cent is allowed on only the original capital, later issues being limited to 7 per cent or less. At the present time the estimated average return to private companies is around 6 per cent.[1] This is due in part to the fact that recent special Acts have fixed the maximum rate at 7 per cent, and also in large part to powers given to the Minister of Health by the Water Undertakings (Modification of Charges) Act of 1921. This Act provides for price complaints to the Minister from customers or from municipalities. If it appears to the Minister that the costs of carrying on the undertaking have substantially altered, the Minister may make an amending order revising the powers of charging, so that the revised maximum charges shall not in any case, however, be less than the statutory maximum charges applicable on August 4, 1914. This Act has since been supple-

[1] From a memorandum supplied by the Ministry of Health, October 27, 1932.

mented by the Water Orders Procedure Rules of 1926. In the case of public utilities which are run by municipal corporations or other public bodies, the profits are restricted by limiting the amount which can be used in relief of local taxation. The growth of administrative authority has brought about more effective regulation and more elastic rate-making.

*Gas Companies*

Many of the things that have been said about water supply apply to gas undertakings[1] as well. In some cases the two services are dealt with in the same Act. Hence our primary purpose should be to point out the differences in the technique of regulation.

"The privately owned gas enterprises," Professor Hormell has concluded, "enjoy a more secure position than that of the other important utility enterprises." It is true that municipal trading has not entered this field as rapidly as certain others, but nevertheless over 40 per cent of the country's gas undertakings are now publicly owned. A considerable part of the investment in private undertakings is in the form of large combines such as the Gas, Light, and Coke Company of London. At the present time 317 public authority undertakings represent an investment of £62,650,000, as compared with 465 private companies involving an invested capital of £109,336,000. However, "in no case can a municipal supply be started to compete with that of a company exercising statutory powers." The purchase of a private gas supply by a municipality must be brought about by agreement between the parties. Nevertheless, it may be said to be a general principle of British public utility control that when rival schemes are submitted to Parliament by a local authority and by

[1] Gas supply is regulated by the Gas Works Clauses Acts, 1847 and 1871, the Sale of Gas Act, 1859, the Gas and Water Works Facilities Acts, 1870 and 1873, certain sections of the Public Health Act, 1875, the Gas Regulation Act, 1920, and the Gas Undertakings Act, 1929.

a body trading for profit, preference is almost always given to the former.

"It must be borne in mind," writes Keen, "that the manufacture of gas is a business which, if not carefully regulated, may give rise to serious nuisance in the locality in which it is carried on." The Board of Trade has been given important powers which the Ministry of Health does not have, namely the authority to issue Special Orders. The Gas Regulation Act, 1920 (Sect. 10), which deals with Special Orders, is so important that its provisions are here set forth.[1]

The principal duty of the gas officials appointed by the Board of Trade is to maintain the proper quality of gas according to the price to be charged. "In very recent years,"

[1] (a) empower any undertakers to obtain a supply of gas in bulk from any source, whether situated within or without their authorized limits of supply:

(b) empower any undertakers to give a separate supply of gas for industrial purposes within their authorized limits of supply:

(c) authorize any local authority, which may be authorized to supply gas within their district, to supply gas outside the district in any area which is not supplied with gas by any other undertakers, or which is within the area of supply of any undertakers whose undertaking has been acquired by such local authority:

(d) authorize arrangements for the purchase by agreement, joint working, or amalgamation of undertakings, including necessary provisions with regard to the capital of the combined undertakings, the vesting of the property and rights of the purchased or amalgamated undertakings, and other necessary incidents and consequences of purchase, amalgamation, or joint working:

(e) authorize the establishment of superannuation, pension, and other like funds:

(f) authorize the raising of capital or the borrowing of money for any of the purposes aforesaid:

(g) make provision for the purchase or redemption (out of revenue or otherwise) and cancellation of debentures, debenture stock, mortgages or bonds, or of obsolete or unproductive capital, or capital not represented by available assets:

(h) modify or amend the provisions of any special Act or other provision relating to the undertaking affected by the special order as may be necessary to provide for the proper and efficient conduct of the undertaking;

(i) make such supplemental and consequential provisions as appear necessary to give full effect to the order.

Points (h) and (i) deserve particular notice. For comment, see the 1921–22 *Municipal Year Book*.

states Keen, "it has become usual not to require the undertakers to conform to a fixed standard of calorific value and charge for the actual quantity of gas supplied, but to allow them to declare from time to time the calorific standard they will adopt, and then to charge for the number of units of heating value in the gas supplied." This alteration was brought about by the Act of 1920, which changed the standard of regulation from costs and profits to "therms," i.e. the amount of heat absorbed in raising the temperature of 1,000 gallons of water 10 degrees Fahrenheit. This has entailed periodic testing by local gas examiners, who are appointed by the local authorities concerned. Where no provision has been made for local examiners there is no enforcement whatever. The central government has not assumed the primary responsibility for enforcement. However, when local inspection officers do discover that the company's standard has fallen below the agreement, the case is reported to three Gas Referees, who are appointed by the Board of Trade. A final appeal may be made, but rarely is, to the Chief Gas Examiner, who is also appointed by the Board of Trade. Both the Gas Referees and the Chief Gas Examiner are appointed for a short term and are therefore not part of the permanent personnel of the department. The Act of 1920 (Sect. 6) provides for specific penalties and fines for the violation of agreements. Any order of the Chief Gas Examiner relative to calorific value, purity, pressure, or composition of gas is held to be conclusive evidence of the liability of the undertakers. The Gas Undertakings Act, 1929, supplemented the provisions of the 1920 Act.

The method of regulating prices differs between private and public undertakings. Since 1875 private companies have been placed under a system wherein the price is regulated according to a sliding scale of price and dividend, but local authorities are usually dealt with by the imposition of a maximum price. The sliding scale provides that dividends may increase beyond a standard figure in proportion to the reduction in the price of gas below a fixed standard price. Conversely, prices may rise if dividends fall. The sliding scale principle is supposed to be a stimulus to more efficient management. Under this plan dividends vary from 5 to 10 per cent. Since the legislation of 1920 the Board of Trade may permit the maximum price per therm and the maximum dividend to be raised if it can be shown that there has been an increase in the cost of coal or of some other factor.

As a result of the Statutory Gas Companies Act of 1925, it has been provided that gas companies may undertake electricity supply as well. Despite misgivings to the contrary, gas undertakings appear to have held their own so far in competition with electricity supply. It is quite generally agreed, though, that the consumer's interests are not as well protected in the case of gas supply as they are in water company or tramway regulation. This criticism is based, in large part, upon the fact that regulation of gas supply is not nation-wide or standardized. Some of the principal defects of gas regulation have recently been considered by the Joint Committee on Gas Undertakings, which reported in 1932. At the present time some of the obsolete statutory restrictions on gas companies, financial and otherwise, are in the process of removal, but there is no doubt that they have seriously hampered the development of the companies in competition with electricity.

*Tramway Undertakings*

A brief discussion of local transportation systems will round off our consideration of some of the older public utilities, and it will also reveal additional characteristics of the framework of public regulation.

The great majority of British tramway undertakings, although in most cases they were begun by private enterprise, are owned by public authorities. In 1930 municipal corporations owned 160 out of 217 tramway systems in England and

Wales.[1] This represented a capital outlay of £82,000,000 or approximately 80 per cent of the net investment in tramways and other forms of local transportation. In 1931 these municipal transport systems contributed £172,976 in relief of local rates.

Local transport administration, both public and private, is subject to the control of the Ministry of Transport. This important department of the central government was established by the Ministry of Transport Act, 1919, which transferred from other departments all powers and duties relating to railways, light railways, and tramways, canals, waterways, inland navigation, roads, bridges, ferries, and "vehicles and traffic thereon." This grouping of responsibilities is a model of functional reorganization. Among his numerous powers, the Minister of Transport may connect existing services, provide "through runs," and even undertake new services himself if existing enterprises are unwilling to do so .

We shall be concerned with these and with additional powers of the Ministry of Transport in our discussion, shortly to follow, of the London Transport problem and in the next chapter, which deals with national transportation.

The powers and obligations of the tramway undertakers in England and Wales are derived from the Tramways Act, 1870, the Light Railways Acts, 1869 and 1912, and Provisional Orders granted under these and later Acts. The Minister of Transport is the sanctioning authority for the raising of loans by a local authority operating tramways, and this enables him to call for accounts and to scrutinize plans more easily than in the case of companies; the powers which he exercises are the same in other cases, i.e. relative

---

[1] (1932) *Municipal Year Book*, 755. The latest and most important information relating to municipal transport will be found in the *Final Report, Royal Commission on Transport*, "The coordination and development of transport," 96–109, Cmd. 3751, 1931. This report is a valuable source of information on transport utilities generally.

to safety, granting of leases, laying out mains, approval of bye-laws and so forth.

The municipality is able to exercise control at several points over private companies desiring to operate local transportation services. When a private company applies for a franchise to establish a new service, the consent of the municipal corporation must be obtained, unless the lines run into two or more districts. In this case the company will not be compelled to obtain the consent of a local authority which controls a third or less of the projected line. Most of the local authority's jurisdiction is derived from its responsibility as Road Authority. The principal ancillary powers thus obtained, in addition to the limited veto which has been mentioned, are the following, namely, control of the breaking up and replacement of roads; usually, authority to approve plans of construction; removal of a tramway not being worked; expropriation of a private company after twenty-one years or purchase sooner by agreement (subject to approval by the Minister of Transport); and power to make bye-laws relative to speed and other details of operation.

As regards profits, the situation is much the same as in the case of water supply, that is, early Acts usually permitted a return of 10 per cent, but later provisions have ordinarily stipulated 7 per cent or less.

In recent years local authorities have been confronted with the necessity of supplementing their tramway lines with omnibus and trackless trolley services, or else face ruinous competition from other quarters. The margin of profit has been small. The average fare on municipally-owned tramways is only 1·35d. Systems which have not kept pace with the development of improved transportation have suffered losses. But in most cases the necessary obsolescence is being frankly faced. The Royal Commission on Transport, 1930, concluded that "tramways, if not an obsolete form of transport, are at all events in a state of obsolescence, and cause much unnecessary congestion and considerable unnecessary danger to the public. The commission therefore recommended that (a) no additional tramways should be constructed, and (b) that, though no definite time limit can be laid down, they should gradually disappear and give place to other forms of transport." In 1931 ten tramway systems were not being operated at all. Many municipalities are changing to railless methods of traction; in 1931 trackless trolley undertakings were being operated by twenty-one municipalities and by two companies. "Municipal motors" is a slogan heard in all parts of the country. Bus routes are either being established as "feeders" to the tramways, or, in some cases, complete motor bus routes have been introduced.

The British citizen unquestionably gets more local transportation for his money than passengers in almost any other country.

With the exception of the four great railway undertakings, most of the public utility companies, such as the water, gas, and tramway companies just described, are local in character. What has been said about local public utility undertakings will not exactly delineate, in all respects, the principles according to which companies operating on a national scale are regulated. Variety is one of the principal features of British public utility control; new problems have required varying forms of regulation. But the general features of regulation exercised over company and local authority undertakings will give one a fair idea of the general law and practice relative to monopoly privileges, the process of incorporation, the extension of public ownership and operation, the administrative control of Whitehall, and the methods of rate regulation. The valuation of public utility properties for rate and expropriation purposes will be discussed shortly, and other principles of public utility regulation, such as equality of treatment, service requirements, and safety provisions will be illustrated in later chapters.

### THE PUBLIC UTILITY TRUST

So far we have dealt with two of the three types of public utility organization, namely the public authority and the private statutory company. The remaining form of public service enterprise is the public utility trust, or, as it is sometimes called, the ad hoc public board. This creation of recent years has been received with great enthusiasm in powerful quarters. The public utility trust has been called the ideal form of public utility undertaking. As we have already suggested, its proponents claim that the public utility trust, as represented by the Central Electricity Board, the British Broadcasting Corporation, or the Port of London Authority, is the effective instrument which will bring about a successful compromise between *laissez-faire* and socialism. At this juncture it seems desirable that a setting for the C.E.B. and the B.B.C. should be created. The general features of the public utility trust will be explained, followed by two examples of the plan, namely the P.L.A. and the London Passenger Transport Board.

"The best method of conducting large undertakings owned by the Government and run in the public interest" (according to the Liberal viewpoint,[1]) "is by means of an ad hoc Public Board analogous to a Joint Stock Company, in which the capital is owned and the directors are appointed by the State." Professor Ramsay Muir prefers to call this type of undertaking a "Public Trust." Parliament creates it, defines the principles of its conduct, stipulates the methods of choosing directors, exercises ultimate control over its actions by means of the right to revise the terms of the Act under which the Public Trust was created, but the management is wholly independent regarding internal operations.[2] Although this general analysis applies to the three major examples of existing public trusts, namely the P.L.A., the

[1] *Britain's Industrial Future,* 457.
[2] Ramsay Muir, *Politics and Progress,* 49, London, 1923.

C.E.B., and the B.B.C., it is difficult to generalize too much because each of the undertakings differs in certain respects from the other two.

Lord Wolmer, who states that the public utility authority is "the modern conception of dealing with monopoly," brings out additional characteristics of the ad hoc authority. The three existing boards, i.e. the P.L.A., the C.E.B., and the B.B.C., he says, have the following features in common: "Each of them is a perpetual corporation, having a common seal, capable of owning property, and of suing and being sued. Their status is different from that of a joint stock company; different again from that of a Minister of the Crown or a Department of State. Each of them is, within the limitations originally imposed, master in its own house. The limitations are precise and impose considerable restrictions upon their operations."[1]

It may help to bring out the essential characteristics of the public utility trust by comparing it with the private concern. The public trust is a special form of legal creation; its directors are appointed by the Government, by local authorities, or in certain cases by the users of the service; the undertaking is a legal monopoly; the stockholders are all creditors of and not partners in the undertaking; and the amount and disposition of its earnings are strictly limited by statutory provision. The public utility trust is non-profit-making. The principal respect in which it differs from a government department, on the other hand, is in the absence of continuous ministerial control over its operations.

The P.L.A. was the first important example of the public utility trust, and its creation established a precedent for later adaptations of the same principle.

### The Port of London Authority

The P.L.A. was established by Parliament in 1908, after the port had been administered under five different forms

[1] *Post Office Reform*, 277, London, 1932.

of organization.[1] About 40 per cent of the total trade of Great Britain passes through this single port. It is the largest and oldest of sixty ad hoc bodies which administer harbors and docks.[2]

According to the Act of 1908, the duties of the P.L.A. are "to take into consideration the state of the river and the accommodation and facilities in the Port of London, and ... to take such step as they may consider necessary for the improvement thereof." Amendments to the Act of 1908 were later added, and all of the legislation was finally unified by an Act of 1920. It is specifically provided, among other things, that the Authority may carry on dock undertakings, load, unload, and warehouse goods, construct wharves, locks, etc., and any necessary buildings in connection therewith, and generally control the organization and equipment of the Port. In case of the dispute with traders over charges or other matters a complaint may be taken to the Minister of Transport.

The Board consists of from twenty-eight to thirty members, who are either elected or appointed. Eighteen directors are elected (under regulations made by the Ministry of Transport) from the various interests represented at the Port. Seventeen of these elective members are selected by traders paying dues, and one is chosen to represent wharfingers. Payers of dues are given from one to fifty votes, according to the amount of dues paid. Owners of river craft receive from one to ten votes, depending upon the number of vessels they possess. It may readily be seen where the final power is vested.

[1] Sir Joseph G. Broodbank, "The appropriate type of public authority," (1926) 4 *Pub. Admin.*, 309–317; also, the *History of the Port of London*, London, 1921, by the same author.

[2] Out of 177 Harbor undertakings, 10 are worked by government departments, 43 by local authorities, and 60 by ad hoc authorities not trading for profit. The twenty largest out of the last-named category have an aggregate capital of about £100,000,000. *Britain's Industrial Future*, 68. The control of harbors and docks was investigated by the Royal Commission on Transport, 1930, and their report and recommendations are found in *Final Report*, 1931, op. cit., 125–135.

Ten members are appointed by the following bodies:

The Admiralty, one member.
The Ministry of Transport, two members.
The London County Council, four members.
The Corporation of the City of London, two members.
Trinity House, two members.

The Act stipulates that one each of the representatives of the Ministry of Transport and of the London County Council should represent labor and be appointed after consultation with labor organizations.

In addition to these twenty-eight members, the Board may appoint the Chairman and Vice-Chairman from without its own membership. At the present time the Chairman is so appointed. The term of office of all members is three years, but they are subject to reelection or reappointment. Salaries may be paid to the Chairman, Vice-Chairman, and Chairman of Committees, but in practice the Chairman is usually the only one who is remunerated.

Most of the Board's work is done through committees, which are appointed by and report to the Board. The most important one is the Dock and Warehouse Committee, which is primarily responsible for operating the docks. The committee system results in a great deal of devolution. The Chairman is supposed to bring about the necessary coordination.

The financial responsibilities of the P.L.A. are impressive.[1] The Authority took over the stock of the companies it superseded and issued its own in exchange. It has power to borrow for approved purposes up to £43,000,000 and to obtain temporary advances up to £1,000,000, or, with the approval of the Minister of Transport, up to £2,000,000. Its outstanding liabilities are in the neighborhood of £35,000,000. The retirement of the bonds is brought about by a sinking

---

[1] The following data will be found in the *Annual Report of the P.L.A.*, March 1931; (1932) *Municipal Year Book*, 359, 1089; and *Royal Commission on Transport, Final Report*, 1931, op. cit., 128–131.

fund arrangement, and if receipts in any year are insufficient the Minister of Transport may order additional dues to be collected. In 1928 the trade handled by the Port of London amounted to £693,000,000. The net tonnage arriving and leaving through the Port during the year was 55·4 million tons, and of this 60 per cent used docks belonging to the Authority. In 1931 the expenditure aggregated £6,279,036, including provision for sinking fund and interest requirements. Maximum charging powers were provided in the Special Act creating the P.L.A., but since the war the Minister of Transport has been given power to vary the statutory charges. The minimum rate of return on P.L.A. stock is 3 per cent and the maximum is 5 per cent. This limit cannot be exceeded, and any additional surplus cannot be paid out as profits.

A former member of the Board of the P.L.A. concluded after seventeen years of service that although the Authority has "adequately fulfilled the intention of Parliament that it should improve the Port, . . . it is slow in action and administration, whilst traders feel the oppressiveness of dues and charges which have increased considerably. These drawbacks cannot be attributed to inefficiency on the part of the personnel of the Authority. They were inevitable in the nature of things and were foreseen."

The principal defect is said to be that the P.L.A. is a mixed administrative and commercial body, at one and the same time regulating the interests of many others and also managing its own docks and interests. However, it should be recorded that very few disputes have been taken to the Ministry of Transport, which is an alleged indication of general satisfaction. The consensus of opinion holds that the contingency of using this power has been an important factor in obtaining justice from the Board.

The best authority on the subject comes to the conclusion that "The merits of public institutions as such cannot be judged by the transactions of a few years, and I would urge the careful weighing of all the circumstances before the constitution and powers of the P.L.A. are taken as the model of a public utility undertaking."[1]

Although the P.L.A. furnished the example, the structure and operation of the B.B.C. and of the C.E.B. differ from each other and from the former in several important respects. The latest public trust which has been created, namely the London Passenger Transport Board, reveals even more striking variations, indicating the high degree of flexibility which is possible under the public board form of utility organization. Considerable importance is attached to the problem of solving London's transport difficulties, not only because the largest city in the world suffers so acutely from traffic congestion, but also because the solution may indicate the manner in which future problems of public control may be resolved.

*The London Passenger Transport Problem*

The London passenger transport scheme was adopted by Parliament in 1933, after alternative plans of solving London's traffic problem had been strenuously contested for many years.[2] No other large city in the world is said to possess such a ramified transport system as London, and no other city has had to cope with more difficult problems of traffic control. The reasons for this are easily understood. London has developed without a plan, haphazardly, resulting in narrow, tortuous streets. As a result of the increasing public preference for motor transportation, London's congestion problem has become as much a question of roads as of conveyances. Moreover, in late years there has been a phenomenal growth of population around London's periphery. Over nine million people, almost one-fifth of the population of the country, live within a twenty-five mile radius of Charing

[1] Broodbank, op. cit., 4 *Pub. Admin.*, 314.
[2] 23 Geo. 5, chap. 14; Herbert Morrison, *Socialization and Transport*, London, 1933.

Cross. This is the most important fact that might be mentioned because it underlies every problem of transportation and of communication. Moreover, the circle of population is being constantly extended. The center of London is thinning out, numerous housing estates have been established on the outskirts, and inadequate transportation alone will check the tendency of people to go further into the country. It is no exaggeration to say that adequate cheap transportation has become as necessary to the Londoner as a satisfactory water supply.

The problem has been too large for existing governmental subdivisions. The area of the London County Council is 117 square miles and the effective area of London traffic is approximately 1,800 square miles. Proposals have been made to create a Greater London, but the idea has not made much headway. Within this area there existed in the neighborhood of ninety transport services, a few large and many small, which had to be considered in bringing about coordination. Competition has resulted in inconvenience and delay to passengers, over-expansion in certain cases, cut-throat competition, and financial timidity due to future uncertainties. Because of the uneconomic competition the underground has been unable to raise new capital for extensions, without a government guarantee, although extensions are admittedly necessary. It costs £800,000 to £1,000,000 per mile to build tubes. As G. J. Ponsonby has concluded in *London's Transport Problem*, "The simple fact that a proper development of London's transport system requires the growth of all facilities, and that if any one link in the chain falls short of requirements the whole will suffer, is self-evident."

The transport services which entered into the new combine consist of tramways, main-line railways, Underground railways, and omnibus systems. In 1929 the transport facilities of Greater London accounted for 4,000,000,000 passenger journeys, or an average of $1\frac{1}{3}$ journey per head of the population per day. The gross receipts from the suburban

traffic, of the four main-line railway companies total about
£10,000,000 a year, or about one-sixth of the total passenger
receipts of the four amalgamated railway companies. The railways' interests have been taken care of by a traffic pooling
arrangement. Over 80 per cent of the tramways were
owned by public authorities, representing an investment of
£18,000,000. All except one of the underground companies
and practically all of the principal omnibus routes were owned
by the same interests, the London Underground group.
Permission to pool the resources of the omnibuses and the
tubes was obtained during the war. "They were potential
competitors, but when that consent was given, for the first
year the tubes kept the omnibuses going. Afterwards, the
conditions of traffic changed. The motor omnibus was introduced and from that time until now the omnibuses of London have kept the tubes alive. The omnibuses contribute no
less than £500,000, a year," it was pointed out in the House
of Commons. This illustrates the close relationship between
all forms of transport. All of the transportation facilities
involved in the combine, exclusive of the railways, reach the
staggering total of £100,000,000.

The recent history of the proposal to unify London's
traffic resources really began in 1924. Since that time
animosity between interested parties has been almost constantly aflame over the issue. In 1924 the London Traffic
Act gave the Minister of Transport power to limit the number
of omnibuses plying for hire on certain streets. This helped
the tramways, and also improved the conditions of labor.
The Road Traffic Act of 1930 provided further restrictions
leading towards monopoly. The creation of the London
Traffic Advisory Committee, prior to this, brought into
being an expert body which held extensive hearings and
worked out plans of coordination. In 1928 and 1929 private
bills were introduced which would have coordinated London
transport under a joint unified management controlled by
the principal combines. These were killed by a Labor-

Liberal coalition at the third reading. The Liberal party favored municipal ownership and operation and the Labor party advocated national control under a public board.

In 1931 the Labor party introduced a bill providing for the complete amalgamation of existing transport services under a board of five members appointed by and responsible to the Minister of Transport. Security holders were to be given stock in the new undertaking, but with no option of demanding cash instead. The bill passed the second reading and emerged successfully from the joint committee stage[1] with only the Metropolitan Railway interests dissatisfied. Then there was a change of government.

All three political parties favored coordination, but disagreed upon the nature of the control which should be established. The Conservative party's objections to Labor's bill were couched in the following terms:

"This House, whilst again willing to consider any sound scheme for the coordination of London traffic, declines to give a Second Reading to a bill which provides for the nationalization of London passenger transport; deprives local authorities of control in respect of their various undertakings; takes the property of private owners out of their control; gives them no option of sale; vests in the Minister of Transport bureaucratic powers; and constitutes him, and not a judicial tribunal, the court of appeal in such important matters as the provision or withdrawal of traffic services and facilities."

When Parliament met in the fall of 1932, the National Government secured permission from the House to bring up Labor's Transport Bill at the next session, at which time only the final reading was to be allowed.

The Act which was finally passed differed in only one important respect from the Labor Government's bill. The alteration related to public control. It has been provided that the Minister of Transport shall set up a body to be called "Appointing Trustees," to whom will be entrusted,

[1] The most illuminating discussion of the bill occurred at this stage. See particularly the introductory and concluding speeches of Mr. Wilfrid Greene, Select Committee on the London Passenger Transport Bill, *Proceedings*, May 12, May 13, and July 17, 1931. Stationery Office publication.

instead of to the Minister, the crucial duty of electing the Board. The Appointing Trustees will consist of the Chairman of the London County Council, a representative of the London Advisory Committee, the Chairman of the London Clearing Bankers, the President of the Institute of Chartered Accountants, and the President of the Law Society. Unlike the original bill, neither the appointing officials nor the operating board are responsible to the Minister of Transport. Disputes regarding service and rates will be taken to the Railway Rates Tribunal, a quasi-judicial body.

A rebellious Conservative summarized his objections to the bill by pointing out that the system of indirect appointment has twice removed the managing officials from the searchlight of public criticism and control. The Board will not be responsible to Parliament nor to the people in the London traffic area, acting through their representatives. Herbert Morrison, who as Minister of Transport fathered the original bill, has concluded that

"This method will, of course, destroy all public accountability. The Minister will not be responsible, and questions in Parliament will be futile. The press or the public at large can grumble, but each of the Appointing Trustees can feel quite impersonal about it because, after all, the Trustees will be responsible as a whole, and not individually. Criticism against an individual Trustee will probably meet with the answer: 'Well, you must remember that I was not the only Trustee, and one cannot always get one's own way.' The device seems almost to invite backstairs influence . . ."[1]

On the other hand, the appointment of Lord Ashfield and Mr. Pick, the successful Underground executives, as the chief operating officials of the new combine, has caused reassurance.

All three political parties have, at one time or another, advocated the public utility trust. However, it is difficult to generalize, because there has been so much difference of opinion among individual members of all the parties. The Conservative party has not only approved the principle, but

---

[1] *Socialization and Transport*, 161, 162.

has been responsible for the creation of the Metropolitan Water Board, the C.E.B., and the B.B.C. Conservatives often argue that the public utility trust will protect investors from the arbitrariness of future governments and safeguard commercial management. The Liberal party has declared that the public trust constitutes the ideal form of public utility control; and it was responsible for the creation of the P.L.A. Liberals discover in the public utility trust a reconciliation of public ownership with efficiency of performance and enterprise. Prominent members of the Labor party hold that the public utility trust is preferable to any existing method of operating public commercial undertakings. Within recent months, however, many members of the party have expressed scepticism regarding some aspects of the development—particularly those relating to the adequacy of labor representation and the sufficiency of public control. The public utility trust may be a step toward socialism, they say, but the form of control leaves much to be desired in the interval.

### PUBLIC UTILITY VALUATION

One of the questions which has created a great deal of difficulty in connection with the purchase of the London transport facilities is the price which should be paid, in other words, what constitutes the proper value of the existing services. This issue is a very important one because since the 1870's a large percentage of private utility companies have been acquired by public authorities, either by negotiation or by expropriation. The right to expropriate a public utility company is an important form of public control.

The circumstances surrounding the forced sale of a public utility property, viz. the price which must be paid and the upkeep and modernity of the plant, are determining factors in the ultimate success or failure of public commercial undertakings. There have been many striking examples of this truth in Great Britain. For example, in the course of the debate on the London Passenger Transport Bill, a member stated that he hoped the Government would "not allow this great enterprise of London traffic to be weighed down as the London Water Board was, and as the Port of London Authority has been all its life, by immensely exaggerated capital charges." An official of the Board of Trade, who has been in close touch with the public acquisition of privately-owned utilities, stated to the writer that in several instances in which it had been provided that the local authority might take over the undertaking at the end of twenty-one years, the private owners refused to make replacements due to deterioration during the last several years of the life of the company, with the result that the municipality "found a pile of junk on its hands."

In the United States one finds a vast amount of material relating to the valuation of public utilities for rate-making and dividend-earning purposes. "A fair return on a fair value" is a common maxim. The British have spared themselves endless disputes regarding the proper theory of valuation underlying the rate-base.[1] Where it has been provided that a maximum rate of interest may be paid upon an investment, the amount referred to is invariably the face value of the outstanding securities. The law regarding the theory of valuation applicable to purchase is also well settled. Each Act defines the basis of valuation, leaving no room for dispute except on questions of fact. Certainty relative to valuation theory is one of the principal reasons that public utility issues do not occupy a more important place in British discussion.

The basis of valuation in Great Britain has been laid down by Parliament in a large number of cases extending over many years. Therefore the courts have had relatively few valuation controversies before them, and the rule to be

[1] Sir Henry Bunbury, "The economic regulation of public utilities," (1926) 4 *Pub. Admin.*, 208.

applied has never been seriously in doubt. This may be shown by characteristic statutory provisions and by court decisions.

According to Section 43 of the Tramways Act of 1870, "Promoters shall sell to them (local authorities) their undertaking ... upon terms of paying the then value (exclusive of any allowance for past or future profits of the undertaking or any compensation for compulsory sale or other consideration whatsoever) of the tramway, and all lands, buildings, works, materials, and plant of the promoters ... said value to be in case of difference determined by an engineer or other person nominated by the Board of Trade." When this provision came before the courts it was held that value includes "all real and movable property belonging to the 'promoters' necessary for conducting the tramway traffic and all proprietary rights attaching thereto ... as successfully constructed and in complete working condition, after deduction of a proper sum for depreciation; but not of the rights of user, such rights being conferred upon the 'promoters' of the undertaking for the time being by the statute itself and not by the vendors."[1] From the above quotation it may be

[1] Edinburgh Street Tramways Co. v. Edinburgh (Lord Provost), London Street Tramways v. London County Council, 63 L.J., Q.B., 769. In determining what constitutes the "then value" it has been held, where disagreement has arisen before arbitrators, that parliamentary costs and expenses incurred in obtaining the right to construct and work the undertaking may be included, but costs incurred when the company opposed applications for powers by rival companies cannot be allowed. Manchester Carriage & Tramways Co. v. Ashton-under-Lyne Corp., 68 J.P., 576. The entrepreneur may include engineers' fees, subject to depreciation, but the cost of raising the capital must be disallowed. Oldham, Ashton & Hyde Electric Tramway and Ashton Corp., *In re*, 90 L.J., K.B., 828; (1921) 3 K.B., 511. On the results of this rule, see Vesey Knox, "Economic effects of the Tramways Act of 1870," (1901) 11 *Economic Journal*, 493. In evidence submitted to the Royal Commission on Transport, 1930, it was contended that "faced with the possibility of purchase at a comparatively early date, a company cannot develop its undertaking as it should; that the uncertainty of the future is accentuated in consequence of the option of the local authority to exercise their right of purchase recurring every seven years; and that the provisions of the Act have had the effect of preventing the development of the systems and have militated against the modernization of rolling-stock and the adoption of improved methods by the tramway companies." The companies suggested that the

seen why the British rule of valuation is frequently compared to the "prudent investment" theory of Mr. Justice Brandeis.[1]

The theory of present value less depreciation is well expressed in Section 2 of the Electric Lighting Act of 1882, where it is stated that "the value of lands, buildings, works, materials and plant shall be deemed to be their fair market value at the time of purchase, due regard being had to the nature, then condition, . . . repair thereof, and to the circumstances that they are in such a position as to be ready for immediate working, and to the suitability of the same for the purpose of the undertaking." In actual practice, however, the results in certain cases have been hard to distinguish from the reproduction cost theory.

The advantages of the British practice with regard to valuation are at once apparent. Its principal virtue is definiteness, resulting in certainty for all parties. Although not subject to the extreme fluctuations of the "reproduction cost" theory, it does permit consideration of the changes which have occurred in the general index level. On the other hand, as regards "original cost"[2] it emphasizes depreciation and successful management. True, it imposes a great deal of power upon arbitrators and engineers, but this is to be preferred to judicial logic. The simplicity and fairness of the valuation procedure have gone a long way to keep British public utilities, and the courts, out of the political arena. Nevertheless, the system is by no means free from defects, as we shall have occasion to point out later.

tenure provisions of the Act of 1870 should be repealed, and that a period of, say, forty-two years should be given to existing undertakers to allow them to develop and modernize their systems, the local authority being given an option in the first instance to purchase the undertaking if it so desires. *Final Report*, op. cit., 100.

[1] This theory was first advocated by Mr. Justice Brandeis in the case of Southwestern Bell Telephone Co. *v*. Public Service Comm., (1923) 262 U.S. 276.

[2] For an analysis of the conflicting theories referred to, see E. C. Goddard, "The evolution of cost of reproduction as the rate base," 41 *Harvard Law Rev.*, 564 (March, 1928), and J. C. Bonbright, "The economic merits of original cost and reproduction cost," Ibid., 593.

So far a great deal of our analysis of the outlines of British public utilities has dealt with the law of the subject, both as developed by Parliament and by the courts. As a concluding consideration, it appears desirable to analyze the position of British public utilities in the framework of the central administration. True, we have already referred to some of the functions of the Ministry of Health, the Board of Trade, and the Ministry of Transport, but further explanation is necessary as a background for further discussion.

### PUBLIC UTILITY CONTROL BY WHITEHALL

Like other countries with a monarchical-parliamentary tradition, Great Britain has not looked with favor upon delegated supervision. It is a striking fact that outside of the United States so-called "independent commissions" are almost unknown. Whereas the United States has created scores of regulatory tribunals, in Great Britain the only tribunals of this nature are the Railway and Canal Commission, the Railway Rates Tribunal, the Electricity Commission, and the Traffic Commissions. In France, Germany, Switzerland, Sweden, Norway, and in certain other countries, advisory committees which assist the responsible Ministers may be found, but the independent quasi-judicial commission is conspicuous by its absence. Its lack of vogue in other countries is sufficient reason for Americans to examine the underlying assumptions of their own regulatory methods with great care, and to view the alternative devices of other leading countries with open-minded interest.

One reason for not finding a greater variety of administrative forms among the regulatory mechanisms of other countries is found in the greater extent to which municipalization and nationalization of essential economic services have occurred. For example, it is estimated that in Great Britain almost two-thirds and in Germany around three-fourths of the electric power industry is owned by public bodies. The point is that the administrative aspects of regulatory control have shrunk in importance as the administrative problem of management has gained headway.

In Great Britain during recent years there has been a definite struggle to revive the effectiveness of regulation. Realizing that non-regulation of monopoly services would not be tolerated and that greater socialization has gained numerous adherents, those with conservative inclinations have devoted unprecedented labor to effect a compromise, namely the improvement of the form and variety of regulation.

A casual analysis of the result will indicate that the independent commission has not been favored. This may not necessarily prove that the railway tribunals have been tried and are found wanting. Later analysis will attempt to throw light upon that question. But it is a fact that when new machinery was needed for the public control of radio broadcasting, the national development of electricity supply, the expansion of the Port of London, and the unification of the London transport system, an operating rather than a regulatory instrumentality, namely the Public Utility Trust, was evolved. The general features of this significant new development have already received attention. It remains to suggest the bearing of the public board development upon the general problem of administrative organization and control.

In the first place, its effect is to bring about decentralization, to remove the utility from direct governmental control. In this the public utility trust may be compared to the railway tribunals. Moreover, the responsibility for protecting the consumer's interest is imposed upon political officials who already have their immediate departments and their special work to occupy the major portion of their time. The nominal ministerial jurisdiction over the C.E.B. is exercised by the Minister of Transport, while the Postmaster-General acts in a general supervisory capacity toward the B.B.C. Theirs is an ex-officio duty.

There is no direct, continuous control. Hence both with respect to Ministerial responsibility for policy and execution, the public utility board development runs counter to the traditions of the British administrative system. This need not be taken as a condemnation of it.

The traditional theory may be stated as follows. Since the Government is responsible to Parliament, all regulation in the public interest must be performed by the head of one of the Departments of State in order that he may be made answerable to Parliament for what he does. Hence, for the most part and until recently, administrative regulation in Great Britain and on the Continent has been left to the Ministers who are concerned with industrial and commercial affairs, not to the detached tribunals or boards.

In Great Britain the departments most concerned with public utility matters are the Post Office, the Ministry of Health, the Board of Trade, and the Ministry of Transport. Only two of these, namely the Post Office and the Ministry of Transport, will appear prominently in the balance of the book. In chapters ii, iii, vi, and vii, where the railways and electricity are considered, the Ministry of Transport will be found to possess a certain degree of relationship with the railway tribunals and with the electricity authorities. In chapters iv and v the Post Office will be seen administering vital public services according to the traditional method, namely as a Department of State. Finally, in chapter viii the Postmaster-General's relation to the B.B.C. will again raise the question of ministerial supervision over public boards. The remaining chapter will deal with any general observations or conclusions which may be hazarded as a consequence of the study.

SUMMARY

In the period since the war, public utilities have assumed a position of great importance, particularly as a result of national developments in the fields of electricity, broadcasting, national transport, and telephone administration. There has been a tendency for action to outstrip policy, so rapidly have new problems of public utility organization and control arisen. Moreover, British public utilities have emerged from a *laissez-faire* industrial background, and not until recent years has the term "public utility" been applied to regulated monopolies. Parliament may grant any powers or impose any restrictions it pleases upon public service undertakings, and, unlike the United States, the courts will not attempt to modify or nullify the legislature's control. Legislative supremacy has resulted in three important differences between public utility control in Great Britain and in the United States: in the first place, the public utility concept and the category of undertakings which may be called public utilities are not as clearly defined in Great Britain as. in the United States, where the law has been developed primarily by the courts; secondly, due to the fact that greater elasticity has been possible in Great Britain, a wider variety of forms and of methods of public control over public service undertakings has resulted; finally, responsible government in Great Britain has made it traditional for Parliamentary Ministers, rather than for independent regulatory tribunals as in the United States, to exercise primary control over public utilities. American public service commissions are a "fourth department" of government, whereas the principle of responsibility in the British system has made it natural that the British railway commissions (the nearest approach to American public utility commissions) should be drawn closely to the judiciary. Regulation has shrunk relatively in importance as municipally-owned public utilities have increased in number and variety. It has been possible for municipalities to expropriate privately-owned utilities on a "prudent investment" basis, but in many cases the cost of reproducing the enterprise seems to have been paid.

The greater variety of organization and control of public utilities makes a study of British developments extremely interesting and suggestive. Three types of public service enterprise have been distinguished: the statutory company under regulatory control is illustrated by the national railways, or by the water, gas, and local transport undertakings; the British Post Office, which administers a large number of vital services, among them the telegraph and telephone systems, is in a class by itself: it is a department of the central government and one of the oldest public service undertakings in the country; the third and newest public utility development has been called the public utility trust, and great interest has been aroused in this form of large-scale enterprise by the creation of the Central Electricity Board, the British Broadcasting Corporation, the London Passenger Transport Board, the Port of London Authority, and the Metropolitan Water Board.

These developments represent the efforts of the British to adjust a strongly individualistic economic structure to the requirements of a socialized age. The most vital public issues are at stake: the choice between competition and cooperation, *laissez-faire* and planning, investors' profits and increased returns to labor and consumers, commercial management versus socialized administration. Intelligent citizens are speculating as to whether the public utility developments of recent years represent the deep trenches of vested interests or the first furrows of Social Democracy.

## CHAPTER II

# THE RAILWAY PROBLEM

## THE PRESENT POSITION OF THE RAILWAYS

The position of railways in most of the countries of the world has become a source of serious concern. Their large fixed charges cannot be adjusted to cope with the exigencies of depression, and yet their financial well-being constitutes one of the main pillars of the industrial and financial system. About sixty per cent of British railway costs consist of fixed charges which cannot be materially altered when revenue is declining. With the development of road competition an increasingly large portion of the railways' business has been lost beyond recovery. Since 1921 the railways have been going through a process of reorganization, but the reforms which have been undertaken so far are only a first step in the more complete integration that seems to be necessary.[1]

Although England pioneered the steam railway, she has probably suffered more from railway problems than any other important country, due in part no doubt to the persistence of extreme individualism and also to the fact that in the early stages of development she was not in the position to profit by others' mistakes. The regulation of British railways in the period between 1844 and 1888 not only established the principles of public utility regulation for other public service undertakings in Great Britain, but it became the model for the United States and for countries in other parts of the world. A *laissez-faire* Parliament, after much delay and many mistakes, contrived to make railway con-

[1] The best general sources of information on British railways are C. E. R. Sherrington, *Economics of Rail Transport in Great Britain*, 2 vols., London, 1928; C. D. Campbell, *British Railways in Boom and Depression*, London, 1932; Howard C. Kidd, *New Era for British Railways*, London, 1929; K. G. Fenelon, *Railway Economics*, London, 1932; and *Royal Commission on Transport, Final Report*, Cmd. 3751, 1931.

trol the principal avenue of State intervention in economic development. The fate of railway regulation and the future of public utility regulation as a whole are therefore closely connected.

When the British railways were returned to private operation after the war they were amalgamated into four main groups, and their rates were fixed at a level which was intended to yield the same net revenue as that of 1913. Standard rates have since been reconsidered annually. Although rates are now almost 60 per cent higher than in 1913, the "standard revenue" (based upon the 1913 earnings) has never been earned and dividends have fallen to little or nothing. The standard revenue, as determined by the Railway Rates Tribunal, is approximately £50,000,000 per annum; but the railway net receipts have fallen far below this figure as the following summary indicates:

*In millions*

| Year | | | £ | Year | | | £ |
|------|--|--|----|------|--|--|----|
| 1922 | .. | .. | 47 | 1928 | .. | .. | 41 |
| 1923 | .. | .. | 43 | 1929 | .. | .. | 45 |
| 1924 | .. | .. | 39 | 1930 | .. | .. | 38 |
| 1925 | .. | .. | 37 | 1931 | .. | .. | 33 |
| 1926 | .. | .. | 19 | 1932 | .. | .. | 26 |
| 1927 | .. | .. | 42 | | | | |

The result has been that reserve funds have been continually depleted during the past decade, earnings on ordinary stocks have almost disappeared, and a considerable proportion of preference capital must go without dividend. The return on ordinary stocks in 1923 was 5·55 per cent; in 1929, 3·97 per cent; in 1930, 2·23 per cent; and in 1931, 0·95 per cent.[1] In 1932 no less than £260,000,000 of railway capital went without any dividend. Under these circumstances the ability of the railways to raise new capital must inevitably become impaired, thus deferring improvements which might assist the railways to compete with road transport.

[1] Decision 164, *National Wages Board*, 97, January 1933.

A summary of the financial results for the four amalgamated companies, based upon official returns for 1923–31, will reveal recent railway tendencies:

Receipts:—

| 1913 | 1923 | 1924 | 1925 | 1926 | 1927 | 1928 | 1929 | 1930 | 1931 |
|------|------|------|------|------|------|------|------|------|------|
| 100% | 172 | 171 | 168 | 145 | 175 | 168 | 169 | 161 | 147 |

Total expenditure:—

| 100% | 216 | 218 | 216 | 200 | 219 | 211 | 208 | 204 | 188 |
|------|------|------|------|------|------|------|------|------|------|

Railway costs had risen from £84,000,000 in 1913 to £158,000,000 in 1931. Nevertheless, a decline of over £50,000,000 in railway receipts has been offset by a reduction in expenditure amounting to more than £35,500,000.

In recent reviews of standard and exceptional charges,[1] the Railway Rates Tribunal has expressed the pessimistic view that "deficiencies not necessarily as large but substantial in character are likely to continue" and that nothing appeared on review "which established that under present conditions any modification or modifications would enable the companies to earn their respective standard revenues. . . ." Nothing has transpired since that time to improve prospects; as a matter of fact they are considerably worse.

Trade revival, drastic cuts in operating costs, the restriction of road competition, a revision of standard revenue provisions based upon capital reorganization, or nationalization are possible ways out of the serious financial plight of the railways. The first three remedies seem to hold out little hope of immediate relief, but the likelihood of the respective alternatives may better be judged after a more complete analysis of the causes of the present difficulties has been afforded.

---

[1] (1930) *Proceedings of the Railway Rates Tribunal*, 137; (1931) Ibid., 128; (1932) Ibid., 255.

E

British industry has been handicapped by the unfortunate circumstances accompanying the development of the railways. The drawbacks of the railway heritage have been felt mostly in the lean post-war years, because for almost a century prior to that time the railways had been, despite their handicaps, the principal medium of commercial expansion. No railway system in the world has been weighed down by more adverse factors. American companies were granted fabulous subsidies of land and money, and could build up the vast expanses of a rapidly developing continent; British railways not only received no State aid but paid exorbitant prices for their initial fixed capital, while the distances to be traversed were short. Railway economy depends largely upon long hauls, but no point in Great Britain is more than ninety miles from a port. The geography of the country is ideal for motor superiority.

British railways are said to represent a capital investment of £1,085,000,000, but it is generally admitted that this figure is not based upon their present or prospective earning capacity. For example, Mr. A. G. Walkden, representing the Railway Clerks' Association, suggested to the National Wages Board on December 2, 1932, that "if a capital reconstruction were fairly arranged and the capital written down to £500,000,000 instead of £1,000,000,000, and a lot of dead capital were got rid of, the public would be much more ready to subscribe."[1]

If the question of expropriating British railways comes to an issue, the problem of fair value will present almost

---

[1] *Manchester Guardian*, December 3, 1932. "As regards watered capital, the nominal addition to the companies' capital rank for interest, the shares issued to cover them are of a perpetual character, and those shares do not represent any money put down by anybody whatever, but are in the nature of a bonus addition to the share capital. In the case of the London and North-Eastern Railway Company, nominal additions amount to £52,000,000...." Evidence, *Decision of National Wages Board*, 86, January 1933. The companies contended that all the watered capital has been removed. Ibid., 56.

insuperable difficulties. "It should be remembered," writes Sherrington, "that the unduly high first costs of our early railways can never be eliminated and they will always remain a permanent charge against the industrial efficiency of this country. . . ." The British railways are the most highly capitalized system per track mile in the world. The English railway capital was £54,152 per route mile in the United Kingdom, £64,453 in England and Wales, whereas the Prussian railways cost £21,000 per mile and the American less than £13,000.[1] The preliminary expenses including surveying and legal costs have been put at £4,000 per mile, and land costs ranged from £4,000 to £8,000 per mile. Land was valued for the London and Birmingham railway at £250,000, but cost three times as much. Many similar instances might be cited. The fundamental difficulty arose from the fact that the early railways were opposed by the landed gentry who were allied with the canal and turnpike interests. Due to the restricted franchise, the affairs of Parliament were almost wholly in their hands, and as a result many burdens were imposed upon the railways which are still borne today.

The existing standard revenue was computed primarily on the earnings of 1913, which was considered one of the best pre-war years. The pre-war prosperity of the railways was based largely upon the coal industry, which has suffered acutely in recent years. The total tonnage of goods traffic originating in 1930 was 17·8 per cent less than in 1913, while the decreases for general merchandise, coal, and other minerals were 22·1, 15·9, and 19·7 per cent respectively.[2] Passenger receipts have fallen in about the same ratio. At the same time, the general level of wages and salaries was 117 per cent higher in 1932 than it was before the war; the average wage of railwaymen in 1914 was only 28s. 5d.

---

[1] L. C. A. Knowles, *The Industrial and Commercial Revolutions in Great Britain during the Nineteenth Century*, 257, London, 1926.

[2] Campbell, op. cit., 63.

per week. Finally, road competition has made great inroads on rail traffic, especially since 1926. These factors will receive further attention.

Great Britain is a short-haul country, which militates against the success of the railways. Shorter hauls result in relatively greater costs. The average haul per ton is around 60 miles in Great Britain, while it is over 330 miles in the United States. This factor, combined with the other dis- advantages of British railways, results in an average charge per ton mile almost three times as great as in the United States.[1] The effects of high railway rates upon British com- merce cannot be precisely measured, but they are known to be serious. The rail charges on pig iron, for example, accounted for 25 per cent of the market price in 1914, 29 per cent in 1925, and 38 per cent in 1931. In its 1931 review of standard charges the Railway Rates Tribunal referred to industry's belief that "it is really a drastic altera- tion of the level of railway rates which is necessary if the trade of this country is to recover." Can effective regulation supply the necessary reform?

### THE PRINCIPAL STAGES OF REGULATORY CONTROL

The period of railway experimentation during which such exorbitant capital costs were incurred lasted from 1821 to 1844. At the close of this era Parliament was forced to admit that the control of railways was a necessity. Three major phases of railway regulation have occurred since 1844. During the first period, 1844–88, the railways were not effectively controlled, but by 1888 permanent regula- tory machinery, the Railway and Canal Commission, had been established. The years between 1888 and 1921 saw the growth of railway unions and the emergence of a move- ment to nationalize the railways; during the war period the railways were commandeered by the State. The current

[1] Kidd, op. cit., 47.

era dates from the Railways Act, 1921, by means of which the railways were returned to private operation, extensive amalgamations were effected, and new regulatory legislation was enacted. Since 1921 the primary responsibility for regulating railways has been fulfilled by the Railway Rates Tribunal, while the conciliation of labor questions has been entrusted to a hierarchy of tribunals.

By 1840 Parliament began to realize that through their "superior accommodation and cheapness," compared with canals and roads, the railways had "acquired command of the travelling in their district," but nevertheless there was a nervous anxiety not to interfere with private enterprise and initiative. In 1842, however, the powers of the Board of Trade were enlarged and Parliament announced that no new railways were to be opened without previous notice to the Board of Trade, which might appoint officers to inspect every new proposal. In the same year the railway interests formed the Railway Clearing House, "a sort of federal council for the English railway companies." The first railways to join it were the first ones to amalgamate. In 1844 Parliament enacted that there could be a revision of railway charges if the dividend of any railway was more than ten per cent. The Treasury was empowered to acquire by compulsory purchase, if the Government so decided, any railway built after 1844. These provisions were motivated by the canal interests, and were meant merely as a warning. They were not acted upon in any way. In the same year a commission was appointed to make preliminary reports to Parliament on railway charters, but after a year the work was discontinued.

During this period Parliament was forced to realize that the conditions of railway labor had become "shocking," and as early as 1846 a select committee recommended a principle which was the forerunner of the Workmen's Compensation doctrine. Although the management's responsibility for their employees' safety was not recognized at this time, company liability toward the travelling public was established. The railways came to be recognized, contrary to their desire, as "common carriers," and therein lay the legal foundation of later regulation.

In 1846 Parliament set up a special tribunal of five paid commissioners. Their function was to scrutinize proposed amalgamations, encourage competing schemes, and generally take over any supervisory powers of the Board of Trade. The plan proved a failure. In 1851 the commission was dissolved and the Board of Trade again assumed nominal control. Three years later undue preferences were made illegal, and the railways were ordered to provide facilities for through traffic. This period was characterized by the consolidation of short lines and the formation of trunk lines. Canal competition was ineffectual, and by 1870 Parliament had become alarmed about monopoly. The railways were sometimes forced to purchase the canals in order to get rid of the opposition they offered to projected railway bills in Parliament.

## THE RAILWAY AND CANAL COMMISSION

The inauguration of more effective control began with the creation of Railway Commissioners under the Regulation of Railways Act of 1873. This body was the forerunner of the Railway and Canal Commission. The Commissioners were originally appointed for a term of only five years, but were not superseded by the Railway and Canal Commission until 1888. The Act of 1873 provided that the Commission should consist of not less than three members, one of whom was to be a judge and one a railway expert. The Commissioners took over some of the powers of the Board of Trade and were enjoined to enforce the Act of 1854. In addition, the Commission was given special jurisdiction over railway amalgamations, the purchase of canals by railways with the purpose of stifling competition, undue preference between traders or areas, disputes between railways, and the reasonableness of through rates and terminal charges.

The deficiencies of the Commission were soon apparent. "It has power to annoy the railroads," concluded Hadley in 1886, "but not power enough to help the public efficiently." Although complaints regarding undue preference decreased, dissatisfaction with rates grew very rapidly. The Commission was helpless, because differing rates had been specified in the thousands of special Acts creating the railway companies. By 1866 railway law was contained in 1,880 Acts, modified by 1,300 amendatory Acts. Not until 1867, moreover, did Parliament order the railway companies to keep their accounts in a specified form. Railway rates were not only high, but they differed so much that merchants felt sure they were being "done" no matter what they were charged. With rates so confused, the railway tribunal found it impossible to establish reasonable through rates.

There was considerable disillusionment concerning the Commission itself. The traders, who had succeeded in getting the tribunal established, thought that it would act promptly, that it would be easy of access, and that its procedure would be informal and inexpensive. In most of these respects the proponents of the specialist tribunal were destined to be disappointed. The legal fraternity, jealous of its prerogatives, saw to it that the tribunal was styled a "court," and later experience proved that the Commission was to become affiliated closely with the personnel, the procedure, and the atmosphere of the law courts. Litigation was expensive. A complainant before the Commission was said to be "a marked man" and the court was powerless to protect him from the vengeance of the railway companies.

The historical importance of the commission idea was, nevertheless, very great. The railway board of 1873 was the first semi-administrative tribunal which England had ever established for regulatory purposes.[1] Its creation recognized the necessity of relying upon technicians in government, and it marked the State's entrance as a positive force into economic affairs. The first tendency to modify "departmentalism" and parliamentary responsibility was set in motion. Independent commissions were not destined to become numerous in Great Britain, but in the United States scores of State regulatory tribunals and the famous Interstate Commerce Commission which was established in 1887, have owed their germ idea to the example afforded by the railway tribunal of 1873.[2]

The Railway and Canal Traffic Act of 1888 corrected several of the defects of the 1873 legislation. It really ushered in the modern era of regulatory control. The Act provided for the revision of the whole system of charging, with the result that by 1893 maximum rates and revised schedules and rates had been fixed by Provisional Orders for all of the railways. This was a prodigious task, and the consequences were epoch-making. As viewed by an economic historian, Professor Knowles,

"The State had hitherto limited its activities in the control of industry to fixing hours for women and children and seeing that the wages agreed on were properly paid. It now began to fix the prices of services. It had previously fixed maximum tolls for the use of the road because it had permitted railways or canals to appropriate property under compulsion and in many cases had fixed maximum rates, but it had made no attempt to see that these tolls or charging powers were adhered to until the Railway and Canal Commission was founded. . . . When, after 1888, the State fixed maximum rates with a view to being fair to the traders, the railways, and the public, and also with a view to simplification and publicity, it repudiated *laissez-faire* and entered upon the great struggle to limit the profits of monopolies."

The most important feature of the 1888 legislation was the creation of a new Railway and Canal Commission,

[1] Parliament's reasons for favoring the commission system have been discussed by W. A. Robson, *Justice and Administrative Law*, 92–95, London, 1928.

[2] I. L. Sharfman, *The Interstate Commerce Commission*, I, 16, New York, 1931.

which was established on a permanent basis. Although the tribunal was given a more distinct judicial flavor, Parliament plainly revealed its misgivings regarding the judicial technique. Efforts were made in the Act to ensure speedy redress and a cheaper procedure outside of the Commission. Complainants were given the right to lay their cases before the Board of Trade, which would thereupon attempt to reach a friendly settlement between the parties. During the fifteen years ending 1903 some 3,126 cases had been dealt with by the Board of Trade under this section of the Act. Failing to effect a satisfactory solution, the Board of Trade transferred cases to the Railway and Canal Commission.

The judicial characteristics of the Railway and Canal Commission are striking, and the tribunal may properly be classed with the higher law courts. The Act of 1888 provided that a judge of the High Court should ex officio be a member of the tribunal, and that of the other two members sitting at any time one should possess railway experience. The Act stipulated that the Commission shall be a court of record, have an official seal which shall be officially noticed, and sit in the Royal Courts of Justice. The judicial member presides over the deliberations and dominates the procedure. The other two members appear to be, and are largely in reality, merely consultants. This result has followed largely in consequence of the stipulation in the Act that the judge's "opinion upon any question which in the opinion of the Commissioners is a question of law shall prevail." Counsel addressing the tribunal disregard lay members, and address their remarks to "My Lord." On any question of law an appeal may be made to the Court of Appeal. The Commission may issue injunctions and writs of attachment, and inflict heavy penalties for disobedience. Finally, "It shall be lawful for the Lord Chancellor, if he think fit, to remove for inability or misbehavior any appointed Commissioner."

The commercial interests, who since 1873 have favored

an informal tribunal composed of railway and business men, were effectively forestalled by the conservative legal profession, suspicious of any development that might lessen its authority.

The procedure of the Railway and Canal Commission is not as formal as that of the high courts, but it is infinitely more stilted than that of American railway tribunals. The same observations apply to the nature and admissibility of evidence. The Act provides that

"The Commissioners may from time to time, with the approval of the Lord Chancellor and the President of the Board of Trade, make, rescind, and vary general rules for their procedure and practice under this Act, and generally for carrying into effect this part of this Act."

The general rules which have been issued periodically since 1889 do not differ materially from the ordinary rules of common law procedure.

Most of the Railway and Canal Commission's jurisdiction over railways was transferred to the Railway Rates Tribunal by the Railways Act of 1921. In recent years the Railway and Canal Commission has heard on an average only two or three railway cases a year. It is not popular with the railway companies or with the traders' organizations. As a matter of fact, representatives of trade associations stated candidly to the writer that it was largely their objection to the legalism and formality of the Railway and Canal Commission, and the subordination of expert opinion, that led to the creation of the Railway Rates Tribunal.

There is now no satisfactory reason for maintaining two railway tribunals in Great Britain. The small amount of business transacted by the Railway and Canal Commission is mostly concerned with coal mines and special cases arising under the Local Government Act of 1929 and other legislation of recent years. There is general agreement among the railway and commercial interests that the entire jurisdiction over railways should be consolidated in the Railway Rates Tribunal. That such action may soon be forthcoming is evidenced by the following conclusion reached by an important House of Commons committee in 1932:

"Your Committee have considered whether the continued concurrent maintenance of both the Railway Rates Tribunal and the Railway and Canal Commission is necessary and economical. New duties have been placed on the Commission, principally in connection with mining, since the Tribunal was set up under the Railways Act. 1921, but your Committee are of opinion that the total volume of business does not warrant its continuance at a cost of approximately £7,000 a year. They recommend that the legislation necessary for a redistribution of its functions should be obtained as quickly as possible."[1]

The abolition of the Railway and Canal Commission would throw the whole weight of regulating the railways on the Railway Rates Tribunal. Before we can judge how capable it is of assuming this responsibility, we must analyze the events which led up to the Railways Act of 1921.

In the period prior to the outbreak of the war, the general condition of the railways was favorable for investors but unsatisfactory to labor. Railway costs began to increase significantly in 1909, and in 1913 the railways were granted a four per cent increase of rates. The average dividend on British railways in 1913 was 4¼ per cent. Prior to the beginning of the war further amalgamations had occurred, but over two hundred companies remained in existence. In 1911 an official inquiry into amalgamations concluded that "the era of competition between railways is passing away and it was recognized by witnesses on behalf of the traders that this could not be prevented."[2] The tendency to diminish competition led to a proposal to unify and extend the canals, but this movement did not go very far.

The campaign to nationalize the railways, on the other hand, had become a burning issue when the war broke out in 1914. The Taff Vale decision of 1906 and the railway strike of 1911 had put the unions in fighting trim. A strike was imminent when the war broke out. The strike of 1911

[1] *Second Report*, House of Commons Committee on Estimates, 1932, Par. 7.
[2] *Report on Railway Amalgamations*, 7, Cmd. 5631, 1911.

had resulted in the establishment of the largest and most comprehensive union in the country. The workers advocated the nationalization of railways and a share in their management, a position which they continue to hold to this day.

During the war the railway system was commandeered by the State. No charge was made at the time for transporting the supplies and passengers of the Government, and the actual administration of the lines remained in the same hands. The "Railway Executive Committee," consisting of General Managers, became the ruling body for the railways. The Lloyd George Government was sincerely anxious to improve the lot of railway labor. Wages were increased and the eight-hour day was established. During the war the deterioration of the lines was accelerated and of course replacements were not made. The problem of railway reconstruction presented many difficult questions. The Railway Act, 1921, attempted to supply the solution of past and of future difficulties.

### THE RAILWAYS ACT, 1921

The coordinated management of railways between 1914–21 had demonstrated that economies were possible under unified control. During the war a certain amount of reorganization was effected, such as the introduction of common user of rolling stock and the inter-availability of tickets between certain common points. There was general agreement that the railways should not be returned to private operation without preserving the benefits of coordination, standardization, and improved labor conditions. The railway managements faced the future with an uncertainty that required an overhauling of the railway system. Moreover, the American Congress had just adopted far-reaching reforms in the form of the Transportation Act of 1920; this legislation provided an example for the Railways Act of 1921, as a comparison of the two Acts will readily reveal.

The Railways Act of 1921 served three definite but related purposes: in the first place, the railways were compensated by the Government and were amalgamated into four major groups under private management; secondly, important changes were made in the responsibilities and the actual administration of the companies; finally, the provisions of law relating to rates and labor were considerably expanded, and permanent administrative machinery was created in order to carry out the new legislation. Moreover, as Sir Eric Geddes, the Minister of Transport, stated,

"The Railways Act is really a 'Traders Charter' and with the great trading organizations which exist they can afford, and will afford, the best brains and the greatest skill to enable them to take advantage of that charter. The companies can now induce the cooperation of the trader by offering lower rates whenever the trader will help them to work more cheaply."

The Act was also a charter for labor, because it firmly established the principle of collective bargaining and virtually made it impossible to return to the wage conditions of 1914. The Railways Act of 1921, stated Sir William Acworth, "recognizes that the wages and conditions of employment of the staff engaged in an essential service can no longer be regarded as a matter of private bargain—still less a matter for mere employers' dictation—and establishes a hierarchy of councils and boards culminating in a National Wages Board in which representatives of the public have the final voice."

During the war the Government took all the receipts, met all the working expenses, and made up to the companies annually the same net income as they had earned in the year 1913. In other words, the war receipts enabled the guaranteed income of railway stockholders to be paid. In consequence of the Railway Act of 1921, the Government paid the railway companies a lump sum of £60,000,000 as compensation for deficiencies in net receipts, repairs, and renewals. This settlement was certainly generous, and coupled with rate increases in 1923, the railways appeared to be in a favorable position.

Part One of the Railways Act of 1921 dealt with the reorganization of the railway system.[1] It provided for the amalgamation of the numerous independent companies into four groups "with a view to reorganization and more efficient and economical working of the railway system of Great Britain." The more important companies in each group were termed constituent companies and became the nuclei of amalgamations. The "Big Four" have been called the Southern, the Great Western, the London Midland and Scottish, and the London and North-Eastern. The stockholders and debenture holders of the constituent companies exchanged their securities for corresponding holdings in the new group. The remaining companies allotted to a group were called subsidiaries and were absorbed by the purchase of their stock. The Act provided that each group was to submit its amalgamation scheme to the Minister of Transport on or before January 1, 1923, and these were to be examined by a "Railway Amalgamation Tribunal" consisting of three commissioners. Should the companies fail to submit an agreed scheme, the tribunal was empowered to devise a compulsory solution. Only two companies had failed to reach agreement by the specified time, and hence the tribunal was dissolved in 1923. In effecting the combination only a small transfer of cash was necessary.

A railway monopoly was not created, but competition was curtailed and provision was made whereby it could be reduced still further. The significance of Parliament's action will be appreciated when it is recalled that for a century Parliament had been suspicious of railway combinations. The Act of 1921 makes unification possible, because provision was made whereby further amalgamation may take place through purchase, lease or working,

[1] 11 and 12 Geo. 5, ch. 55.

or the reduction of competition through allocation or pooling of traffic, subject to the consent of the Minister of Transport.

The Act purposely provided that each of the four groups should not have a monopoly of their respective territories. Sir William Acworth stated in 1923 that "The effect of the new statutory grouping is to leave the bulk of the territory of Great Britain non-competitive but the bulk of the traffic still competitive." This view has proved to be too sanguine, because competition has not been eliminated even to that extent. Although the four amalgamations dominate their respective areas, their lines are by no means confined to definite geographical regions, but invade each other's territory. In short, the respective groups penetrate into each other's areas both directly and indirectly by means of running powers. The grouping did not effect a geographical redistribution or consolidation of natural traffic areas because there was a desire to link up weak units with strong units. This consideration was particularly true in the case of the two northern companies which serve the great manufacturing centers of the Midlands. The disadvantages of competition in this area have already become convincing, and steps have been taken to reduce it to a minimum.

In July 1932 an agreement was reached between the L.M.S.R. and the L.N.E.R., the two northern companies, whereby about 50 per cent of their traffic receipts will be pooled for a period of fifty years.[1] The Minister of Transport appointed the members of the Railway Rates Tribunal as the committee to hear the case. During the course of the hearings witnesses representing no less than one hundred commercial and labor organizations were given an opportunity to present their respective viewpoints. The Traders' Coordinating Committee alone, a permanent organization through which business negotiates with the railways, represents over eighty commercial undertakings. Eventually only

[1] *Report of the Railway Pool Committee*, Stationery Office, 1932.

two traders' associations and the three major railway unions[1] expressed dissatisfaction with the agreement which the Committee recommended to the Minister of Transport. The pooling plan is expected to effect an annual operating saving of not less than £100,000 and perhaps considerably more.

The drawbacks of the remaining competition, and the possibility of effecting greater economy and standardization, have convinced some observers that the amalgamation of the two northern routes is the next logical step. Others favor the unification of all four companies under national administration, a proposal which we shall consider at a later point.

When the Railway Act of 1921 was passed, estimates of economies which could be effected through amalgamation ranged from £20,000,000 to £45,000,000. Everyone was convinced that amalgamation would certainly bring about considerable reductions in rates and fares. The Minister of Transport declared in 1921 that "within a very measurable time we can look forward to immense prosperity in the railway industry and to a reduction of charges to users." With railway charges 60 per cent higher than before the war, Sir Josiah Stamp estimated in 1929 that savings of £20,000,000 had been effected, but his figure included the whole of the fall in the cost of materials, for which the railways can take no credit. During 1931 the companies were able to effect savings of over £11,000,000 but about half of this sum was due to wage and salary cuts.[2]

The way in which savings have been effected and the

---

[1] The companies announced their willingness to undertake that they would not, as a result of the pooling arrangement, dismiss any of their staff included in the conciliation or salaried grades, although they reserved the right to accelerate the retiring age and to reduce employees to an inferior grade. The unions rejected the proposals because they were said to provide less protection to employees than Parliament had guaranteed under general laws. *Report,* Ibid., 23–27, 32–34.

[2] "Future of the British Railways," *Manchester Guardian Commercial,* January 7, 1933.

possibility of bringing about additional reforms may best be judged by a discussion of the broad outlines of railway management.

### THE GENERAL ADMINISTRATION OF BRITISH RAILWAYS

The question of the organization and management of the four amalgamations is closely related to the problem of reorganizing British railways. It is commonly said that the railways "must put their own houses in order" before they can justifiably complain of the burden of competition.

The railway companies of Great Britain were created by specific statutes of Parliament instead of under the Companies Acts as are most joint stock companies. The management is controlled by the stockholders, who elect the Board of Directors and the auditors.[1] The Board acts through numerous committees, such as Finance, Traffic, and Legal Matters. The minutes of each committee must be submitted to and approved by the Board of Directors. The auditors, usually two in number, are appointed by the shareholders, and act in their behalf rather than for the Board. The form in which the accounts and the balance sheet must be prepared, as in the case of the American companies, has been stipulated by Parliament.

The chief officer of the company, who is usually called the General Manager, is responsible for executing the general policies determined by the Board of Directors. In the past he was really a combined operating and commercial manager, without complete responsibility over the engineering and the finance departments. As such he was necessarily concerned with a considerable amount of operating detail, and as a result coordination and planning suffered. In recent years the General Manager's position

[1] Wood and Stamp, op. cit., ch. 7, provides the best account of general administration.

F

has been made more analogous to that of the permanent head of a Department of State. The objective of the modification is to coordinate the policy of the several departments of the service through the General Manager, although leaving most of the responsibility for technical matters with the engineering officials. This change has naturally increased the Manager's influence with the Board.

In 1927 the L.M.S.R., the largest corporation in the country, adopted a plan of organization which was patterned after American railway administration. A President (formerly General Manager) and three Vice-Presidents form an Executive Committee which is responsible to the Board. Each Vice-President controls, and acts in the capacity of director of a number of departments, divided along functional lines. The Vice-President concentrates on one of the main branches of railway work—commercial and operating, technical, or finance. There is a continuous chain of delegated responsibility down to the lowest grades.

The L.M.S.R. and the Southern have adopted a "departmental" system according to which the whole of the staff in one department, through the district and divisional officers, is responsible to the chief of that department. This is the Civil Service system. The L.N.E.R. is organized partly on a departmental and partly on a regional basis. The L.M.S. is the only system that has completely absorbed its constituent companies under a unified administration: the managements of the other three amalgamations are weakened, in the view of impartial observers, by the fact that they have simply created an administrative superstructure on top of the old company organizations.

The L.M.S.R. has created an independent officer for all staff and labor questions. The example of the establishment officer in the Civil Service was consciously followed. The other companies have a corresponding official who is attached to the office of the General Manager.

There is reliable evidence to show that administrative

reorganization and greater coordination have played some part in effecting the economies of recent years. One important instance of this is the reduction of manufacturing and repair stations. The number of these has been reduced to ten, and their productive capacity is still greater than the demand warrants. Although constant pressure is brought to bear on the railways by manufacturing interests, the railways have found it advisable to continue the manufacture of their own rolling stock and equipment. If it were possible to unify all of this work an important additional saving could undoubtedly be effected. Although a considerable amount of reorganization has occurred in some cases, a great deal more is necessary if all four amalgamations are to become completely unified and smoothly operating systems. More attention to administrative reorganization would undoubtedly produce greater efficiency.

## RAILWAY EFFICIENCY AND SERVICE

The railway systems and their operation are under the nominal supervision of the Minister of Transport.[1] The responsibility for enforcing reasonable service and adequate facilities is shared by the Railway and Canal Commission, but as has already been said the tribunal is now called upon very rarely to exercise these powers. In comparison with the Interstate Commerce Commission's active and comprehensive control over service requirements and general operating standards, the attitude of the British administration appears to be passive. The Transportation Act of 1920 virtually made the State a partner in the railway industry, and hence responsible for making suggestions and improvements; the Railways Act of 1921 placed the State more nearly in the position of an auditor or a trustee:

[1] An excellent analysis of the Ministry of Transport's powers over railways will be found in (1929) *Minutes of Evidence, Royal Commission on Transport*, I, pars. I 23–164.

generally speaking, power is not used unless something goes wrong. The nominal character of the Ministry of Transport's control over the railways is clearly revealed by the fact that there are only seven railway inspectors of the Ministry in the entire country, while in the Headquarters establishment there are only twelve employees who devote their full time to railway matters.

The responsibilities of the Minister of Transport over railway operation are very few and relate primarily to safety regulations. Various Acts provide for an inspection by the Minister prior to the opening of any new, additional, or deviation line on which passengers are to be carried. The Minister's powers in this respect are confined to giving or withholding permission for new railways or works to be brought into use and do not relate to subsequent maintenance.[1]

The inspections referred to are carried out wholly with the idea of public safety. In addition, railway companies are required to report to the Minister "all accidents causing personal injury; all derailments and collisions in which passenger trains are involved, and any other accident of a kind prescribed by the Minister," who has power to hold inquiries into the causes of such accidents. The reports of these hearings are made public, and they sometimes contain recommendations. However, the Minister has no statutory power to compel companies to carry out his advice. "We are glad to learn," stated the Royal Commission on Transport, "that in practice it seldom happens that a company declines to adopt, or at any rate to test such recommendations."

Most of the above observations also apply to the safeguarding of railway employees. In this case the Minister is empowered, and has made Rules. The scope of the power is broad, applying to any matter which the Minister considers may cause avoidable danger to persons employed on

[1] *Royal Commission on Transport, Final Report*, 18–21, Cmd. 375, 1931.

railways. Here again the machinery of enforcement has been reduced to a minimum. Not until recent years did British railways begin to install air brakes, and the transformation still has a considerable way to go. This factor not only affects safety, but it diminishes the speed of trains —a consideration which is vital to competition with road transport. The employment of private wagons, accounting for nearly half of all freight cars, has seriously retarded the installation of air brakes.

The Minister of Transport has important powers relative to standardization of equipment and rolling stock, but these powers have not been widely used. The Railways Act of 1921 provided that the Minister of Transport may require the companies gradually to standardize their equipment and to adopt schemes for cooperative working or common user of rolling stock, or other facilities, unless the railways can satisfy the Railway and Canal Commission that the capital involved would prejudice the interests of their stockholders. Moreover, any order enforcing standardization except by agreement with the companies concerned, must be referred to a committee consisting of representatives of each of the groups, together with three other persons selected from panels set up under Section 23 of the Ministry of Transport Act of 1919.

The development of standardization has been achieved almost wholly by voluntary action, but much remains to be desired. The complete interchange of freight cars, which the Interstate Commerce Commission was authorized to enforce under the Transportation Act of 1920,[1] has not been effected in Great Britain, nor is it wholly possible to do so under existing circumstances. Under the present system of private ownership of wagons, of which there are something like 700,000, a great deal of empty haulage and unnecessary waste are involved. These private wagons belong mostly to coal and colliery owners, but ownership is distri-

[1] Sharfman, op. cit., I, 235–244.

buted among at least 5,000 firms. About two-thirds of the coal traffic is conveyed in them, and the majority of the wagons have a capacity of between 10 and 12 tons, which is less than half that of the Continental coal wagons. Sir Ralph Wedgewood, General Manager of the L.N.E.R., calculated that the elimination of private wagons would result in a saving of £600,000 to £1,000,000, but the "great bulk of operating opinion is inclined to the view that the savings effected would be vastly greater."[1]

Despite these handicaps, a considerable degree of standardization and coordination has been brought about by means of the Railway Clearing House, a central organization which is controlled by a board representing the railway companies. "The Clearing House," states Fenelon, "has been of the greatest importance in facilitating proper coordination of British railway traffic and in promoting the rationalization of the railway industry." In 1850, eight years after its creation, the Clearing House was given a legal status and granted power to sue debtor companies; in 1897 it was reincorporated; and in the Railways Act of 1921 its powers were again recognized and extended. The organization, employing 2,000 persons, is divided into Secretarial, Merchandise, and Coaching Departments. The Clearing House is the neutral ground on which meetings of general managers, engineers, and other employees are held. These conferences sometimes produce standardization schemes. The primary object of the organization, however, is to facilitate the sending of through carriages and wagons from one railway system to another and to provide a method for the division of through rates among the companies concerned. Railway companies are still entitled to payment for the use of common user wagons passing over another company's line. The Clearing House administers this highly complex system by means of junction employees, and debits and credits the several companies on a monthly basis. One

[1] *The Times*, May 16, 1932.

of the advantages of unifying the railways would be the elimination of the administrative complication and the over-head cost involved in the work of the Clearing House.

The obligation of railways to afford reasonable facilities for traffic and the prohibition against undue preference were placed upon the companies by the Railway and Canal Traffic Act of 1854. Jurisdiction over this class of complaints was bestowed upon the Railway and Canal Commission in 1888. The fact that there are few cases does not necessarily prove that grounds of complaint do not exist; it may indicate instead that the present machinery of enforcement is inadequate. The principal difference between railway regulation in Great Britain and in the United States is with respect to the vastly greater control which American railway commissions exercise over service and facilities.

During the last few years a large number of branch lines and railway stations have been closed by the British com-panies. Between 1928 and 1932 some 730 miles of branch line were closed to passenger traffic. This policy will un-doubtedly be expedited as road competition increases and as the railways are able to cover larger adjoining areas by ancillary motor services. Referring to this development, the Royal Commission on Transport stated,

"We are somewhat concerned with the consequent disappearance of facilities for travelling. Speaking generally, it appears that railway companies do not require express authority to close the lines or stations; the matter is one governed for the most part by the obligation of the companies to provide 'reasonable facilities,' and persons who feel that the closing of a particular line deprives them of a 'reasonable facility' may, if they wish, take the matter before the Railway and Canal Com-mission—a proceeding which we fear would involve a certain amount of expense."

As a matter of fact, since the war only two attempts have been made to challenge the railways' right to close lines, and both failed. In the more recent case, decided in 1931, the Railway and Canal Commission stated that it would be unreasonable to demand that a railway company "should provide some particular service for which there was so little demand that it could only provide it at a dead loss; the company is entitled to carry on its own business in its own way, but if it chooses to carry on a certain traffic, this court has jurisdiction to see that reasonable facilities are granted in respect of that traffic."[1] The expense of bringing an objection, and the well-known solicitude of the tribunal for the financial difficulties of the railways, are probably the principal reasons that more cases involving facilities are not taken to the Railway and Canal Commission. In the United States no branch line can be closed without the permission, preceded by an investigation, of the Interstate Commerce Commission.

Few administrative regulations regarding railway passenger facilities have been adopted in Great Britain, and as a result crowding on suburban and short-distance railway trains has become a common complaint. The Royal Commission on Transport heard many such objections and came to the conclusion that

"A railway company is apparently under no obligation to find a seat for a particular passenger on a particular train, and, therefore, it is more or less a matter of chance whether that passenger travels sitting or standing. . . . We do not suggest that railway companies should be placed under a statutory obligation to find a seat for each passenger desiring to travel by a particular train, but we do recommend that they should be placed under a statutory obligation to provide a seat for each passenger who joins a main-line train at its starting point. With regard to passengers joining a train at other stations on the route, we think that the companies should make greater efforts to find this accommodation, the lack of which causes much discomfort."

With reference to the general facilities and efficiency of the railways, other than those matters which have been mentioned, the Royal Commission on Transport brought

[1] Winsford Urban District Council v. Cheshire Lines Committee, decided July 23, 1931 (unreported), following the leading case of Darlaston Local Board v. London and North-Western Railway Co., (1894) 8 *Railway and Canal Traffic Cases*, 216.

out many interesting facts, of which the high-lights may be summarized as follows:

"it cannot be denied that in the days of their monopoly (i.e. prior to road competition) the railways had in some ways insufficiently studied the needs of the public, and that their policy had become unduly conservative; it is in the short and moderate distance journeys that the railways have lost passenger traffic by failing to make full use of their capacity for speed. It is remarkable that there has been practically no improvement in locomotive speed in this country during the last eighty years; the average load for general merchandise is only 2·94 tons, a factor which greatly increases costs; finally, it is not yet possible to give a considered opinion as to what extent, or in what directions, amalgamations have affected the railway companies, either in the matter of economics or in that of services."

"The truth of the doctrine," stated the Commission, "that facilities create traffic appears to have been forgotten." However, the railways were congratulated on the following improvements: the use of containers to avoid unnecessary handling of fragile goods; the electrification of a large proportion of its lines by the Southern; the development of rail motors; and, if it is not carried too far, the extension of ancillary lorry services.

The railways have, in varying degree, considerably improved their public relations technique during late years. The L.M.S.R. has been outstanding in this respect. Keen competition from the roads is indirectly responsible for the new policy of the railways, which aims at anticipating the wants and pleasures of the travelling public. This is an important gain, and in any future reconstruction safeguards should be taken to preserve this attitude.

SUMMARY

The British railways have suffered severely as a result of years of depression. Their financial position has gone from bad to worse. In 1932 the railways earned only slightly over half of their standard revenue requirements. Although the railway system has been improved by reorganizations which commenced in 1921, railway transport has received a severe setback as the result of road competition, which has become very acute since 1926. Moreover, the modern railway system inherited the weaknesses of exorbitant first costs and the confusion of organization which marked the maze of companies in existence before the amalgamations of 1921. The new alignment into four great units has not completely settled down; the process of reorganization has not been concluded. Unification may be the necessary next step.

Parliamentary policy relative to railways has been strongly *laissez-faire* or else suspiciously restrictive. A more positive attitude has commenced to appear since 1921. However, the Railway and Canal Commission, which was established in 1888, has exercised very little control over railway service and efficiency, and its influence is very small today. The Ministry of Transport's relation to the railways is one of nominal control—its powers are kept in reserve. Railway regulation has been "timid" and negative. In the days of their prosperity a passive policy on the part of the State did not matter much, but, faced by problems like those of the present, the railways require a definite policy vigorously pursued.

## CHAPTER III

# THE FUTURE OF RAIL TRANSPORT

## THE RAILWAY RATES TRIBUNAL

The regulation of railways in Great Britain must be judged, in the last analysis, by the work performed by the Railway Rates Tribunal. The control exercised by the Ministry of Transport is, for the most part, either delegated or limited in scope.[1] The Railway and Canal Commission, with jurisdiction over general questions of service, is rarely appealed to, and has no authority to make investigations and regulations on its own responsibility. The National Wages Board is concerned solely with the labor conditions of railway employees. The Railway Rates Tribunal, by means of its periodic review of standard revenue and rates, possesses a continuous responsibility for the financial health of the railways. Then, too, the Railway Rates Tribunal is the principal agency through which there is hope of obtaining more favorable rates. Parliament's confidence in the tribunal is indicated by the provision in the London Passenger Transport Bill which gives the Railway Rates Tribunal authority over the charges and revenues of one of the world's largest transport combines.

We must attempt to see whether the Railway Rates Tribunal is free from the defects which turned the business community away from the Railway and Canal Commission. Has the Railway Rates Tribunal been able to satisfy the railways, the traders, and the consumers? Is effective regu-

[1] "A right to enforce common standards may be valuable in the last resort. In practice, however, in matters relating to the commercial and technical side of railway operation and development, we tend to keep such powers as the State possesses in reserve for matters of national scope and importance and to refrain from the detailed and constant intervention in management. . . ." Sir Cyril Hurcomb, permanent Secretary to the Ministry of Transport, "The new transport and its administrative problems," (1931) 9 *Pub. Admin.*, 197.

lation even possible when service, rates, and labor costs are under the control of separate administrative bodies? These are simply the general questions which an examination of the Railway Rates Tribunal is bound to raise. In addition, we shall be interested in the specialist, as compared with the judicial characteristics of the Tribunal; in its speed, costs, and procedure; and in the general results and conclusiveness of its determinations.

The Railway Rates Tribunal consists of three permanent members, one of whom must be a business man, one a railway expert, and the third, the President, a lawyer. They are jointly selected by the Lord Chancellor, the President of the Board of Trade, and the Minister of Transport, but in actual practice the last named is principally instrumental in making the choice. Before appointments are made it has been customary for the Minister to consult the principal interests concerned. Of the present members, the railway representative was formerly a Vice-President of the L.M.S.R., the trading representative was connected with the iron and steel industry, and the President was a lawyer for the railways and appeared frequently before the Railway Rates Tribunal. Despite the President's intimate association with the railway interests, the traders' organizations unanimously endorsed the appointment because of his expert knowledge of the railway industry and his independence of mind. However, in several instances the view was expressed to the writer that the precedent established was somewhat unfortunate, inasmuch as the success of interest representation in adjudication depends primarily upon the chairman's complete freedom from partisan predilection. After their experience with the Railway and Canal Commission, however, the trading interests unhesitatingly prefer an expert, whose past experience has been as a special advocate, to a lawyer whose general practice has trained him to excel in the technicalities of law and procedure but not in railway economics.

Provision has been made to add to the membership of the Tribunal for the hearing of particular cases whenever the Minister of Transport or the interests affected desire it. Two panels have been set up, one consisting of representatives of trading, labor, passenger and agricultural interests, and the other of representatives of the railway interests. So far this means of increasing the representative character of the Tribunal has never been used.

Although the Act refers to the Tribunal as a court, the commission bears less resemblance to the judiciary than does the Railway and Canal Commission. The room in which the Rates Tribunal convenes is part of a temporary structure and hence the surroundings are informal. The white wig of the judge is conspicuous by its absence. The customary salutation to members is "Sir" instead of "My Lord." The two railway and trading members ask questions of witnesses and of counsel as freely as does the President, the legal expert. The observer gets the impression that all three commissioners consider themselves equal in status and hence they confer frequently and freely. The atmosphere is refreshingly informal, and technical objections and disputes regarding evidence are not tolerated.

Proceedings before the Railway Rates Tribunal are usually brief. A representative of an important trade association told the writer that in his twelve years' experience he can recall only half a dozen cases that have been strenuously contested by prolonged arguments. A study of the decided cases corroborates this observation. Outside of its annual review of standard revenue and rates, most of the Tribunal's time is devoted to the formal approval of agreements which have been made outside the court. This statement requires an explanation. In the first place, most applications are made by the railways, who make monthly applications for the approval of exceptional rates in order to meet motor competition. The receipts from exceptional rates now account for almost 80 per cent of railway revenue. About 90 per cent of the total rates granted are within the discretion of the companies to alter, subject merely to reporting them. In 1928 the railway companies were adding to their exceptional rates by about two thousand to three thousand a week. Frequently the railways have been induced to apply for lower rates by the Traders' Coordinating Committee, which bargains with the railways for the principal commercial interests. Other trade associations, such as the Federation of Iron and Steel Manufacturers, carry on their negotiations directly with the Railway Companies' Association, the legal, public relations, and lobbying agency of the railways. Agreement is usually reached by this means. Occasionally, complaints are made to the Minister of Transport or to the Board of Trade, in which case applications are sent directly to the Railway Rates Tribunal. But it should be noted that the private negotiations of interest groups constitute by far the larger part of rate determination.

The vital part of the Tribunal's work is to see that agreements which have been reached outside are consonant with the principles and standards which have been laid down in the statutes or in the past decisions of the Tribunal itself. Administrative standards, like rules of law, tend to become fixed. But administrative adjudications produce more "new" cases than do most fields of law, because the exercise of discretion and the making of new law by means of administrative standards becomes a necessary and recognized part of the process.[1] Frequently the duty of the

[1] A few cases will illustrate the point. It was held by the Court of Appeal, affirming the decision of the Rates Tribunal, that the ordering of interrogatories by the Rates Tribunal is discretionary, since the Tribunal is not bound by the practice of the High Court, and "the Court of Appeal will not interfere with their discretion except when it is shown that there were no grounds on which it could have been exercised." Lord Mayor of Bristol v. Great Western Railway Co., (1931) 20 *Railway and Canal Cases*, 28. A principle which the Railway Rates Tribunal has developed is this: "A rate is not necessarily excessive because a railway company is not handing back on balance to the

Tribunal is to establish a standard that will result in equality of treatment between parties and regions.[1]

Proceedings are brief because most of the Tribunal's work consists of an examination of very complete written applications, evidence, and pleadings. This material must be presented to the commission well in advance of the actual hearing. The really important work of the commission is performed at this stage.

In the hearing of cases the members of the Tribunal frequently interpose. Speeches by counsel are discouraged and seem out of place. The principal part of the public hearing consists of question and answer between the members of the railway court and the person or persons who are conducting the case. The Act of 1921 gave the commission power to make its own rules,[2] a fact that unquestionably accounts for the dispatch and informality of the procedure. For example, the Rules provide that "No proceedings before the court shall be defeated by any formal objection."

---

traders all the savings that they are making in reduced expenses."·M. and South Wales Coal Owners' Association *v.* Great Western Railway Co., (1925) 18 Ibid., 1; Manuf. Confectioners' Alliance *v.* Caledonian Railway Co., (1923) 17 Ibid., 135. The discretion of the Tribunal relative to classification is not a matter of law and will not be disturbed, it was held, on appeal, in Railway Standard Charges on Coal, Etc., (1928) 19 Ibid., 163.

[1] Compare the following cases. "The fact that equal rates were formerly charged from two competing points to a common market unequally distant from them, whereas the corresponding standard charges are unequal, is not a ground on which the Railway Rates Tribunal will grant a new exceptional rate so as to restore the equality." Dowlow Lime and Stone Co. *v.* L.M.S.R., (1931) 20 *Railway and Canal Cases*, 41. On the other hand, "it was not intended by the Railways Act, 1921, to establish the principle of equal mileage rates for all places, and the consequent adoption of exceptional rates based on competition by water or road as the standard for all rates, whether such competition exists or not, and therefore the existence of a low exceptional rate (not being in fact an undue preference), while in fact to be considered, is not alone a sufficient ground for ordering the reduction of a rate for goods in competition with those having the benefit of the low rates." Port of Manchester Warehouses Ltd. *v.* Cheshire Lines Committee, (1923) 17 Ibid., 95. This policy has undoubtedly caused the extension of road competition. A claim for allowance on the ground of inequality of service was denied in the case of Good & Sons Ltd. *v.* L.N.E.R., (1928) 19 Ibid., 191.

[2] Railway Rates Tribunal, Statutory Rules and Orders, No. 906, 1922.

It is not surprising that Mr. Justice Scrutton, on an appeal from the Railway Rates Tribunal, stated:

"The first thing it is necessary to understand is the position of the Railway Rates Tribunal. Fortunately for themselves, they are not bound by any rules in either the White or Red Book, on which I congratulate them. They have power given to them by statute to make certain rules of their own, and the rule they have made is this. 'Where not inconsistent with these Rules the general principles of practice or any particular practice of the Superior Court may be adopted and applied at the discretion of the court to proceedings before them.' That leaves the Railway Rates Tribunal an extremely free hand in a subject-matter with which they are very familiar, and in my view this court should not interfere with the discretion of the Railway Rates Tribunal unless there are no materials on which that discretion could be exercised."[1]

The cost of taking cases to the Rates Tribunal is moderate, and all charges are definitely stipulated in the Rules. For example, the daily charge for a hearing is only £2 for ordinary cases and £5 5s. od. for disputes between railway companies. Costs are not assessed against one party only, unless in the court's view the case is "frivolous and vexatious." The employment of special counsel is unusual, because most arguments are conducted by the full-time employees of the respective companies or associations, as a part of their manifold duties. Every interest may be effectively and cheaply represented except the small merchant who is outside a trade association, and the unorganized body of consumers.

A high degree of finality attaches to the judgments of the Railway Rates Tribunal. There has been only one reversal out of a half-dozen appeals since the court was created.[2]

[1] Lord Mayor of Bristol v. Great Western Railway Co., (1931) 20 *Railway and Canal Traffic Cases*, 35, 36.

[2] This case was of considerable importance because it involved the expenses and earnings of the ancillary services of the railway companies and the treatment they should be given by the Rates Tribunal in arriving at the total standard revenue of the railway companies. The Tribunal had supported the railways' contention that all receipts and expenses in respect of railways, sidings, and warehouses within the area of railway-owned docks were to be treated as "railway" receipts and expenses. The Court of Appeal, reversing the Tribunal, held that as a matter of "law" the line of demarcation between railway and dock accounts must be drawn so as to include under dock admin-

The decision may be reached by a majority of all members present, including those selected from the panels; but there has been no case in which there was not unanimity, although occasionally reservations have been expressed. The Rules (par. 53) of the Tribunal provide that:

"No appeal will lie from the court upon a question of fact, or upon any question regarding the *locus standi* of an applicant or the right of audience. An appeal will lie from the court to a Superior Court of Appeal upon a question of law. . . . The decision of the Superior Court of Appeal will be final; provided that where there has been a difference of opinion between the Superior Courts of Appeal, the Superior Court of Appeal in which a matter affected by such difference of opinion is pending may give leave to appeal to the House of Lords on such terms as to costs as such court shall determine. Save as above stated, an order or proceeding of the court is not to be questioned or reviewed, or to be restrained or removed by prohibition, injunction, certiorari or otherwise, either at the instance of the Crown or otherwise."

The Rules also provide (par. 49) that the Tribunal may review, rescind, or alter its own decision or order in case of surprise, submission of further evidence, some substantial wrong or miscarriage, or mistake or inadvertence.

The Railway Rates Tribunal, like the best regulatory commissions in the United States, is "a model for judicial reform." But there are definite limits to what the Tribunal can accomplish. Its jurisdiction is not as broad and its discretion is not as great as that of American railway commissions.

The jurisdiction of the Railway Rates Tribunal is concerned primarily with the classification and standardization of rates, but the Tribunal also took over other powers which formerly belonged to the Railway and Canal Commission. For instance, the Tribunal may determine "The reasonableness or otherwise of any conditions as to packing of articles specially liable to damage in transit or liable to cause damage to other merchandise." Further powers relative to service

istration all the different operations which, under statutory provisions, go to make up the business of a dock undertaking. Manchester Ship Canal *v.* Amalgamated Railway Companies, (1928) 19 *Railway and Canal Traffic Cases*, 74.

and public convenience were provided in the Railways (Road Transport) Act of 1928 and the Local Government Act of 1929. It is to be hoped that these provisions may be the entering wedge which will result in Parliament's transferring the remaining railway powers of the Railway and Canal Commission to the Railway Rates Tribunal.

The technicalities of the rate structure will not be dealt with here, but they have been amply discussed by other writers.[1] However, we cannot form a sound estimate of rate regulation without reference to the Tribunal's most important function, the annual review of standard revenue and rates.[2]

The Railway Rates Tribunal began the annual review of standard revenues in 1928. It will be recalled that the Act of 1921 provided that the Railway Rates Tribunal should establish such rates as would, together with other sources of income, guarantee each railway the same net revenue as it earned in 1913, the standard year. Whether this provision was wise or its accomplishment possible may

[1] Fenelon, op. cit., ch. ix; Sherrington, op. cit., II, 62–120. The following account gives the most important information. "A new classification of merchandise has been made containing twenty-one classes (excluding coal, coke, and patent fuel) instead of the eight classes contained in the old classification. New charges—known as 'standard charges'—were approved by the Tribunal in relation to the new classification, and railways were placed under an obligation to charge these standard charges without variation either upwards or downwards 'unless by way of an exceptional rate or an exceptional fare continued, granted, or fixed under the provisions of this Part of the Act or in respect of competitive traffic in accordance therewith.' This last provision is, of course, of great importance, since flexibility of charging powers is essential for the proper and satisfactory working of a railway. Substantially, a company may quote exceptional rates in respect of the carriage of merchandise provided those rates are not less than five per cent nor more than forty per cent below the standard rate. If a company wish to quote exceptional rates outside these margins, the consent of the Tribunal must first be obtained. Considerably greater latitude has been given to the companies in the matter of fares charged for passengers, and a company may now charge fares below the standard fares in such circumstances as they may think fit. All exceptional rates charged below the ordinary fares must, however, be reported to the Minister of Transport, who, in certain circumstances, may refer the matter to the Tribunal." (1931) *Final Report, Royal Commission on Transport*, 25.

[2] (1929) *Proceedings of the Railway Rates Tribunal*, 222; (1930) Ibid., 137; (1931) Ibid., 126; (1932) Ibid., 253.

well be doubted, but in any case the rate base was made definite. With reference to the Tribunal's responsibility for fixing the standard revenue William A. Robson has written,

"Here was a truly Herculean task. The mere discovery of the standard net revenue of 1913 took the Tribunal many months of hard work to ascertain: much cerebral activity on the part of the companies and their legal and financial advisers was directed toward getting the figure fixed as high as possible; and on the part of the consumers of transport services towards keeping it as low as possible."

In the period following the Railways Act of 1921 trade experienced a short-lived boom, which undoubtedly affected the amount of standard revenue the commercial interests were willing to countenance. Moroever, the trading community was convinced that substantial rate reductions would be forthcoming and hence did not seriously question the basic assumptions underlying the standard revenue of approximately £50,000,000.

The exact provisions of the Railways Act of 1921 relating to standard revenue are of such vital importance that they should be fully explained. The Act (Sect. 58) stipulated that charges for each amalgamation should be fixed so that together with other sources of revenue they would yield an annual net revenue equivalent to the aggregate net revenues of the constituent and subsidiary companies in 1913, together with (a) a sum equal to five per cent on the capital expenditure, which formed the basis on which interest was allowed at the end of the period during which the railways were in the possession of the Government; and (b) an allowance for additional capital expended so as to enhance the value of the undertaking since January 1, 1913, and not included above; and (c) a reasonable allowance in respect of capital expenditure [not less than £25,000 in each case and not included in (a)] on works enhancing the value of the undertaking, but which had not become fully remunerative in 1913; and (d) an allowance up to 33⅓ per cent of any economies that might be effected through amalgamation. The

Act further provided that the Tribunal might, on any subsequent review, raise or lower the allowance for "the revenue which would be produced by any such business" in the case of ancillary services over which the Tribunal has not been given jurisdiction.[1] Finally, if in any year there should be a surplus over the standard revenue 80 per cent of this is to go to the reduction of charges and 20 per cent may be retained by the company. The Rates Tribunal was instructed to review the rates, exceptional and standard, at the end of each successive year.

With reference to the method followed in the annual review, the Railway Rates Tribunal has stated, "It has been our task to follow the development of the companies' case and see that their methods are correct; to test the results of the companies' calculations and listen to all objections." Under the existing circumstances, no other course is open to the Tribunal. Unlike American commissions, the Rates Tribunal has no staff of examiners, engineers, and financial experts in its own employ. The Tribunal may call upon the Ministry of Transport for certain information, but it has had occasion to do so only in the case of the annual review of standard charges.[2] In addition, the Minister of Transport may send a representative to appear in any case that is being heard by the Rates Tribunal. But it should be made

[1] The railways have invested in steamers, docks, canals, electric power stations, hotels, and road services, a capital sum of approximately £110,000,000, (1931) *Official Railway Returns*, 10. In case the Tribunal decides that the profits of these ancillary services have not been sufficient, the only course open is to reduce the amount the railway lines will be permitted to earn.

[2] Practically all of the data are obtained from statistical reports which are furnished by the railway companies. "The Ministry of Transport Act, 1919," states Sir Cyril Hurcomb, "enabled the Minister to obtain a wide range of returns and statistics from the railway companies; and these powers were fully exercised and were made permanent by the Railways Act, 1921. As a result, the Rates Tribunal has constantly before it a broad picture of the operating efficiency of the railway companies so far as that can be supplied by comparative statistics. There is, of course, a risk that statistical computations may become stereotyped and cease to stimulate thought; they need, therefore, to be looked at afresh from time to time." Hurcomb, op. cit., (1931) 9 *Pub. Admin.*, 196.

clear that the Tribunal is not an appendage of the Ministry; the two are distinct and independent. No confidential information is supplied by the Ministry; every report is made available to all interested parties. In other words, the Railway Rates Tribunal is not an investigative, originating body; it must be sought, and in reaching conclusions it depends upon sources of information not its own. The expert judges supposedly possess sufficient knowledge and experience to reach a salutary judgment on the basis of the evidence presented.

Although the Railway Rates Tribunal deserves commendation, several circumstances conspire to make important aspects of railway regulation in Great Britain generally impracticable and ineffectual. It appears to the writer, as it has to many others, that the railways have a dubious right to earn the present standard revenue even if it were possible for them to do so. The following objections to the standard revenue provisions appear on candid examination:

(1) A large part of the capital investment existing in 1913, quite irrespective of exorbitant first costs, is irreconcilable with the competitive value of rail transport today. It is socially unjustifiable to maintain railway capitalization arbitrarily. The turnpikes and the canals were not permitted to burden the national development by artificially protecting investments in them.

(2) The year 1913 was one of the best pre-war years for the railways, and it is out of harmony with prevailing or prospective conditions.

(3) When obsolescence has occurred, for example when stations or branch lines have been closed, the nominal value of the railways has not always been diminished although there is every reason why this should be done.

(4) The railway companies have invested £10,000,000 or more in road transport, and as the Royal Commission on Transport stated, they are feverishly extending their investments on motor services; the railways are permitted to increase their capital and their revenue by this means, although the companies themselves loudly insist that road competition is destroying the earning power of the railways.

So long as the railways are earning only what the traffic will bear, it may be asked, is not the question of standard revenue unimportant or at least untimely? A thorough reconsideration of standard revenue requirements is necessary for at least three important reasons. The presumption regarding standard revenue requirements has an important bearing on those basic (heavy) industries which have no alternative means of transport and hence must pay higher rates as gross traffic falls:[1] the existing standard revenue is used as the principal argument in attempts to reduce railway wages; and it largely underlies the effort to check road competition.

Assuming that railway problems may still be solved by more effective regulation (an extremely doubtful assumption), the following reforms are suggested:

(1) The valuation of the railways on the basis of their earning capacity. (A rough approximation is all that would be possible.)
(2) The effective regulation by the Rates Tribunal of ancillary services owned and operated by the railway companies, where such jurisdiction would not conflict with other regulatory authorities.
(3) The transference of the remaining railway powers of the Railway and Canal Commission to the Railway Rates Tribunal, thereby unifying the control over service and rates.
(4) A grant of power to the Railway Rates Tribunal whereby it may conduct field investigations on its own initiative.

Whether or not it would be wise or expedient to give the Tribunal jurisdiction over railway wages (because they are a vital element of costs) raises a question which cannot be answered without further consideration.

### THE POSITION OF RAILWAY UNIONS

Until the end of the nineteenth century railway unions played only a small part in the general trade union movement, but once they were thoroughly organized the unions became exceedingly powerful and today their bargaining power is not excelled. The railway companies employ

[1] The railway companies have secured an increase of 41 per cent in gross receipts over 1913 for carrying less than three-quarters of the 1913 tonnage.

approximately 575,000 persons whose wages and salaries amount to £100,000,000 a year, which, allowing for the change in the cost of living, means that the average pay is about 50 per cent higher than before the war. Although the railway managements have made strenuous efforts to reduce the wages bill, reductions of only £4,430,000 have been obtained since 1919. In 1932 the railways attempted to secure a 10 per cent wage cut, but their effort failed. As a result of the National Wages Board's decision in January 1933, one thing appears clear: there will not be a return to 1913 wage standards. The independent Chairman of the National Wages Board found that

"The wages of railway servants were at the beginning of the war unduly low; the new (1919–20) standards of pay were intended to remedy this position and were related to the skill necessary for and the responsibility of the work; the new standard salaries and rates of pay were agreed as permanent standards."[1]

The victory of railway labor is attributable to the aggressive leadership of the three powerful unions, the National Union of Railwaymen, the Associated Society of Locomotive Engineers and Firemen, and the Railway Clerks' Association with respective memberships of 450,000, 11,000, and 85,000. The strong position the railwaymen occupy today is largely explained by agreements which were made during the war.

The new charter for railway labor was secured in 1919 and 1920 largely as the result of a strike in which the Government intervened as mediator. Prior to that time the progress of the unions had been slow. Although the first railway union was formed in 1865, the companies did not officially recognize trade unions until 1907. By that time the unions had become so large that the companies were forced to establish a conciliation system and to meet certain demands of the employees. However, a nation-wide strike occurred in 1911 and another was imminent when the war broke out.

[1] Decision 164, *National Wages Board*, 99. January 1933.

Between 1913 and 1920 the average weekly wage for all grades increased from less than 30s. to 85s. This increase took the form of an actual hourly rate advance, a reduction in hours by the inauguration of the eight-hour day, and the standardization of working conditions among employees. In 1919 a complete arbitration system was established, and in 1920 standards of employment were definitely set up and accepted, forming the basis of present-day agreements.[1]

The machinery of negotiation was recognized and enlarged by the Railways Act of 1921. Provision was made in Part IV of the Act for the establishment of conciliation boards similar to the Whitley Councils which were set up in other industries and in the Civil Service. The hierarchy of railway conciliation consists of local Departmental Committees, Sectional Councils, Railway Councils, the Central Wages Board, and the National Wages Board. The several boards, including the National Wages Board, are not bound to reach legally binding decisions, but with one or two exceptions compromise decisions have been possible. In recent months relations have become considerably more strained, however, and it appears that the system as a whole will not continue to work satisfactorily.

The Local Departmental Committees consist of four representatives of each side, and they exist in all stations and depots where the number of regular employees exceeds 75. The local committees deal with all questions affecting conditions of employment and they give the employees a wider interest in and knowledge of the administration. In case of disagreement, matters are referred to the Sectional Councils, which represent various groups of grades. Here again the companies and the workers are equally represented and the employees' representatives are elected by the

[1] The principal items in the agreement were a fixed schedule of wages, a guaranteed day and a guaranteed week of 48 hours, overtime for night and Sunday duty, and provision for rest periods and holiday observance. Wood and Stamp, *Railways*, ch. vii; Fenelon, *Railway Economics*, ch. v. For alterations of standard agreements which took effect in 1931, see Fenelon, Ibid., 76, 77.

unions. The Sectional Councils are concerned with the local application of national agreements and with broad questions affecting labor conditions. The final court of appeal in the framework of each of the four railways is the Railway Council, consisting of ten representatives from each side. The Railway Council deals with submissions from the Sectional Councils and with general questions affecting the system as a whole.

The Central Wages Board and the National Wages Board are the upper rungs of the conciliation hierarchy. These two bodies, which have been in operation since 1921, will probably be superseded by new conciliation machinery in 1934. The Central Wages Board consists of eight representatives of the companies and eight representatives of the trade unions, four of whom are selected by the National Union of Railwaymen and two each by the two smaller unions. The Board may consider questions relating to rates of pay, hours of duty, and other conditions of employment. In case of disagreement either side may refer the matter to the National Wages Board, the apex of the conciliation hierarchy.

The membership of the National Wages Board is drawn from wider sources, and an independent Chairman is appointed by the Minister of Labor; but, like the subordinate tribunals, the Board is not under legal compulsion to reach a binding decision. Agreement between the companies and the unions is the slender reed upon which the success of the plan depends. The Board, in addition to the appointive Chairman, is composed of six representatives of the railway companies, six representatives of the unions, and four representatives of railway users, two of whom have labor sympathies. The four interest groups designated are the Trades Union Congress, the Cooperative Union, the Association of British Chambers of Commerce, and the Federation of British Industries.

The success of the plan depends upon compromise. The

Board has heard 164 cases and only one of them, the latest, has led to a complete impasse. This situation arose out of a claim by the railway companies in December 1932, that the pay of 420,000 employees should be reduced 10 per cent, thereby effecting a saving to the companies amounting to £5,000,000 a year. The minimum wage for adult workers would have been reduced from 40s. to 38s. a week. In March 1931 the employees had accepted a decision of the National Wages Board which provided for a tentative cut of 2½ per cent on all salaries within the "conciliation" grades, i.e. all employees except shopmen and railway police. Out of a total of 575,000 employees, 420,000 are subject to the conciliation machinery under discussion. The application for the substitute 10 per cent reduction was more ably and hotly contested than any case which has ever been brought before the Board. The Chairman recommended a compromise reduction of 4⅛ per cent; the representatives of the railway companies clung to their original application in their written conclusion, but afterwards indicated their willingness to accept the Chairman's suggestion; the representatives of railway labor claimed a complete victory, and served notice that the Chairman's recommendation left matters just as they were before the hearing; while the four representatives of railway users divided evenly between the employers' and the employees' positions.[1]

After the decision most observers prophesied that the 1921 conciliation machinery would break down. This verdict seems to be borne out by the fact that on March 3, 1933, the railway companies served formal notice of their decision to withdraw from the National Wages Board and the Central Wages Board. In accordance with the 1921 legislation, twelve months must elapse before the notice of withdrawal takes effect. The companies made it clear that the existing machinery for local and sectional conciliation will not be affected. In the meantime wage conditions will probably

[1] Decision 164, *National Wages Board*, 106–119.

remain unaltered, and attempts are being made to prepare a new scheme that will be acceptable to both sides.

During the hearings it clearly appeared that railway labor is not prepared to make further wage concessions. Their representatives advocated a drastic reorganization of railway capitalization and finance, followed by nationalization. Failing in their effort to reduce railway wages, the companies have turned with increased vigor to the attack upon road competition.

## ROAD COMPETITION

Apart from the unsatisfactory condition of the nation's trade, the rapid development of road competition since the war has clearly been the chief cause of the railways' recent plight. These two causes of railway distress are by no means the only ones: the effect of the internal weaknesses of the railways and the paralyzing result of tariff policies also deserve, but rarely receive, prominent consideration. Again, one cannot accurately measure the proportion of diminished railway receipts that is accounted for by the diversion of passenger and freight traffic to road haulers. Certain observations may be made with assurance, however, and fairly reliable deductions may be drawn therefrom.

Between 1923 and 1930 the number of motor passenger vehicles, private and public, more than doubled and motor goods vehicles increased from 173,363 to 334,237. In no country in the world is the number of cars so great in relation to area. During the general strike of 1926 scores of passenger and freight lines appeared on the roads, and a large proportion of the traffic which was diverted from the railways at that time has never been recovered. In distances of less than 50 miles motor companies have clearly established their supremacy, and the closing of railway branch lines is clear evidence of this fact. Due to the speed, economy, frequency, elasticity, and comfort of motor transport over the shorter distances, it would appear that the railways have permanently lost this important source of revenue. Moreover, it has been demonstrated that motor vehicles can compete successfully over longer distances, especially if national highway construction is furthered. Finally, the railways are bound to haul all classes of goods submitted to them, while the road haulage companies can skim off the most remunerative part of the available traffic. It is not surprising that railway stockholders should conclude that competition must be eradicated and that the national economy demands the coordination of road and rail.

If transport by road should prove generally superior to transport by rail, why interfere with the eventual collapse of the railway structure? In the view of a business observer,

"The railways must be saved from collapse in the interests of the public, not in the interests of the stockholders, who took their own risks in making their investments. They must be saved because (1) Transport by rail is far the best form of transport for large classes of goods, and almost invariably the best for long-distance traffic; (2) Transport by rail gives employment to at least two million people, taking into account railwaymen and their dependents; (3) The railway companies have the inestimable advantage of large and unimpeded arteries of communication running right into the centers of our large cities. In short, the public utility of railways is far from exhausted, and no alternative means of transport now in sight seems likely to make the railways useless."[1]

But it is one thing to say that the railways should be saved, and quite another thing to determine the conditions of their convalescence. The struggle between the rail and the road interests has caused more lobbying and propaganda than any clash between interest groups since the railways fought the canals and the turnpikes. A former Parliamentary Secretary to the Ministry of Transport recently wrote, "For some years past the question of Road v. Rail has been boiling up to such a pitch that if you mention the subject today you will find the public divided sharply into

[1] "Future of the British Railways," *Manchester Guardian Commercial*, January 7, 1933.

two camps who hold extreme views on either side, and few trying to hold the balance between these warring forces and to see how a middle path can be secured."

The question of competition between road and rail has been the subject of investigation by a Royal Commission[1] and by a committee representing rail and road interests.[2] The latter inquiry, which resulted in the Salter Report, is particularly apposite because it sought to determine the fair share of road expenditure that should be borne by commercial vehicles and to establish a fair basis of competition with the railways. This report seems merely to have fanned the flame of antagonism, and any action taken by Parliament on the basis of it is sure to cause strong resentment. In "The Case of Trade and Industry against the Report of the Conference on Rail and Road Transport," most of the principal commercial, agricultural, and road transport organizations of Great Britain thoroughly disapproved of the methods and conclusions of the Salter Committee, stating that the document was "partial and incomplete, and definitely biased in favour of the railways."

An extensive consideration of the merits of the case presented by the Salter Committee is out of the question, but the principal issues should be suggested. The main proposals of the Conference on Rail and Road Transport were' that the burden of taxation should be readjusted in such a way that commercial vehicles would bear a much larger percentage of the total taxation, and that mechanically propelled road vehicles should be taxed £60,000,000 a year instead of the then £58,500,000. Unfortunately, none of the evidence taken by the Salter Committee has ever been published. The conference of traders, after observing that the Salter Committee had "trespassed into the consideration of the taxation of road (passenger) trans-

[1] *Royal Commission on Transport*, 1929–31. Cmd. 3751, 1931.
[2] *Conference on Rail and Road Transport*, Stationery Office, 1932.

port, for which it was ill-constituted," reached the conclusion that £40,000,000 is the maximum sum that should be levied on motor vehicles. The Salter Committee recommended that "commercial" vehicles should contribute £23,500,000 a year and that all other vehicles including private cars, coaches, buses, and taxis should be taxed £36,500,000 a year. The conference of traders pointed out that commercial vehicles, both goods and passenger, already contribute £31,200,000 a year and that if private cars and ratepayers were to pay their fair share of road building and maintenance the existing amount of taxation borne by commercial vehicles would be considerably reduced. Moreover, the Salter Report subsidizes seriously for a period of five years one form of transport, namely, compression-ignition-engined vehicles, at the expense of petrol-using vehicles, especially when these vehicles are competing with the railways; and as a corollary they fail adequately to safeguard the interests of trade and industry. "The distribution of the amount to be raised by the taxation of mechanically propelled road vehicles under the report," concluded the representatives of trade and industry, "is open to objection as unfair and prejudicial, is based upon erroneous particulars, and is inaccurate even on the principles laid down in the report."

The Salter Committee advocated that road traffic should be more meticulously regulated, in order that public safety might be increased and in order that the railways should not suffer from unequal disabilities. The Committee dealt primarily with the hours of duty, the rates of pay, and the conditions of employment of drivers, the fitness of the vehicle, and a much more drastic restriction of the number of vehicles in use upon the roads. The conference of trade and industry concluded that further regulation may be necessary, but that adequate machinery already exists; whereas the new proposals would be "impracticable, inequitable, and arbitrary" and would create "prejudice and uncertainty among the providers and users of commercial road transport."

A writer in a recent number of the *Manchester Guardian Commercial* has summarized the objections to the Salter Committee's proposals as follows:

"(1) the only conceivable object of the report is to drive some traffic back from the roads to the railways by making road transport more expensive; (2) the report assumes that motor traffic should pay the whole annual upkeep of the roads, including the service of loans raised in future for road works. This assumption is completely oblivious to the fact that a road increases enormously the rateable value of the property through which it passes; (3) the figure of £60,000,000 a year for the cost of the roads is grossly excessive; (4) motor transport already pays in taxation more than the total annual cost of making and mending roads; (5) the remedy for any public nuisance caused by motor traffic is surely not to drive heavy traffic off all roads but to schedule certain roads as the only arteries which such transport is permitted to use!"[1]

The railways have attempted to meet the competition of their new rival by going on the road themselves. Over £10,000,000 have been invested in new motor services or in existing companies, and the average return on capital invested has varied between 5½ and 7 per cent. Half of this amount was invested in one year, 1931, the railways having only been granted power to undertake road services in 1928.[2] At December 31, 1931, however, the railway companies and the local authorities combined owned only 11·67 per cent of all public service vehicles.[3]

[1] "Future of the British Railways," *Manchester Guardian Commercial*, January 21, 1933.

[2] At the end of 1931 the ownership of road vehicles by British railways was distributed as follows:

| | | | | | Passenger | Goods and Parcels |
|---|---|---|---|---|---|---|
| L.M.S. .. | .. | .. | .. | .. | 210 | 1,840 |
| L.N.E. .. | .. | .. | .. | .. | 40 | 798 |
| Great Western | | .. | .. | .. | 73 | 1,324 |
| Southern | .. | .. | .. | .. | — | 351 |
| | | | | | 323 | 4,313 |

(1931) *Railway Year Book*, 11.

[3] (1931–32) *First Annual Report of the Traffic Commissioners*.

When the Railways Act of 1921 was being drafted and almost continuously until 1928, the railways sought the right to establish motor services. The various proposals were strongly opposed by the road transport industry and by most of the trading interests, who feared the result of a potential monopoly. This move of the railways hastened the amalgamation of road transport services. The Minister of Transport also objected to the proposals because of the difficulties of regulating charges and because of the uncertainty regarding the effect upon standard revenue requirements. Committees that were appointed to investigate the subject pointed out that greater efficiency would be possible if the railways were permitted to establish "feeder" and "pick-up" motor services, but agreement was not reached as to the restrictions and form of control until 1928.[1] The establishment and regulation of railway motor services are shared by the Minister of Transport and the Traffic Commissioners, the latter having been created under the Road Traffic Act, 1930.

### THE PROBLEM OF NATIONAL COORDINATION

The regulation of road traffic was comprehensively inaugurated by the Road Traffic Act, 1930.[2] The licensing provisions of this Act transferred the functions which had been exercised by over 1,300 separate and local licensing authorities to Area Commissioners in the twelve districts into which the country outside of London was divided. The Metropolitan Traffic Commissioner controls services between London and outside points. In the twelve provincial areas the commissions consist of three members, one of whom, the Chairman, devotes his whole time to the duties of his office. The other two commissioners are unpaid and are

[1] The history of the agitation between 1921 and 1925 has been covered by K. G. Fenelon, *Economics of Road Transport*, ch. xvi, London, 1925.

[2] 20 and 21 Geo. 5. ch. xliii. Sir John Brooke, "The administration and control of road traffic," (1930) 8 *Pub. Admin.*, 148–163.

appointed from two panels of persons nominated by the
local governments. In the Metropolitan Traffic district
there is a single full-time Commissioner. He frequently
cooperates with the Commissioner of Police, who still
controls purely local traffic.

The jurisdiction of the Traffic Commissions provides
room for more discretion and skill than does any other
case of administrative control over public utility undertakings. In the licensing and regulation of public service
vehicles, as defined in Parts IV and V of the Road Traffic
Act, the Commissioners are called upon to decide such
matters as whether an application will conduce to the
coordination of all forms of transport; whether if a new
license is granted, existing services can be maintained at a
reasonable profit; whether the proposed service will be
necessary, regular, and adequate; whether vehicles are fit
and in proper repair; whether rates are reasonable; whether
conditions of employment laid down in the Act are observed;
and whether, and under what circumstances, licenses should
be revoked.

One of the most difficult provisions of all states that
"where desirable in the public interest the fares shall be
so fixed as to prevent wasteful competition with alternative
forms of transport"—a stipulation that pits the railways
against almost every new application. With reference to
the powers accorded to administrative officials by the Road
Traffic Act, the Secretary to the Ministry of Transport has
written, "I would ask you to note the marked degree of
administrative discretion which is accorded to and indeed
enjoined upon the Traffic Commissioners. They must, of
course, act impartially and in a judicial manner and spirit.
The statute itself gives guidance, in considerable detail—
but much is left to their skill and common sense in solving
their problems."

The Minister of Transport has power to issue general
directions to the Commissioners, and appeals may be taken

to him from the decisions of the several commissions. During the first year the plan was in operation seven appeals against refusals of certifying officers to grant certificates of fitness were received, and of these three were withdrawn, three were dismissed, and one had not been disposed of. Two appeals were received against the refusal of Commissioners to grant public service licenses; one of these was withdrawn and the other dismissed. Of twelve additional appeals on other grounds, only one case was decided in favor of the appellant.[1] "The most difficult task which lies at the threshold of any system of enforcement," states Sir John Brooke, a former Secretary to the Ministry of Transport, "is the determination of a standard." After pointing out that the coordination of long-distance omnibus services with the main-line railways is an uncharted sea, the same writer observes:

"I see no criterion by which the need for a road service between, let us say, Bristol and Birmingham or London and Manchester, can be tested except the inclination of the passengers. No ground exists for branding such competition as unfair unless the road service is not contributing its proper share to road maintenance or rates and taxes, and that can be adjusted by older methods without the assistance of the Commissioners."[2]

So long as this view obtains, the public may be assured that the national economy is being soundly and fairly developed.[3]

[1] *First Annual Report of the Traffic Commissioners*, op. cit., 4.

[2] Brooke, op. cit., (1930) 8 *Pub. Admin.*, 160.

[3] A recent instance of the difficulties of giving satisfactory weight to the coordination of national transport facilities may be of interest. An existing coach service applied to the Metropolitan Traffic Commissioner for permission to transport ships' crews between London and Liverpool at the rate of 20s. round trip. The demand had been created by sailors who sought cheaper means of returning to their homes; full coaches were guaranteed and it was conceded that the company could make a reasonable profit. The existing bus rate was 27s. 6d. and the regular railway fare was 49s. 6d., but the Railway Rates Tribunal had authorized an exceptional rate of 33s. in order that the railways might cater for the traffic. Counsel for the railways contended that if the application were granted, the railways would lose all of their traffic from that source, because of the "uneconomic" rate. They relied upon the coordination provision of the Act to defeat the application. "What is the public interest?" demanded the attorney for the coach operators. "Is it the travelling

Attempts to bring about the effective regulation and coordination of existing forms of national transport are almost sure to prove ineffectual so long as rail and road services are competitive and are under the control of different tribunals. The Railway Rates Tribunal stated recently, "It is difficult to see how the standard revenue can be realized now that a rate-cutting struggle has been forced upon the railways." At the same time road operators constantly complain that the railways attempt to undercut them as soon as new rates have been fixed.

The Royal Commission on Transport, 1929–31, concluded after a thorough investigation of the results of competition that "It appears to us that without unification —however it may be accomplished—no attempt to bring about complete coordination would be possible." Four different methods of unification suggested themselves, namely, nationalization, rationalization, a combination of both of these, or the formation of a public utility trust. Although it was impossible for all twelve of the members of the Commission to agree on one solution, the report states "We are all impressed with the immense importance of internal transport as the handmaid of British industry, and we are all agreed as to the necessity of making it as cheap and easy and efficient as possible. Some of us hold strongly that this can best be done by the adoption either of nationalization or, alternatively, by the formation of a National Transport Trust."[1] Three members of the Commission

public or the railways? I submit that the standard revenue requirement of the railways is an irrelevant consideration." However, the application was refused on the ground that so great a reduction would be injurious to the regular services of existing operators. The Commissioner, who said he attached great importance to the principles laid down in this case, concluded that "The evidence convinces me that adequate and convenient facilities . . . have for many years been provided by the railway companies, and that if the present application were granted, the general effect would not be to create new traffic, but to divert traffic from the railways to the applicants, and that the tendency of granting reduced fares in services of this character would be to injure the standard fares of regular road and rail facilities." Application of J. Pearson and Sons, dismissed by Metropolitan Traffic Commissioner, February 1933.                                   [1] *Final Report*, 172–174. Cmd. 3751.

developed their ideas further in an Appendix and suggested principles which are likely to carry great weight in future years. As the inevitable result of existing conditions, they submitted,

"(1) Competition is not a possible solution and is incompatible with coordination; (2) Coordination can only be attained by unification; (3) Unification, through the preponderance of one form of traffic over another, in a given area, is not desirable, and would not have the support of public opinion; (4) Consequently, unification which is desirable in the public interest can only be brought about through some form of public control or ownership; (5) Public ownership combined with commercial management should operate through a National Transport Trust, perhaps in the form of a statutory corporation, free from all political and governmental interference. It should manage the coordinated transport facilities in the interest of national industry and trade: in other words, it should operate for service rather than profit."

## CONCLUSION

Railway regulation is weakened by the multiplicity of administrative agencies and the consequent division of responsibility. The Railway Rates Tribunal has proved an efficient organization, but its jurisdiction is limited and its utility has been circumscribed by the economic impossibility of meeting the standard revenue requirements established in 1921. Rate regulation is unavoidably chaotic. Uneconomic capitalization is seen in the comparatively high level of charges which must be borne by industry and by the travelling public.

Regulation might be improved by readjusting the revenue expectations of the railways in accordance with a reduced capitalization, by amalgamating the work of the Railway and Canal Commission and the Railway Rates Tribunal, and by increasing the powers of the Rates Tribunal. But it is extremely doubtful if more effective regulation would get at the roots of the transport problem. Conditions have radically changed in ten years.

Since the war the adjustment of disputes between the

companies and the employees has been effectively settled by a framework of collective bargaining boards. The wages and conditions of railway labor have been substantially improved since 1913. In recent months, however, the apex of the negotiation structure, the National Wages Board, has failed to satisfy the companies and therefore a new plan of national conciliation must be created. The future of railway labor relations appears to be unsettled and strained.

Minor adjustments will not solve the plight of the railways. If their financial structure were completely overhauled, if unification took place, and if great improvements in operating efficiency were brought about, the problems of competition and coordination would remain. Road competition has completely altered the problem of railway regulation. The community will never permit the railways to obtain financial control of road transport, and not for long would it permit rival forms of transport to be weighed down by onerous burdens and restrictions. National coordination of transport facilities under some form of unified control is a likelihood of the next few years. Fortunately, the British are more adept at the art of public administration than they are at the tactics of regulation!

## CHAPTER IV

# POST OFFICE TELEGRAPHS AND TELEPHONES

## IMPORTANCE OF THE POST OFFICE

Measured by the number of its employees, the impressiveness of its financial responsibilities, the variety and importance of its functions, and the use made of its services by all classes of the population, the Post Office is one of the most significant undertakings, either public or private, in Great Britain. In 1932, following a twelve-year period of severe retrenchment, the Post Office staff still numbered around 230,000. Almost two-thirds of the British Civil Service are engaged in this enormous public commercial undertaking. The effects of Post Office policy are far-reaching, because every remote part of Great Britain is served by the postal organization.

The Post Office, as in many other countries, possesses a monopoly of all forms of communication. Any communication service that the Post Office does not operate itself, therefore, can merely be secured by others in the form of a concession. With the exception of broadcasting and international cables, all of the communication facilities of the country are administered by the Post Office. The importance of efficient postal, telephone, telegraph, and wireless services to the business and social life of the nation requires no explanation. The functions performed by the Post Office enter so closely into the lives of the people that the department's successful operation under popular control is a matter of major significance.

An idea of the size and complexity of the undertaking may be suggested by figures recently published by the Post Office. The financial importance of the telephone and the telegraph services is indicated by the fact that out of a total capital of over £152 millions, telephone expenditures have accounted for more than £118 millions, and telegraphs represent a capital sum of almost £10 millions. Revenues collected on all services for the year 1931–32 amounted to more than £71 millions, and the net surplus contributed to the Exchequer was £10,631,794. Each year the Post Office transmits about 7 billion postal communications, 160 million parcels, 56 million telegrams, and handles almost 1½ billion telephone calls. Post Office Savings Bank deposits amount to almost £300 millions: and these are simply the department's major functions!

The British Post Office renders a more numerous and important group of services than any other national postal organization, with the possible exception of the German. The ambit of its present functions may be visualized by reference to the principal stages of its expansion.[1] A brief historical survey will also show how the telegraph and telephone services were absorbed by the Post Office. Since we are not attempting to study all branches of the Post Office, however, many points which might otherwise be of interest may be disregarded.

In 1482 the King's dispatches were carried for the first time by arrangements made by officers of his household. Although the posts were "farmed" to private entrepreneurs until 1677, an Act of 1609 made the carriage of letters a State monopoly. In 1657 the office of Postmaster-General of England and Comptroller of the Post Office was created for the first time, and by an Act of 1711 a General Post Office was established for the three Kingdoms and the Colonies. Shortly after this, part of the revenues of the Post Office began to flow into the general funds of the Government, whereas formerly they were either farmed by individuals or were the King's revenue.

The Money Order system was put into operation at an early period, in 1792, and for many years it was carried

[1] *The Post Office: An Historical Summary*, Stationery Office, 1911. Sir Evelyn Murray, *The Post Office*, ch. i, London, 1927.

on as a private concession. The Treasury, in 1839, was given the important power of fixing Post Office rates. Two years later provision was made for Registered Mail. In 1861 the Post Office Savings Bank was established, and in 1864 the department was given the responsibility for a State system of Annuities and Life Insurance.

By the Telegraph Act of 1868, the Postmaster-General was authorized to acquire the inland telegraphs. This same Act was the foundation of an extremely important court decision in 1880 which held that telephones are a State monopoly.[1] Soon after this the Post Office began to operate a limited telephone service, but licensed private companies and municipalities were also permitted to establish exchanges. In 1896 the State purchased all of the trunk lines, giving the Post Office control over future expansion. Not until 1905, however, was agreement reached to take over the operation of the private combine, the National Telephone Company, and the actual administration of a nation-wide service by the Post Office did not commence until 1912.

The parcel post was started in 1883, and three years later insured letters were added to the facilities offered the public. Finally, in 1909 the Postmaster-General was ordered to administer old-age pension payments.

Although the above dates provide the high-lights of Post Office expansion, the list of its present duties is not entirely complete. Within this supplementary list there should be included the telegraph service with the Continent; telegraph money orders; postal orders; postal drafts; the cash on delivery system; the inspection of ships' wireless installations and wireless operators; the Post Office register of government stocks and bonds for small investors; the payment of widows', orphans', and Army and Navy pensions; the sale and management of national savings certificates (of which £381 millions have been issued); the sale of unem-

[1] Attorney-General *v*. Edison Bell Telephone Co. of London, *Law Reports*, (1880) 6 Q.B.D., 244.

ployment insurance stamps; and the sale and issue of local taxation licenses, wireless receiving licenses, and motor licenses.

In addition, as has been suggested, the Postmaster-General has important powers and duties in relation to the British Broadcasting Corporation.

The above enumeration of functions reveals the comprehensive and vital nature of the services performed by the Post Office. Moreover, it should be observed that the citizen must pay for services rendered, and that in some cases the services are competitive and the demand for them is elastic. This is especially true of telephones and telegrams. These are factors which clearly establish the commercial character of the Post Office.

In this chapter the relationships, organization, problems, and accomplishments of the telegraph and telephone services will be considered. The Beam wireless controversy will be discussed incidentally, as it bears upon the problem of the telegraph service. In the next chapter, the general constitutional and administrative problems of the Post Office as a national public utility will be more fully examined. Does the Post Office, the only Department of State supplying commercial services to the public, require reform, and if so, what should be the nature of the changes? The merits or demerits of the communication services will furnish a sound basis upon which to formulate a valid judgment.

### CONTROL AND ORGANIZATION

Since the Post Office is clearly a public commercial undertaking, in most of its important functions at least, many people believe that it does not possess the administrative and financial autonomy which such an enterprise should have. Ministerial control of the Post Office has been increasingly criticized in recent years, and it has been suggested that the Post Office should be completely transferred from government operation. This proposal of certain Members of Parliament led to the first general examination in British history of Post Office organization and administrative principles—the recent Bridgeman Committee inquiry.[1] The committee concluded that the constitutional status of the Post Office should not be altered, but that it should be given greater freedom along certain lines.

The ultimate master of the Post Office is the House of Commons, which exercises control by means of the annual debate on the Estimates and by questions addressed to the Postmaster-General. These instruments of control are based upon the underlying reality of the Postmaster-General's responsibility to Parliament.

From the standpoint of constitutional theory and practice the position of the Post Office does not differ materially from that of any other government department. The Postmaster-General is a member of the Ministry, and occasionally he is admitted to the Cabinet. The Cabinet's control is largely exercised through the Treasury, which acts upon rates of charge, fixes the amount of all appropriations, determines all salaries, and approves the amount and the more important items of proposed capital outlay. This is done in cooperation with Post Office officials.

One of the important points that should be comprehended is that the Post Office is treated by the Government as a Revenue Department. No other factor raises more problems concerning the future of the Post Office than the use of a public commercial undertaking as a means of balancing the national budget. Revenue and expenditure are kept entirely separate, the former being paid over intact to the Exchequer, and the latter, with certain exceptions, being voted by Parliament on the Annual Estimates. Moreover, no payment is made to the Post Office for most of the services it renders to other departments, and correspondingly it is not debited for work done by them.

[1] Cmd. 4149, Stationery Office, 1932.

As a going concern the Post Office relies upon other services of the central government in two very important respects. Private businesses are also dependent upon outside concerns, for that matter, but this point is usually over-looked in discussions of the Post Office and its relations. The Office of Works is responsible for the provision and main-tenance of Post Office sites and buildings of the first class and the larger rented premises. The Stationery Office has been given most of the department's printing, and the transference of postage stamp and security printing is being considered.

The supreme head of the Post Office is the Postmaster-General, who, as a member of the Government of the day, is responsible for carrying out the general policies of the Cabinet in so far as they relate to the Post Office. Men who have attained considerable prominence, such as Sir Austen Chamberlain, Sir Herbert Samuel, Lord Stanley, Mr. Neville Chamberlain, and Major C. R. Attlee, have occupied the office within the last generation. Inasmuch as the responsibilities of the Postmaster-General do not usually involve broad political questions or controversial issues, it must be said that promising men rather than distinguished figures are generally given the post. The degree of influence which the Postmaster-General is able to exercise depends largely upon the personality of the individual occupying the office. Postmasters-General come to the office without previous special training: frequently it is their first minis-terial position; and the average tenure is less than two years. As Lord Wolmer concludes, "He must be a remarkable man if he is to master and bend the machine in that period." On the other hand, it may be noted that the Postmaster-General has more time to devote to departmental work than many other Ministers. Since 1909, except for a few intervals, the Postmaster-General has been aided by a politically appointed Assistant Postmaster-General.

The Post Office Advisory Council, which was originated

a few years ago, is an additional connecting link between the department and the public. Prior to its reorganization in January 1933, the Council represented commercial interests only, met infrequently, and had no authority to determine the agenda of the meetings, which were presided over by the Postmaster-General, Since the recent reform the board has been made more representative by the inclusion of labor and women members. It will meet regularly, and members will be expected to raise suggestions and criticisms. This alteration is one of the first constructive results of the Bridgeman Committee Report of 1932.

The foundation of the Post Office structure consists of Civil Service employees. The Secretary is the permanent head of the organization. He is the principal adviser to the Postmaster-General and, assisted by the Second Secretary and the Headquarters Staff, is responsible for the entire organization and the functioning of its component parts. Since 1899 there have been only five Secretaries, and the present incumbent, Sir Evelyn Murray, has been in office since 1914.

Under the Secretary and his deputy, the Second Secretary, there are two Directors, the Director of Postal Services and the Director of Telegraphs and Telephones, the latter of whom controls the telephone, telegraph, and wireless services. The Secretary's Office is divided into eight Divisions, each under an Assistant Secretary who is responsible either to the Second Secretary or to one of the Directors. The division is as follows:

1. Mails.
2. Inland Telegraphs.
3. Overseas Telegraphs.
4. Telephones.
5. Establishments (numbers, organization, and pay of staff).
6. Staff (personnel, recruitment, promotion, discipline).
7. Buildings and Supplies.
8. Chief Clerk.

The Second Secretary is in direct charge of the four last-named Divisions, which are really the only functional units in the Secretarial organization. The eight Divisions, plus the Investigation (detective) service, the Publicity bureau, the Solicitor, and the Chief Medical Officer, complete the Secretariat Branch proper.

In addition, there are Headquarters Departments which are parallel with the Secretariat branches, but, in some respects, subject to their general authority. These are headed by the Comptroller and Accountant-General, the Engineer-in-Chief, the Controller of the Savings Bank, and the Controller of the Money Order Department.

These officials constitute the hierarchy at Headquarters, St. Martin's-le-Grand. There are two additional systems of organization, the metropolitan and the provincial. In London the three services, namely Posts, Telegraphs, and Telephones, operate along independent lines. Each is headed by a Controller, who is subject to the authority of the Secretary at St. Martin's-le-Grand, acting through the Directors of Postal Services and of Telegraphs and Telephones.

In contrast with the organization at Headquarters and in London, the provincial administration is based upon geographical considerations, wherein the same official is responsible for all three services, namely, postal, telegraph, and telephone. There are thirteen Surveyors in charge of country districts and nine Postmaster-Surveyors in charge of large towns. A special administration has been provided for Scotland. The provincial administrations are subject to a large degree of control from the Secretary's Office.[1]

It must be admitted that the outline of Post Office organization appears to be somewhat complicated and illogical. Perhaps it is. But paper organizations sometimes create a more unfavorable impression than is warranted by the facts of the actual administration. Yet, if unsound basic

[1] See diagram on page 127.

principles are incorporated into an organization, no amount of tinkering will rectify the weakness. In the following pages we shall see how the administrative system works.out in the two great Post Office utilities, telegraphs and telephones.

Although the telegraph and telephone organizations are unified at the top by the Director of Telegraphs and Telephones, as operating services they are almost entirely independent of each other. Even if the telegraph and telephone divisions were amalgamated on the operating side, as the Bridgeman Committee proposed, it would be necessary to consider each administration separately in order to understand the basic problems of the Post Office communication services.

In recent years the telegraph branch has attracted attention primarily because of the financial losses sustained by its operation. Although its annual deficit is more than offset each year by the earnings of the postal and the telephone services, the problem of putting the telegraph service on a paying basis has been, during the past ten years in particular, the subject of frequent internal and external investigations. The deficit of the telegraph service, which stood at £1,380,000 in 1927–28, was reduced to £1,005,000 in 1930–31, 'and to £809,000 in 1931–32. Although traffic has continued to decline, the telegraph service has brought about very noteworthy efficiencies.

An understanding of the present and of the future problems of the telegraph administration will be best obtained by reference to the outstanding factors in its development.[1] As has been stated, the telegraph companies were taken over by the State in 1870, at a cost of about

[1] *Bridgeman Committee Report*, op. cit., 10–12; *Report of the Lever Committee on the Inland Telegraph Service*, Cmd. 3058, Stationery Office, 1928; *The Post Office: An Historical Summary*, op. cit., 66–88.

## ADMINISTRATIVE ORGANIZATION OF THE GENERAL POST OFFICE

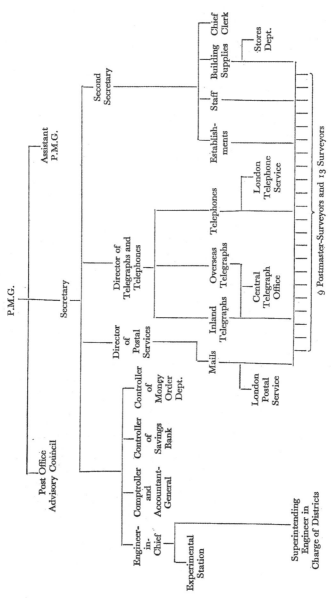

£8,000,000. However, in the next three years it was necessary to spend an additional £2,130,000 on extensions and improvements. The cost of the subsequent capital outlay has been voted annually by Parliament on the Post Office Estimates.

In addition to the original cost of acquisition, the Post Office assumed an added liability which has had an important bearing upon later financial difficulties. When the telegraph companies and the railway companies, which had formerly operated the service, were bought out, contractual liabilities in perpetuity were entered into with the railway companies. It was agreed that the railway undertakings should enjoy a perpetual right to send annually without payment a fixed number of messages subject to a limit placed on the number of words. It is estimated that these messages, if paid for, would provide a revenue of £94,000 a year.

It has sometimes been asserted that the later difficulties of the telegraph service were due in large part to the excessive purchase price paid to the former owners. Sir Evelyn Murray has replied to this allegation as follows:

"The compensation terms were certainly liberal, and in many cases excessive. But it is fair to remember that the companies had been operating, not as licensees, but as pioneers in a free market, and that they had successfully tided over the lean years and were reluctant vendors of a business which was showing rapid expansion and growing dividends. Contemporary estimates indicated that even allowing for the inflated purchase price, the tariff could be reduced and a satisfactory service still maintained. What was not foreseen was the rising curve of operating expenses, and particularly wages, which, combined with the introduction of the sixpenny telegram, converted the anticipated profit into a permanent deficit. But it is a fallacy to suppose that the existing telegraph deficit is attributable to the excessive price paid for the system; it has in fact nothing to do with it. The plant was revalued in 1912 and for the last fifteen years the capital charges debited in the telegraph accounts have been based upon the value of the plant so ascertained, as modified by subsequent additions."

For the first ten years the business expanded and operated at a profit, but in 1883 the introduction of the 6d. telegram turned the profit into a loss. The number of telegrams rose from 30 millions to 50 millions, but it involved a loss of revenue of at least £170,000 a year, and a capital expenditure of £500,000. The 6d. charge was not altered until 1915, when it was raised to 9d. and finally in 1920 to 1s. for 12 words with an extra penny for each additional word. Between £7,000,000 and £8,000,000 of the capital costs were written off in 1912, leaving a depreciated value of approximately £4,800,000.

Frequent comparisons have been made between the British and American telegraph services, the purpose usually being to show the vast superiority of the latter. Such a comparison will prove very little, due to the important differences between the two countries. In America there are great distances to be covered, making the telegram an indispensable means of communication. In Great Britain a letter will be delivered anywhere within the country in less than twenty-four hours, at a fraction of the cost of a telegram. In 1900 the local or short-distance telegram constituted an important part of telegraph traffic. Today that business has practically disappeared owing partly to the telephone and partly to the excellence of the mail service. Due to the efficiency of the postal service, a letter posted in the inner London area at noon will be delivered in the London area by tea-time, and one dispatched before four o'clock will be delivered the same evening.

There are many factors, other than those mentioned, which account for telegraph deficits. In past years a substantial loss of revenue has been caused by the exceptionally low rates granted to newspaper telegrams. The estimated annual loss from the press traffic in 1888 was £200,000, in 1895 it had reached £300,000, and in 1931 it was still £230,000. The loss will clearly diminish, but only because the newspapers are relying more and more on the telephone. There is a wide-spread belief that any government which attempted to raise rates on newspaper traffic would be swept out of power. There can be no doubt that the cheap rates granted to newspapers have resulted in a certain amount of public benefit, viz. more complete news, but the policy is hard to justify on the basis of business principles.

A flat rate is charged on all inland telegrams, irrespective of distance. After frequent investigations it has invariably appeared that, for a small country like Great Britain, the flat rate is to be preferred to a zoned rate. The consensus of opinion indicates that the existing charging practice on ordinary telegrams is not a cause of telegraph deficits.

The telephone has made serious inroads upon telegraph traffic. Due to its speed, convenience, intimacy, relatively small cost, and the short distance to be covered, the telephone has constantly won public preference. It is a significant fact that in a country as small as Great Britain the distance covered by the average telegram should be 140 miles. The distance has constantly grown, thereby reducing telegraph receipts.

Will the telegraph service never be reestablished on a paying basis, it will be asked? Until recent years the continuance of the subsidy system was taken as a matter of course. The indirect benefits of a cheap and a more extended telegraph service than can be found in any other country were said to benefit business and all classes of the population to such an extent that the intangible assets clearly offset the liabilities. To-day there exists a constantly growing demand that the service should not operate at a financial loss.

An official of the telegraph service stated a few years ago that "there is not the slightest doubt that the service could be turned into a revenue-earning concern."[1] What changes would be entailed? It might mean the closing of a large number of country and suburban telegraph offices. At the present time the Post Office maintains approximately 11,000 offices from which telegrams are received. Over a thousand

[1] G. T. Archibald, "Notes on telegraph practice," (1925) 11 *Telegraph and Telephone Journal*, 59.

of these offices do not pay their way. However, an analysis made by the Accountant-General's Department reveals that only £20,000 a year could be saved by retrenchment at this point. Prior to 1870 the private company worked only the richest fields and neglected the rest of the country. This, in a general way, is true wherever private companies are in operation. Telegraph offices are still opened in Great Britain where the average annual demand for telegrams is in the neighborhood of 300. "No other country is so solicitous for the telegraphing public." When service and not profit is the consideration, who can say categorically if the indirect benefits to trade and to national development make a system which purposely loses money, defensible?

It is sometimes asserted that the telegraph service could be made to pay, if only certain resources were tapped which have not been exploited to the fullest extent heretofore. This could be done, it is argued, by developing new forms of business, largely in accordance with the recommendations which were made by the Post Office delegation which visited the American telegraph companies in 1928. The night letter could probably be made more popular, as illustrated by American experience. Special holiday and greeting telegrams have not been exploited, although they have proved immensely successful in the United States. The letter form and envelope of the British telegram are un-attractive, but so far the 1928 commission's recommendation that they should be made more suitable has not received favorable action. A more cheerful color might help to dispel the popular prejudice that a telegram means bad news. Finally, the telegraph service does not receive its proportionate share of Post Office advertising, which, as will be pointed out, has become extremely effective in the promotion of telephone sales. However, it seems too optimistic to suppose that an annual deficit amounting to over £800,000 could be absorbed by the methods which have been suggested.

In contrast with this rather disappointing picture, the improvement of the internal efficiency of the British telegraph service is a matter of proper pride. As the Bridgeman Committee pointed out, the public is not generally aware of the degree of technical progress that has been made by the Post Office in the last ten years. In the case of the telegraph service the period of outstanding internal development is much less, more like three or four years. The best place to discover what has occurred with respect to operating efficiency is in the Central Telegraph Office, where all of the foreign communications and the greater part of the inland traffic are handled.

## THE CENTRAL TELEGRAPH OFFICE

The Central Telegraph Office (C.T.O.) is the nerve center of the British telegraph system. At the present time the C.T.O. employs a staff of 3,300, and although traffic has fallen considerably during the past ten years, it deals with a daily average of about 160,000 telegram transactions during the summer and approximately 130,000 during the winter. All of the foreign business is carried on from the central office, the average number of daily messages being 20,000. About 750 telegraph offices are in direct communication with the C.T.O., either by direct wire connection or through the telephone system. The C.T.O. is connected with the chief telegraph offices of inner London by pneumatic tubes, of which there are seventy-three, with a total of seventy-one miles.

The telegraph service has greatly improved its efficiency in recent years, in line with a general quickening of initiative throughout the Post Office. Although technical discussions are to be avoided, it will be interesting to consider some of the readily appreciated respects in which the telegraph service has progressed in just the last three or four years. The record of the C.T.O. points to the potential improvement as well as to the shortcomings of governmental administration.

In 1928 the British telegraph service compared very unfavorably with the American companies because of the great variety of apparatus employed by the former. Prior to the close of the war a dozen or more types and makes of machine had been introduced, and until recently different forms of apparatus existed side by side. About ten years ago the teleprinter came into operation. The history of the last ten years consists of the replacement of all other forms of apparatus by the teleprinter, and at present the inland telegraph system is operated entirely by teleprinter and telephone.

Since 1923 there has been a rapid development of the phonogram and the telephone-telegram, thereby necessitating important internal changes. Obsolescence has been a chronic problem. About 9 million telegrams a year are now accepted from the public by telephone and about 7 million a year are now delivered by telephone. Many smaller Post Offices—about 9,000 in all—conduct their telegraph business entirely by telephone. This will give some idea of the close relations which may be expected in the future between the telegraph and the telephone.

Additional illustrations of rationalization and of improved operating efficiency prove that progress has been rapid in recent years and that the British telegraph service now compares favorably with the best foreign administrations.

Whereas in 1871 the average delay in London was 90 minutes per telegram, it is now only 10 minutes, and when improvements now in progress have been completed it is anticipated that the "internal drag" will be reduced to below three minutes. Within the past year the average speed per operator has increased from 62 to 70 words a minute. Service complaints received in 1925 were in the ratio of 1 to 1,500 telegrams handled. In 1930 complaints from customers were 17 per cent less than in 1929, and in 1931 they were 28 per cent less than in 1930, although 1931 traffic was 5 per cent less than in 1930.

The recent history of operating economy is reassuring, because it reveals a progressive policy on the part of the telegraph administration. Between 1928 and 1932 the operating costs, including supervision, had been reduced by almost a million pounds. However, more than half of the saving was achieved by means of wage and salary reductions. Between 1928 and 1932 the cost of living index bonus had declined from 250 to 239 a year for men telegraphists, and from 163 to 151 a year in the case of women telegraphists.

Rationalization on such a scale cannot help but have a serious effect upon the vocational opportunities in the telegraph service. Retrenchment not only involves a continuous reduction of staff, but it makes promotion prospects appear discouraging. For several years the telegraph traffic has fallen off from 5 to 7 per cent a year. Only a significant improvement in trade conditions would bring about any substantial encouragement. When it is learned that a telegraphist usually has little chance of promotion out of his class until he is about forty-five years of age, it is not surprising that a depressed atmosphere is found among many of the employees. It is a tribute to the officials and the staff of the telegraph service that so much improvement has been made in operating efficiency while traffic and pay have been falling.

In recent years more attention has been given to public relations. All complaints are immediately investigated either by the Assistant Controller or by the Outdoor Representative, an office which has been created in late years. In addition to his investigatory duties the Outdoor Representative is responsible for soliciting business, and for sending out advertising for display purposes. For example, a complete telegraph set is sent round to public exhibitions, such as those held at Olympia. The public is given an opportunity to operate the set, hence revealing to them the complicated character of the work done by the telegraph service. This alone has greatly increased public understanding and interest. When it is realized that a comprehensive public relations program is a development of the last few years—just as Post Office advertising is—an additional reason will appear for believing that in the future a more aggressive commercial attitude may be expected from the telegraph service.

### THE IMPERIAL BEAMS

Closely connected with the future of the telegraph service is the bitter controversy which took place in 1928 over the leasing of the Post Office Beam service. A great deal of feeling was aroused when the Conservative party, then in power, turned over to a private combine not only the government-operated Imperial and Continental cables, but also the Imperial Beam service, which had been operated up to that time by the C.T.O. The question deserves consideration at this point for several reasons. In the first place, the alienation of the Beams dealt a severe blow to the financial future of the Post Office telegraph service. The earnings of the Beam service would have substantially reduced the loss on the telegraph service. The first year's profit amounted to £166,000 on an investment of only £240,000. When the foreign branch of the C.T.O. lost the Beams the demoralizing effect was very great. There are now three services to the Continent, namely, the Post Office cables, the Post Office wireless, and the Communications Company's wireless. In February 1928 the Post Office had nineteen wireless stations in operation and several stand-by stations for emergencies.

The action taken by the Government at that time reveals the powerful clash of forces which are at work determining the future of British public utility control. The alienation of the Beam service is one of the few instances in British history of the handing over of a national asset to a profit-making enterprise. Finally, the Act of 1928 created a more or less distinctive type of public utility undertaking, the Imperial and International Communications Company.

As early as the Imperial Conference of 1911 it was agreed that the Dominions should be connected to Great Britain by a chain of powerful wireless stations. The war intervened. In 1924 a special commission on imperial communications recommended that the imperial wireless service should be undertaken by the Post Office.[1] Parliament gave its approval, and negotiations were entered into with the Marconi Company to instal transmitting stations. Soon afterwards the "Beam" principle was announced. The British and Dominion Governments contracted to try the new discovery. The distinctive feature of the Beam is that it is a directive short-wave system of wireless communication. Great distance can be covered with a minute fraction of the power required by long-wave stations. Hence, as experience proved, the advance of science made the new service so cheap that nothing else could compete with it.

The Beam station to Canada was completed in 1926, and those to Australia, South Africa, and India began to operate in 1927. By 1928 it began to appear that at last the Post Office had pioneered an asset which might help to pull the telegraph service out of a financial hole. Astonishing speeds running up to 250 words a minute in both directions simultaneously were obtained, and the development was still in its infancy. The invention was employed with success for foreign and overseas telephone communication. The privately owned cable companies could not compete with such service and were said to be facing a hopeless financial future.[2] In 1927–28 the Beam service was said to have caused a reduction of revenue on the Pacific cable alone of £80,000. Deficits on two other cables amounted to £27,000 and £40,000 in the same year. They had found it necessary

[1] *Report of the Imperial Wireless Telegraphy Committee*, Cmd. 2060, Stationery Office, 1924.

[2] *H.C. Debates*, vol. 223, col. 1803, December 10, 1928.

to reduce their rates in order to compete at all. Hence, as Mr. Ramsay MacDonald said in debate, the Post Office held "the key of the whole situation—the economic key, the business key, and the scientific key." If the cables were not to fail it meant that either the Beam service would have to absorb the private cables, or that the private companies would have to get the key to the situation—the Beams. As late as the Imperial Conference of 1926 government operation had been consistently favored.

The lease of the Beam service to the Cable-Marconi merger was recommended by the Report of the Imperial Wireless and Cable Conference,[1] which represented the British and Dominion Governments. The British Parliament was asked to pass an Enabling Act providing for the sale of the Post Office cables and the lease of the Beam stations, which it did in December 1928. The Beam stations have been leased for a term of twenty-five years, with a basic rental of £250,000 a year. It was stipulated that if, after three years, the profits of the Imperial and International Communications Company exceeded 6 per cent (a fixed standard of £1,865,000), the British Government was to receive 12 per cent of such excess profit, and of the remaining balance one-half was to go to the company and the other half to reductions in rates or improved services. In addition, the Communications Company agreed to a single payment of £60,000, for the costs of disturbance. The Post Office has retained the overseas telephone service. The British and Dominion Governments sold outright three cables: the Pacific, the Imperial, and the West Indian, all of which had usually earned a small profit.

The new company, Imperial and International Communications, Ltd., therefore merged government cables, government wireless, private cables, and private wireless facilities. The sale of the government services was no doubt influenced by the fact that the Dominion Governments were

[1] Cmd. 3163, Stationery Office, 1927.

opposed, at the time, to complete government operation. The private combine was able to buy the government cables at cost less depreciation, with no provision for goodwill or future profits; the private companies were turned into the merger on the basis of their outstanding securities, irrespective of the real value of the properties, i.e. with no consideration of the obsolescence of the cables or of their earning power. The new operating company was capitalized at £30,000,000, from which the British Government received only £2,500,000 on an alleged original cost of £7,000,000. The total capitalization of the merger company, £53,000,000, represented in addition the assets of a manufacturing company which was to work in conjunction with the Communications Company.

One of the most interesting angles of the case was the pressure group motivation. The House of Commons heard a great deal about the alleged influences behind the Bill, but many of these statements were undoubtedly exaggerated. The main point seemed to be missed by most speakers. This was that a revolutionary scientific discovery necessitated some method of rationalization. However, some characteristic criticisms of the Bill will indicate the vital clash of interests underlying the controversy. For example, Lieut.-Commander Kenworthy, referring to the Parliamentary majority, said in the House of Commons, "they looked after their friends. At all costs private enterprise was bolstered up, and the only private interests concerned, the cable companies and the Marconi Company, were allowed to make their own terms. They know how to govern, and how to govern in the interests of their friends, not their personal friends, but the directors and shareholders of the private companies." "Look at the list of directorships held by Members sitting on the Government side of the House," stated a Member of Parliament. "We find that 106 Members hold 568 directorships." Other speakers were more specific in their reference to lobbies. One speaker contended that the financial and chain newspaper interests had most to gain, and that the combination was operating in such a powerful way that it was almost impossible to know where their influence extended. The new monopoly will mean, it was said, that "in addition to the controlling of the press you are going to place the supplying of news into the hands of a few people."[1]

Champions of the Bill replied that government ownership should not be permitted to supplant private business, but should merely supplement it; that Canada had suggested the plan originally; and that the British Government was honor-bound to follow the desires of the Imperial Conference. Furthermore, it was argued that the Beam Service could not guarantee secrecy. Hence, in time of war it would be necessary to rely on the cables, and therefore they should be sustained.

The question of public control raised a vital issue. The Bill provided that the company should nominate and the Government approve two out of the twelve directors. As a writer on the subject has recently said, apart from the unimportant fact that two of the directors, one being the Chairman, are approved by the Government on the nomination of the board, there is nothing to distinguish the merger from an ordinary limited liability company. An Advisory Committee, composed of representatives of the British and of the Dominion Governments, was created, with power to consult concerning general policies and with specific authority to act upon applications for increased rates, the scrapping of any service, and the handling of excess profits. The advisory body has no authority to order lower rates. Although it was provided that the Advisory Committee should have access to information in the hands of the Communications Company, when necessary to carry out its duties, it was agreed that "such information will, of

[1] *H.C. Debates*, vol. 223, col. 1837, December 10, 1928; Ibid., vol. 222, col. 1851, December 6, 1928.

course, be treated as entirely confidential." Moreover, no supervisory power was given to the Postmaster-General or to any other Minister of State, and hence the House of Commons possesses no opportunity to question the policies or the conduct of the company.

What has happened to the interest of the consumer as a result of the transfer? Has the linking up of the inexpensive but very efficient Beam service with the very costly but less efficient cables resulted in any appreciable increase of rates? The following table, which compares the full-rate cost per word for the Beam service under Post Office management and under the present control, tells the story:

| London to | Post Office | Communications Company |
|---|---|---|
| Canada .. | .. 9d. | 9d. |
| Australia .. | .. 1s. 8d. | 1s. 8d. |
| South Africa | .. 1s. 4d. | 1s. 3d. |
| India .. | .. 1s. 1d. | 1s. 3d. |

It will be observed that the rate has remained the same on full-rate messages to Canada and to Australia, but that the increased rate to India more than offsets the reduction in the South African tariff. However, this does not tell the full story. In the first year of operation the Post Office paid off out of revenue something over two-thirds of the cost involved in the installation of the Beam service. There had been very valuable rate reductions. In regard to India, for instance, the press message rate had been reduced from 4d. to 2½d., and there was a reduction of 8d. on full-rate messages. Charges for government wireless, with the exception of the Canadian rates, were as much as 4d. a word cheaper than for cable telegrams on the Empire routes. In the first year of operation 30,000,000 words were sent over the Beam service. There is little doubt that still greater rate reductions would have been possible.

Imperial and International Communications, Ltd., perhaps to an even greater extent than most undertakings, has been hard struck by the depression. The dividend for the year 1930 was only 1¾ per cent. A sum of £216,047 which had been paid by the company on account of unextinguished formation expenses was refunded by the Government to the amount of £216,000 under the Finance Act, 1930. The Imperial Communications Advisory Committee in June 1930, in consultation with the company, appointed a committee "to inquire into the position of this company including the causes and consequences of the discrepancy between standard revenue and current earnings, and to suggest measures to remedy the situation." It may be noted in passing that the "merger" or holding company, namely Cables and Wireless, Ltd., which was formed at the same time, includes among its assets, amounting to approximately £53,000,000, a sum of £11,898,894 for "Goodwill, etc."[1] The two companies have interlocking directorates.

In future years it will be interesting to discover whether the opposition to the solution effected in 1928 will die out, or whether additional chapters will be written in the struggle for control over imperial and international communications.

## THE TELEPHONE SERVICE

Since the transference of the Imperial Beams, the telephone has occupied an unrivalled position as the center of Post Office interest. Every effort is put forth to make the Post Office staff 100 per cent "telephone minded." An aggressive campaign, the object of which is to popularize the use of the telephone, has been one of the outstanding features of Post Office policy during the last few years. The most noticeable change has occurred since the establishment of the Publicity Bureau in the Secretary's Office three years ago. Where formerly there was practically no advertising, today the canvassing and publicity campaign of

[1] (1932) *Stock Exchange Year Book*, 1399. The controversy which has taken place between the Post Office and the Imperial and International Communications Company since 1929 has been discussed in (1930) 110 *Economist*, 312, 515, 699.

the Post Office is one of the most effective in the entire country.

An understanding of the new atmosphere is vital to a comprehension of current problems of telephone administration. The secret of the viewpoint of earlier years is explained by the policy which until recently the Government and the public expected the Post Office to follow. It is expressed in the advice given to the Post Office by the Treasury in 1883, in answer to a proposal that the telephone business should be popularized. The Treasury, stated the memorandum, objects "to anything in the nature of solicitation, and above all personal solicitation." The Post Office must be content to bring its offers "fairly within the knowledge of the public" and thereafter to wait for its demands. What a difference there is today! The technique of the telephone sales force compares favorably with the methods of the most progressive private companies. The results have proved encouraging. During 1931, a year of most intense industrial distress, the British Post Office produced a net gain of 2 per cent in telephone rentals. During the same period most foreign telephone systems sustained heavy net losses. It may be replied that the Post Office telephones could not have progressed if the expansion of the service had been more vigorously exploited in previous years. There is some truth in this criticism, but it may also be stated, as the Post Office contends, that slow, stable growth is preferable to mushroom development, with its severe periodic fluctuations.

The Post Office telephone system has grown into a vigorous maturity, although its formative years were difficult. Only since the war has it had a chance to show what it can really do. The period from the telephone's introduction in 1877 until the establishment of a unified service under the Post Office in 1912 was characterized by competition for local monopolies between the Post Office, the private companies, and municipalities, and the oscillation between one policy and another by Parliament. Briefly, the situation was as follows. The Post Office possessed the legal monopoly, and all other undertakers had to obtain licenses. Moreover, the Post Office controlled all transfer and toll circuits. Although exchanges were established in certain places, Parliament, for thirty years, refused to adopt State operation over the whole country. In 1905 Parliament finally formulated a definite program, namely the purchase of the private company and the establishment of a unified service under the Post Office. The situation at that time has been described by Lord Wolmer as follows: "The Post Office owned and was operating the whole of the trunk lines, under the provision of the Act of 1892; the great bulk of the local exchanges were owned and operated by the National Telephone Company under a license expiring in 1911; in London and in certain provincial centres there were also Post Office exchanges with about 10 per cent of the total subscribers; under the Act of 1899 a limited number of municipalities were experimenting with systems of their own." The National Telephone Company's system began to be operated by the Post Office in January 1912. Only one municipality, Hull, continues to operate its own local exchange.

During the war the consumer's demand increased more rapidly than the Post Office could instal new service, because materials could not be spared. Renewals, estimated to cost £3,000,000, had been deferred; and spare plant in about three-fourths of the country was exhausted. As a result of the fictitious trade boom of 1919–21, thousands of applications from new subscribers could not be met. By the time telephone manufacturers had caught up with the demand the bubble had burst, but many people had formed an unfavorable impression of Post Office service—a misunderstanding that has had to be undone by the slow process of providing a constantly more efficient service. High prices and heavy capital expenditure in conjunction ruled from 1919 to about 1925, and during four years of this period the telephone administration sustained heavy deficits.

The expansion of the business since the war is revealed in the following table:

*In Thousands*

| Year | Number of Telephone Stations | Telephone Calls | | |
|------|------|------|------|------|
| | | Local | Trunk | |
| | | | Inland | International |
| 1920–21 | 979·6 | 785,500 | 57,417 | 185 |
| 1921–22 | 995·4 | 629,000 | 51,998 | 213 |
| 1922–23 | 1,050·7 | 671,000 | 58,842 | 314 |
| 1923–24 | 1,158·5 | 762,000 | 69,608 | 355 |
| 1924–25 | 1,273·8 | 851,500 | 77,288 | 432 |
| 1925–26 | 1,390·2 | 930,000 | 86,001 | 490 |
| 1926–27 | 1,508·8 | 1,006,000 | 94,661 | 598 |
| 1927–28 | 1,631·2 | 1,070,500 | 102,207 | 702 |
| 1928–29 | 1,754·6 | 1,155,000 | 109,554 | 950 |
| 1929–30 | 1,882·1 | 1,204,500 | 117,130 | 1,125 |
| 1930–31 | 1,982·2 | 1,248,000 | 121,670 | 1,139 |
| 1931–32 | 2,054·2 | 1,305,000 | 124,462 | 1,227 |

It will be observed that the progress if not spectacular, has been remarkably constant. In January 1912 Great Britain had only 700,000 telephone subscribers; in 1922 the number had increased to a million; in 1927 it stood close to 1,500,000; and the two million mark has now been passed.

The United States, with about three times the population, has over nine times as many telephone subscribers as Great Britain. This has been a common cause of criticism in the British press. Such comparisons usually possess little intrinsic value. For example, it may be noted that America has about ten times as many automobiles as Great Britain. There are important differences of social structure and consumers' habits which should be weighed before comparing British and American public utility developments. Because the standard of living has been higher in America than in Great Britain, the telephone has been widely adopted by the lower middle class in the United States. It is not so in Great Britain, where, as a rule, only the wealthy and the upper middle classes instal residential telephones. Then, too, manners and traditions have caused an important difference in the acceptance of the telephone. The use of the telephone for social purposes has not progressed nearly so far in Great Britain as in the United States. One of the most striking differences arises over the relative use of the party-line. The British exalt privacy to such an extent that there are only 9,000 party-lines in the entire country. In America the party-line is the most popular form of residential service. This factor alone makes a great difference in comparisons of cost and of relative efficiency.

TELEPHONE FINANCE

The profitability and the success of any business which is expropriated depends in large part upon the price and the efficiency of the assets acquired. In the early years of the Post Office telephones, much of the blame which was showered on the Post Office was really the fault of the private company from which the service was acquired.

The purchase price of the National Telephone Company, as fixed by the Railway and Canal Commission's arbitration, was £12,470,264, as compared with the company's original claim of £20,934,100.[1] Although it is usually agreed that the price paid was not excessive, it is true that the Post Office found the company's system in a bad condition. Arrears of renewal and extension were still being made when the war occurred. "While *in articulo mortis*," states Sir Evelyn Murray, "the company had naturally been

[1] For the theory and the terms of the valuation, see National Telephone Co. *v.* Postmaster-General, 29 *T.L.R.*, 190, appealed 29 *T.L.R.*, 624.

K

chary of spending capital on additional plant, where it was not immediately revenue-producing, and of replacing material which the Post Office was bound to take over. Consequently a considerable portion of the transferred plant was not of a modern or efficient type, renewals on a large scale were necessary, and in many areas there was little or no margin of spare wires or switchboard accommodation." The Chairman of the National Telephone Company admitted that a great deal of the business was conducted "monstrously badly," and yet original investors were making 15 per cent on their investment.[1] Despite the handicap, Post Office telephones have made up a great deal of ground since the war.

Between 1912 and 1931 the Post Office had lost, on balance, about £1,000,000 net during the nineteen years it had operated the telephone service. Most of the gross loss was sustained between 1919 and 1922 when prices went sky-high, with little corresponding increase in rates of charge. However, the annual surplus in the last ten years has averaged around £560,000.

The latest study of telephone finance reveals some extremely interesting data.[2] The balance for 1931, despite the stringency of economic conditions, was £557,000. This represented a return of 5·15 per cent on the capital invested, as compared with an estimated 7·37 per cent on the American Bell System. The American administrative and incidental expenses amounted to 43·8 per cent of the total and absorbed 34·7 per cent of the revenue, as compared with the corresponding British figures of 36·0 per cent and 27·0 per cent, notwithstanding that the British expenses included a sum (£939,000) for pension liability which was, relatively, four times as great as the American companies expended on pensions, sickness, death, and compensation

[1] The best historical treatment has been written by A. N. Holcombe, "The Telephone in Great Britain," (1906) 21 *Quarterly Jour. Economics*, 96.

[2] A. J. Waldegrave, "British and American telephone accounts, 1931," (1932) 19 *Telegraph and Telephone Journal*, 30, 50.

benefits. The British Post Office put aside for depreciation 4·45 per cent as compared with 4·67 per cent in the case of the American companies. "For several years the British telephone revenue has been growing at the rate of about £1½ millions a year, but in 1931–32 it fell to £700,000, an indication that the industrial slump has had a serious effect on the telephone service," states Mr. Waldegrave. However, the Bell System was even more severely hit. There was an actual decrease of nearly twenty-eight million dollars in the operating income, which reflected a decrease of 292,000 in the number of stations and of 393,000 in the average daily number of calls. In the British service there was an increase of 73,000 in the number of stations and of 207,000 in the average daily number of calls, but to achieve a net increase of 73,000 stations, 183,000 cessations had to be made good.

The profit of the American companies was accounted for in part by earnings on the accumulated surpluses of past years. The British telephone service must turn over its balance to the Treasury, which also makes good any losses. This is a feature of Post Office administration which has been severely criticized.

There continues to be a great deal of speculation as to whether the British telephone service is costlier or cheaper than the American. This factor is usually uppermost in the minds of subscribers and of Post Office critics. As in so many other cases, comparisons are hazardous because there are so many differing factors to be considered. The general impression of the British public is that its telephone service costs much more than that of other countries. As a matter of fact, this opinion appears to be unfounded, and the Post Office has now taken steps to rectify the false impression. For example, Mr. H. B. Lees-Smith, a former Postmaster-General, stated in the House of Commons,

"I have been told that the average capital cost of a telephone in the United States is £47 and that in this country it is £76; and I have been told that that is the acid test of the relative efficiency of the two countries in this respect. But the House must take this into account, that undoubtedly the original capital cost is greater in this country than in the United States, largely because the United States has a material part of its system above ground, whereas six-sevenths of our telephones are underground, and the initial cost is very much higher. I would point out, however, that we get the advantage of that initial increased expenditure in smaller depreciation costs and our operating costs are less, so that if you take the all-in annual cost, allowing for depreciation and interest of a telephone in the United States and a telephone in this country, it works out at £9·17 in this country and £10·97 in the United States."

The following comparison, based upon official reports from the countries concerned, appears in the sales booklet issued by the London Telephone Service:

| | Charge for Installation | | | Minimum Annual Charge | | | Number of Calls included in Annual Charge | Charge per Local Call over the Number included in Minimum Annual Charge |
|---|---|---|---|---|---|---|---|---|
| | £ | s. | d. | £ | s. | d. | | |
| London .. | Nil. | | | 6 | 10 | 0 | None | 1d. |
| New York.. | 1 | 0 | 7 | 10 | 9 | 7 | 792 | 2d. to 2½d. |
| Paris .. | 8 | 5 | 0 | 8 | 10 | 0 | 1,500 | ¾d. |
| Berlin .. | 4 | 0 | 0 | 4 | 4 | 0 | 480 | 1¼d. |
| Stockholm.. | 1 | 7 | 6 | 4 | 8 | 0 | 1,200 | ½d.[1] |

The reader will observe that British charges appear favorably in an international comparison. The advantage indicated over American telephone tariffs is probably applicable to most sections of the United States.

When the National Telephone Company was taken over, the flat rate, i.e. a fixed annual payment independent of the number of calls, was in common use, as well as the measured rate. The Post Office considered this "inequitable as between the small user and the large because it entailed overcharging the former to compensate for undercharging the latter." The message rate, i.e. a fixed annual charge

[1] Extra calls in Stockholm must be paid for in blocks of at least 1,300 at a time.

for the installation, together with a uniform fee for each effective local call, was introduced throughout the country in 1921, and it is considered unlikely that the telephone service would ever revert to the old plan. Reductions in the unit charges between 1921 and 1927 resulted in an estimated initial saving to users amounting to £3,000,000. Several years ago Sir Evelyn Murray stated that "The experience of all telephone administrations is that the cost tends to grow rather than to diminish as the system develops. The subscriber gets the advantage, not in the reduction of his charges, but in the greater number of persons with whom he can communicate." The fall in prices and interest, and the technical developments of recent years, have encouraged subscribers to hope for a further reduction of telephone rates.

### TELEPHONE OPERATING EFFICIENCY

In recent years a large part of the criticism of the Post Office has been directed at the telephone service. The reasons for public dissatisfaction are complicated and seemingly deep-rooted. The telephone received such a bad reputation under private operation that many years have been required to overcome the popular prejudice. Then, too, the disastrous experience during the post-war boom has already been mentioned. One of the principal causes of dissatisfaction is the mistaken view that the British telephone service is greatly inferior to most foreign systems. Finally, defects of operating efficiency have caused justifiable irritation and resentment. The public attitude has been improved considerably in recent months as a result of operating improvements and because of greater attention to public relations and publicity.

In certain respects the service rendered by the British telephone administration is outstanding, just as in other respects it falls short of the standard set in other countries. In connection with the comparative tariffs referred to above, for instance, the Post Office emphasizes the following advantages: (1) the initial installation is done absolutely free. The practice of making a charge for installation is common outside Great Britain. (2) No subscriber is asked to pay for any more calls than the exact number which he makes. In most other countries the subscriber must pay for a certain number of calls whether he uses them or not. (3) Ninety-nine per cent of the subscribers in Great Britain are given continuous day-and-night service. In most Continental countries night service is given only in the larger towns. In small and middle-sized towns not only is no night service given but the day service is also restricted. This means that the night service in larger towns is less valuable because fewer places outside can be reached. (4) Practically every rural subscriber in Great Britain is given a service equal in every respect to that given to subscribers in the largest cities. Rural companies abroad which offer very low rates often operate systems of poor construction, employing single wires with earth returns, and giving an inefficient and unreliable service. In some cases the subscribers themselves have to supply part of the plant or arrange for the operating.

Considering the high standard of construction maintained throughout the country, it is surprising that the cost of the telephone to the British subscriber compares so favorably with foreign charges. The Post Office will establish and operate a rural exchange whenever eight subscribers desire it. No other country is nearly so generous. The average loss on these new exchanges for the first few years is £50 to £60 per annum. A private company would undoubtedly close hundreds of these rural exchanges.

Telephone poles and overhead cables have been reduced to a minimum in Great Britain, where six-sevenths of the wiring is underground. The amenities of the country-side are dominant considerations in Great Britain. Post Office cabling has been very expensive. There are few rectangular streets such as are commonly found in America. The telephone cables taper down to the smallest circuit, instead of being transferred to poles. The City of London is built on a watery foundation. Streets are old and costly to replace. These factors largely account for the higher capital cost per telephone as compared with the United States.

The principal difference between British and American commercial efficiency was stated as follows by Mr. William O'Brien, an American expert on public utilities, who, after observing British methods, said,

"But, after all is said and done, it is probably true that there are other reasons than the question of government or private operation. There is the matter of fundamental difference in methods of business in different countries, some rapid, and some easy-going. My experience in England has been that there is no great pressure anywhere at any time. . . . Probably that is one of the strongest reasons why England . . . is still at the foot of the ladder of telephone development."

Direct labor employed by the Post Office accounts for only one-fifth of the capital expenditure of the Post Office construction work. Steps have been taken by the Post Office to reduce telephone construction and maintenance labor costs between 30 per cent and 40 per cent.

The Post Office engineers have won deserved recognition at home and abroad. Several recent technical improvements in the telephone service are due to their efforts. Perhaps the best evidence of the progressive attitude of the Engineer-in-Chief's department is found at the Dollis Hill Experimental Station. This engineering laboratory and training school employs a full-time staff of over 200 and has an annual budget of £75,000. It gives instruction to 1,600 students at the present time. Pure research is emphasized, but specific problems of the postal, telegraph, telephone, and wireless services are also solved. In 1930 the staff undertook 550 experiments and 15 were put into commercial operation. The inventions of the single year resulted in an annual operating saving of £150,000, a 100 per cent return on the research investment. All patents go to the Government, but the individual may sell the foreign rights.

All of the staff are civil servants and there seems to be plenty of incentive despite the absence of the profit motive. For example, a device has been perfected which will automatically turn on a large fan in underground passages and cause a red light to burn in the nearest telephone exchange whenever an underground main contains more than 2 per cent of escaped gas. If this invention had been perfected a few years ago an explosion in the Holborn district which resulted in terrific damage might have been prevented.

Telephone apparatus companies are permitted to instal exhibits at Dollis Hill, and tests are then made to determine whether the Post Office will adopt new forms of equipment. Telephone receivers and other forms of apparatus are similarly tested before installation. Although the Post Office could undoubtedly manufacture much of its own apparatus, it has never done so. The possibility of turning to manufacture has no doubt assisted the Post Office to obtain better terms from the "loose ring" of international manufacturers.

The improvement of the telephone service in recent years has been very pronounced. Not only has the efficiency of the system been improved, but the management has learned to anticipate the desires of subscribers. An aggressive commercial policy and a successful public relations policy have emerged. Instances of these developments may be of interest.

The transformation of manual exchanges to the automatic principle has made rapid progress in late years. The telephone service opened its first automatic exchange in 1912.

"The Post Office policy," Sir Evelyn Murray has stated, "is to instal automatics where new exchanges are required either to provide for expansion or in substitution of manual exchanges which are worn out and due for replacement in the normal course but not to scrap manual exchanges of a modern type which still have an effective life before them. It will therefore be some twenty or twenty-five years before the conversion of the London area is complete. In the transition stage automatic and manual exchanges will be working side by side, and an ingenious apparatus, installed in the manual exchanges, will give intercommunication between them, just as if the whole system was of a uniform type."

So much progress has been made since Sir Evelyn Murray wrote, that present estimates for London provide for the conversion of the remaining manual exchanges in less than ten years. During 1931–32 no less than fifteen automatic exchanges commenced operation in London, including the largest exchange in the country, Mayfair. The accomplishment of the London Engineering Department received just commendation from engineering experts in all parts of the world.

The quality of the telephone service is ultimately determined by the efficiency of its staff. In recent years a great deal of progress has been brought about by giving greater attention to training. A central training school is maintained in London, where advanced as well as elementary instruction is afforded by a full-time staff. It is interesting to note that the student's attitude toward the public and voice training are two important aspects of the course.

Careful tests of operating efficiency are carried out constantly in each exchange. At the present time about 90 per cent of calls are effective at the first attempt, as compared with 75 per cent in 1920; and the answering time, i.e. the elapsed time between taking up the receiver and the telephonist's answer, averages 5 seconds. These results compare favorably with any foreign system which might be mentioned.

Service complaints are now attributable in large part to engineering difficulties, especially where changes to the automatic system are taking place. Probably the chief weakness of the telephone administration at the present time is inadequate coordination between the engineering and the operating divisions of the service. In other words, the principal fault of the telephone service is an administrative defect.

The modern commercial outlook of the telephone administration may be suggested by some recent examples. Three or four years ago the London Telephone Service opened a new exchange in Chelsea, the artistic center of London. The action taken by the management at that time is an interesting index of the public relations psychology which has developed in the service. Because the residents of Chelsea are different and because they were inclined to frown upon anything as mechanical as a telephone, the establishment of a new exchange in their midst required finesse. The new exchange was named Flaxman, in honor of the artist who, among other things, designed Wedgwood pottery. The halls of the exchange have been decorated with his works. This policy has not only resulted in cordial relations with the community, but it has established an admirable *esprit de corps* among the staff. The idea of developing local traditions and atmosphere has begun to spread to other exchanges.

Arrangements have recently been completed for a service which will enable a subscriber to leave his office or his home with the certainty that he will receive all telephone messages that have matured during his absence. Each subscriber to this service will provide a list of friends and business concerns with whom he has dealings, and a licensed company will inform them that, failing a reply to his number, all messages in his absence will be faithfully delivered. Other illustrations of the same sort of thing might be given. The important point to note is that the telephone administration has not only improved its technical efficiency, but its technique of approaching the public has also made considerable headway.

### TELEPHONE ORGANIZATION AND SALES METHODS

The head of the British telephone administration is the Director of Telegraphs and Telephones. His deputy is the Assistant Secretary in charge of the Telephone Service. The London Telephone Service is directed by a Controller, and the twenty-two provincial areas into which the country is divided are supervised by District Managers, who are assistants to the thirteen Surveyors and the nine Postmaster-Surveyors. Parallel to, but apart from the operating administration, there is the engineering organization, which is directed by the Engineer-in-Chief. At the present time cooperation between the operating and the engineering officials depends either upon voluntary consultation or upon cooperation brought about through the Secretary's Office. Greater collaboration between the engineering and the commercial officials is one of the greatest needs of the telephone organization. The Bridgeman Committee concluded that,

"much of the dissatisfaction with the telephone system is due to the general diffusion of responsibility and absence of coordination between those concerned with the various elements involved in the provision and conduct of the service. While the District Manager is, broadly speaking, responsible for the telephone service in his area he has no jurisdiction over engineering and little disciplinary control over the operating staff. The general public imagine that the District Manager is responsible for all questions affecting the telephone, and are not unnaturally exasperated when they find that there is no one authority who can deal with complaints, or ensure that orders are promptly and satisfactorily executed."

Other administrative changes have been proposed. The Bridgeman Committee strongly recommended that the telegraph service should be amalgamated with the telephone service. The writer cannot see how this would improve operating efficiency and it might easily have the opposite effect. Amalgamation would convert the telephone service's surplus into a deficit. Interchange of operating staff would not be feasible. Administrative coordination has already been secured at Headquarters. However, it will be suggested in the following chapter that greater autonomy should be given to the telephone administration as a whole and to its several geographical areas.

The first recommendation of the Select Committee on the Telephone Service, 1922, was that reorganization should take place "on more commercial lines." Until comparatively recent years, failure to adopt a commercial policy had been the greatest defect of the Post Office. This failure to stress sales, advertising, and public relations has now been rectified in the telephone service.

With the establishment of a separate Sales and Publicity Department in the Headquarters Secretariat, the local Contract Branch in each telephone center was renamed the Sales Department—a significant change in viewpoint. In the London Telephone Service the Chief Sales Officer now ranks as an Assistant Controller. He has two chief assistants, one dealing with development and publicity, the other with sales office methods and control. The salesmen have throughout been granted a small commission on the new business obtained by them, in addition to their salary. Special Post Office display rooms have been opened to promote the use of the most modern forms of telephone instrument. All of the salesmen are put through a rigid training at the Sales School which has been created especially for the purpose. The course is conducted by a private concern which specializes in sales and advertising methods. Prospective canvassers are recruited from other divisions of the Post Office, many of them coming from the telegraph branch. One of the best advertising agencies in London has been secured as consultant. The results speak for themselves. It has been revealed that in London alone, despite depression conditions, there was a net increase of 52,581 stations between September 1931 and September 1932.

During the depression years, the British telephone service has outstripped every other country in the extension of its business. Some of its accomplishments may be summarized as follows: during the past year telephone calls increased by fifty millions; public call stations are being established at the rate of two hundred a month; subscribers have been saved £6,000,000 per annum as a result of reductions which have taken place during the past ten years; and it is now possible to communicate by telephone from Great Britain with approximately 95 per cent of the telephone subscribers of the world. A business which can progress in times like these must be on a sound footing!

CONCLUSION

The writer's general conclusion regarding the Post Office telegraphs and telephones is that very considerable progress has been made in the past three or four years, whilst prior to that time the respective organizations were lacking in salesmanship and in a public relations technique. The change began to occur about the time Major Attlee was Postmaster-General, and he undoubtedly had a great deal to do with it. The new attitude can be strikingly observed by anyone who will take the trouble to go down to the Post Office counter training school, where, among other things, employees are taught to meet the public in the best commercial manner.

It has long been recognized that the Post Office possesses certain valuable assets, such as the high standard of education and the fine traditions of its officials. Candid observers have been ready to admit that the Post Office has many qualities which business firms lack and which they would find difficult to acquire. An official of the National Institute of Industrial Psychology, after having made comprehensive investigations in the Post Office and in many private and public utility concerns, concluded that "Business houses ought to follow the example of the Post Office in its methods and the Post Office ought to follow the example of business houses in making the best of itself" (i.e. in salesmanship and public relations). May it not be possible that Civil Service personnel and methods plus commercial advertising and technique (the latter to be supplied by outside experts as at present), will produce the future's most effective form of public service enterprise?

## CHAPTER V

# POST OFFICE REFORM

"It is doubtful whether there is ever any advantage in conducting an industry or a commercial service by the method of direct State control, i.e. by a government department." This was not a Chamber of Commerce resolution, but a significant conclusion expressed by a committee of the Trades Union Congress in 1932. It is indicative of the widespread view that public service undertakings are not best administered as integral parts of the central government, and that the Post Office should not be taken as an example for solving future problems of public control. This assumption which has grown up regarding the type of organization and control which it represents, has usually not been carefully examined. Prejudice, lack of definite knowledge, or the attractiveness of new forms of control seem to have influenced the minds of many who have condemned the Post Office. Our purpose is to analyze the constitutional and administrative problems of the Post Office, as a means of determining the merits and demerits of this form of control, and to ascertain if reforms are possible which might rectify some of the faults attributed to the organization.

There are several aspects of Post Office administration which deserve constructive criticism. Many thoughtful people believe that the interference of the House of Commons in the routine affairs of the Post Office results in an unprogressive, timid policy at St. Martin's-le-Grand. The business community constantly points out that a great commercial service such as the Post Office should keep its own surpluses, determine its own capital outlay, in other words, be free from Treasury control. It has been said that the Post Office would probably improve the quality of its services if it were not required to perform so many dissimilar functions. Since the publication of the Bridgeman Report, a great deal has been said about over-centralization of management, and the red-tape and lack of initiative which are said to result therefrom. Arising out of the same circumstance, it is contended that too much power is vested in London, and that a decentralized system in which regional directors would possess more authority would produce a more satisfactory service. Finally, personnel problems await solution. Are Civil Service conditions detrimental to Post Office development? Should workers be given more voice in management, or is it desirable that Whitleyism should be curtailed? It is suggested that these basic issues, plus the ancillary questions which emerge, deserve complete and candid consideration.

A few Conservative critics favor a radical reform of the Post Office, namely its conversion into a public utility trust. Lord Wolmer's *Post Office Reform* was written to support this thesis. However, the Bridgeman Committee, which was instituted in consequence of Lord Wolmer's persistent criticism in the House of Commons and in the press, concluded that it is not desirable to change "the status of the Post Office to that of a Public Utility Company or Statutory Authority, either wholly or in part." Without wishing to anticipate too much, it may be suggested that the existing form of organization possesses several important advantages over other types of public utility enterprise, but that important reforms in the present system need to be made if these salutary factors are to operate to the greatest advantage.

#### HOUSE OF COMMONS INTERFERENCE

In summarizing his criticisms of the Post Office Lord Wolmer has stated, "Parliamentary control must be held to be the root of all inefficiency in the Post Office. It involves the changing Postmaster-General, Treasury control, over-centralization, Civil Service conditions, and the conversion of a

communications service into a tax-collecting machine."
Not many people support the extreme proposal of Lord
Wolmer, but there is rather general agreement that some
modification of Parliamentary control is desirable.

Parliamentary control, writes a former Postmaster-General,[1]
is responsible for timidity and centralization, thus militating
against the adoption of a public relations technique. The
same writer has suggested other serious defects of House
of Commons supervision. The Minister and his principal
officials, who ought to be concerned with major policies,
are often diverted to deal with matters which owe their
importance to the status of those who bring them forward,
i.e. Members of Parliament. Major Attlee believes that
Parliamentary questions directed to the Postmaster-General
are usually superficial. Frequent changes of Postmaster-
General result in discontinuity of policy and unfitness to
guide such a ramified and complicated undertaking as the
Post Office.

There has been a great deal of uninformed speculation and
loose thinking concerning the effect of House of Commons
control on Post Office efficiency. As a rule, the thinking of
those who would remove the Post Office from House of
Commons criticism follows along the line of the following
syllogism, viz. most business undertakings are not subject
to constant criticism; the policies and actions of the Post
Office—a commercial service—are exposed to such criticism; therefore the House of Commons should release the
Post Office from continuous interrogation. The writer began
with that idea. Is it desirable that the Post Office should
have to explain why two employees were discharged from
a Post Office factory? Should an artist be permitted to object
to the placing of a red telephone kiosk on the bank of the
Thames, where it was said to detract from the landscape?

[1] Major C. R. Attlee, "Post Office Reform," (1931) 2 *New Statesman and
Nation*, 565; and "The Bridgeman Committee Report," (1932) 10 *Pub. Admin.*,
352.

These are actual instances of so-called superficial questions which were recently addressed to the Postmaster-General in the House of Commons. It may appear on first thought that such questions are merely a nuisance, and that small matters are none of the public's business. However, reflection usually reveals that there is a larger issue involved: in the above questions one aspect of the merit system and aesthetic values were affected. Democratic control of public services is desirable if it does not involve losses which clearly outweigh the benefits.

Parliamentary questioning is said to be a waste of time and a burden on administrative officials. This charge appears to be largely unfounded. For example, a former Postmaster-General, Mr. H. B. Lees-Smith, has stated that the time required to prepare questions constitutes a very small item in the time budget of the Minister and of the administrative officials. Civil Service employees usually express the same view.

The House of Commons is said to bother the Post Office by frequent questions addressed to the Postmaster-General, but that it does not really devote sufficient attention to the major policies of the department. In the debate on the Annual Estimates very little helpful criticism is addressed to Post Office problems. In the writer's view, it is desirable that the Postmaster-General should resume the practice of presenting an annual report on the Post Office to both Houses of Parliament. The last report of this nature was presented for the year 1915-16. The Members of Parliament would by this means have better information with which to debate Post Office questions, and they and the public would be better informed on the financial position and the achievements of the Post Office services. Moreover, a special House of Commons committee, composed of members of all political parties, might act as a nucleus of informed opinion when Post Office policy is periodically considered. This committee should not be given authority over financial questions, nor

L

should it be permitted to detract from the responsibility of the Postmaster-General.

Centralized administration is said to be the most objectionable result of House of Commons control. But centralization as such is no fault unless it can be shown that the results produced are unsatisfactory. Large-scale undertakings everywhere have found it necessary to centralize the administration. However, as we shall point out, the Post Office has been able to decentralize to a greater extent than many people seem to think.

There are benefits of legislative control which are usually overlooked. Parliamentary questioning helps to prevent "grooving" in the Civil Service, by raising questions and points of view which might not occur to employees in the ordinary course of their duty. As a writer in a Post Office journal has said, "the knowledge that Parliament lies behind the administration ready to visit the sins of every minor official upon the Postmaster-General, with the usual consequence for the delinquent, is a stimulus to efficiency."

Certain reformers have suggested that the Postmaster-General should be given a fixed term of office or that a non-political appointee should be chosen for the position. This would mean a complete severance of ministerial responsibility. Unless the party in power supported him, the Post Office would suffer as a result of friction. Furthermore, the Postmaster-General might be tempted to infringe upon the Secretary's responsibility for the detailed administration of the Post Office.

The present constitutional relation appears to be satisfactory, but at times greater attention should be given to the selection of the Postmaster-General. Recent governments have done this. The practice of making the Postmaster-General a member of the Cabinet seems to be desirable. The Postmaster-General has an important duty to perform. Since civil servants are not expected to influence public opinion or allowed to defend their actions in public, it is indispensable that the work of the department should be explained by the Parliamentary Ministers. The present Postmaster-General, Sir Kingsley Wood, is said to have achieved more success in this respect than any of his predecessors. He has explained problems, pointed out achievements, and advertised the services of the department. The relation between the Postmaster-General and the permanent head of the department should be analogous to the collaboration which exists between the mayor and the city manager in American cities: public relations is the responsibility of the one; skilled management is the duty of the other.

### TREASURY CONTROL

The greatest need of the Post Office is self-contained finance. This reform was advocated by the Bridgeman Committee, and it has also been supported by writers of all shades of political opinion. Under the present system the Post Office profits are turned over to the Treasury and are therewith absorbed in the general revenue of the Government. Some one has said that "the efficiency of the Post Office is really determined by the ease or difficulty with which the Chancellor can balance his budget." The expenditure of the Post Office is also subject to Treasury control.

The existing relationship between the Post Office and the Treasury must be understood before constructive reform can take place. The Treasury determines the form and method of Post Office financial procedure, the regularity of its transactions, the rates of charge, and the amount, terms, and period of Post Office loans. Despite opinions to the contrary, it would appear that, as a rule, the Post Office has been treated generously where matters of major policy were involved. The chief exception consists of restrictions which have been placed upon Post Office building construction. So far as the telephone service is concerned, the department has probably received as much financial support as the consumer's demand justified.

The Treasury regulates Post Office charges. All important rates must be approved by the Treasury, and in some cases an Act of Parliament is required to sanction new charges. In practice, the wishes of the Post Office with reference to rates and charges have been respected. Treasury approval must also be obtained before the Post Office may engage in "new" services.

The number of employees and their remuneration and conditions of service are subject, in general respects rather than in detail, to Treasury approval. This limiting factor has an extremely important bearing upon Post Office personnel problems, as we shall see later. Although in practice the Post Office enjoys a certain degree of independence regarding staff questions, all regulations must be in conformity with the general policies of the Civil Service, which are determined by the Treasury. In certain cases organizations of Post Office employees may appeal to the Industrial Court. These are the principal respects in which the Treasury exercises control over the Post Office.

The kind of control applicable to an ordinary government department is clearly not suitable to a public commercial enterprise. The Post Office can be judged by results, i.e. by profit and loss accounts, and therefore deserves more freedom. Internal financial control is more effective than external supervision by the Treasury, because the pressure is continuous and is applied all around instead of at just a few points.[1] However, there is room for a great deal of disagreement regarding the particulars in which the Post Office should be granted more financial freedom.

The Bridgeman Committee recommended that the Post Office should contribute a fixed sum to the Treasury and that the department should be granted "some relaxation

[1] Sir Henry Bunbury, "Financial control within government departments," (1924) 2 *Pub. Admin.*, 131.

of the Treasury control over matters of necessary administrative expenditure." In such cases, states the Report, the obtaining of Treasury approval is very largely formal and relates to matters over which the Treasury cannot expect to exercise informed criticism. However, the committee concluded that what may be termed the "ordinary departmental Treasury control" is not "unduly vexatious." The inescapable inference from the Report seems to be that a considerable degree of Treasury control should be perpetuated, but the distinction is vague and the reasoning is undisclosed.

As a general proposition, the writer agrees with those who hold that a satisfactory solution of Treasury-Post Office relations will not be reached until the influence of the Treasury is limited to that of a "trustee for debenture holders." There is general agreement by writers on the subject that the Post Office should be permitted to carry over its own surplus from one year to another. The accomplishment of such reforms must not be thought easy. Parliament is a jealous mistress. Treasury control entails more than it does in other countries. Although the Cabinet as a whole decides a question, the authority and prestige of the Chancellor of the Exchequer is so great that his view is usually adopted. It is difficult for the Postmaster-General to carry his view with the Cabinet against the opposition of the Chancellor of the Exchequer. The accomplishment of self-contained finance will probably occur by degrees and by means of an understanding between the Chancellor of the Exchequer and the Postmaster-General to the effect that the Post Office will be given greater freedom, rather than by an abrupt change.

If then it is agreed that Post Office finance should be made as self-contained as possible, the remaining problem is the amount which the department should turn over annually to the Treasury. The Bridgeman Committee recommended that "a fixed sum of £11,500,000 plus 50 per cent of any excess over that figure" would be an appropriate sum, but that the amount of the contribution should be reviewed after three years. The profits of the Post Office during the past ten operating years have been as follows:

| | £ | | | £ |
|---|---|---|---|---|
| 1922–23 | 4,450,245 | 1927–28 | .. | 7,570,348 |
| 1923–24 | 5,291,022 | 1928–29 | .. | 9,012,764 |
| 1924–25 | 5,429,594 | 1929–30 | .. | 9,371,672 |
| 1925–26 | 6,667,882 | 1930–31 | .. | 9,187,454 |
| 1926–27 | 5,787,598 | 1931–32 | .. | 10,631,794 |

The Bridgeman Committee, after making provision for financial alterations which they advocated, concluded that the net surplus for 1931-32 would have been £12,303,000, while their estimate for 1932-33 was £12,296,000.

The sum of £11,500,000 fixed by the Bridgeman Committee appears to be considerably too large if the existing services are to be properly financed, and if a fair portion of the surplus is to be passed on to the users in the form of reduced charges. "If the Report had been written five or six years ago," Major Attlee has stated, "the amount recommended would no doubt have been about half this sum." The Post Office should be regarded as a business concern serving a public need and should at least have an opportunity of putting back as reserve a due proportion of the profits into the business. Moreover, if more than a fair amount is taken by the Treasury the shrinkage of the Post Office surplus will have a depressing effect upon the Post Office staff, because it deprives them of the hope of increased remuneration. It is not too optimistic to believe that once the larger question of Treasury control has been settled by permitting the Post Office to keep its own financial house in order, minor questions will be solved without much difficulty.

### THE PROPOSED FUNCTIONAL BOARD

We have now dealt with the control of the House of Commons and the supervision of the Treasury—the two principal respects in which it is alleged that the Post Office's efficiency is impaired by lack of freedom. In the balance of the chapter our attention will be focussed upon the chief criticisms of the Post Office's internal administration. This will involve consideration of major problems relating to organization, management, and personnel.

At the present time, the administrative hierarchy of the General Post Office is a composite of two conflicting theories of administrative organization, namely the functional and the "departmental." The latter has been accorded the greater weight. Next to the Secretary and the Second Secretary, the most important officials are those who deal with commodities, namely the posts and the electrical communications. In the Secretariat branches, only the Second Secretary and the Assistant Secretaries who are under his immediate supervision, i.e. Establishment, Staff, Stores, and Chief Clerk's divisions, deal with functional problems.

It is somewhat surprising that such a bifurcated system succeeds as well as it does. The Bridgeman Committee began its summary of the defects of the existing organization by enunciating a principle which has been almost uniformly approved by both Business Administration and Public Administration:

"The present position of the Secretariat contravenes what has come to be recognized as one of the fundamental principles of organization, viz. the distinction between policy and practice, between the administrative and the executive functions. The neglect of this important distinction we regard as one of the main weaknesses of the existing Post Office organization. . . . The Secretariat of the Post Office, as at present constituted, is concerned not only with the framing and the formulation of policy and with the supervision of its execution, but also with the conduct of the daily business of the Post Office services, for which it is unsuited, both by training and experience."

Most of the minor defects of the existing organization could be ignored if a policy-formulating board, chosen along functional rather than operating lines, were established.

The Bridgeman Committee recommended such a board, and the present Postmaster-General has indicated that the plan will be put into effect. A few years ago a board did operate for a short while, but membership was determined by giving representation to the several departments within the General Post Office. This scheme did not succeed because a member rarely felt called upon to participate in the deliberations unless the matter affected his own branch. No one would care to repeat that experiment.

The Bridgeman Committee suggested that the functional board should consist of the Postmaster-General, the Assistant Postmaster-General, the Secretary (to be called Director-General), and representatives of the following functional units, General Operating and Supply, Engineering and Research, Finance, and Personnel. Although a small board is desirable, the inclusion of a member to take care of public relations would appear commendable. As a former Post-master-General has said, "A competitive business needs a well-thought out and vigorously directed public relations policy." Employees' organizations have contended that they too should be represented on the functional board. The staff point of view might then be presented during the initial stages of consideration of policy rather than when that policy has been determined. This proposal seems to be consistent with the purpose of the Whitley Councils, which attempt to bring into Post Office administration "the utilization of the experiences of the staff."

This group of principal officials would be a tactical unifying agency; it would not be expected to interfere with the operating detail or attempt to share the power to issue orders, which would remain in the Secretariat. "The Postmaster-General," stated the Bridgeman Committee, "must have the power of over-ruling the Board in any matter of policy as Minister responsible to Parliament." This is a constitutional necessity, but it is doubtful if the Postmaster-General would ever find it necessary or justifiable to reject the will of the board when there had been fairly general agreement among the members.

The greatest effect of the functional board is likely to be felt in the Secretariat. Joint policy formulation will broaden the confines within which important decisions relative to administrative policy are reached.

## SECRETARIAT CENTRALIZATION

The Secretariat is "the sole source of authority under the Postmaster-General—no executive department of the Post Office can give an instruction to another department, nor can it through its own officers do anything for which it has not Secretariat authority, either general or specific. By virtue of its autocratic position the Secretariat has come to acquire a status out of proportion to that of other Post Office departments." Thus runs the Bridgeman Committee's indictment of Headquarters centralization. There is another side of the question of alleged centralization, namely the geographical concentration of authority which results from the relationship between the provincial units and the Headquarters Staff at St. Martin's-le-Grand. That aspect of the problem will be considered in the next section.

There has been a great deal of talk about the "autocratic" power of the Secretariat, but part of the argument appears to be based upon comparison which is not apposite. "The Post Office Secretariat has come to assume a position which has no parallel in the Secretariat of any other Government Department," reads the introductory statement of the Bridgeman Committee's consideration of Post Office organization. To which it may properly be replied that it is quite natural and desirable that the management of a great commercial organization, with its multiplicity of divisions, should differ from the ordinary political departments.

Recently a former Post Office official has written, "We

entirely agree with the idea of a functional Board, but we entirely disagree with the suggested degradation of the Secretary, for that is what it amounts to."[1] This construction is based upon the Bridgeman Committee's reference to the Secretary as *primus inter pares*, which phrase was undoubtedly not meant to imply absolute equality, much less degradation. But the suggestion that the Secretary's authority must not be impaired is based upon sound reasoning: definitive authority must exist. Operating efficiency requires that the permanent head of the Post Office should have the necessary authority to direct and coordinate the several branches of the business. In a realistic sense the Secretary, the efficient head, is far more responsible for safeguarding the public interest than the Postmaster-General, the temporary chief. For example, a former Postmaster-General stated to the writer that every year the permanent head of the Post Office saves the tax-payers thousands of pounds because of his ability to deal with the myriad private interests which are constantly attempting to foist their wares upon the Post Office. The Secretary is the permanent watch-dog of the public!

The Bridgeman Committee's reference to the Secretary's "autocratic" powers appears rather misleading. Power has not been sought; it has merely been difficult to delegate. Centralization is inevitable and, within limits, is desirable. But along with unified direction and responsibility there should be a broadening of the sources from which major policies will be jointly formulated. Furthermore, the operating services should be given greater independence in matters which relate to their internal administration. Finally, a more effective juxtaposition of the qualities demanded of the coordinating theorist and of the practical administrator should be devised.

The establishment of a functional board should prove to be the most important corrective of policy formulation

[1] G. H. Stuart Bunning, op. cit., 10 *Pub. Admin.*, 369.

within narrow confines. The board idea might also be adopted with profit in the case of the operating services. For example, a joint operating board for telegraphs and telephones would possess many merits. It would force the Secretariat officials and the operating staff to rub elbows, appreciate each other's problems to a greater extent, and tend to make the services more autonomous. If more joint planning took place, a greater degree of independence would be possible in the routine conduct of each service. Moreover, a joint board would provide for greater cooperation between the operating and the engineering sides of the service.

Failure to coordinate the commercial management and the engineering technicians more effectively is one of the greatest organizational defects of the existing arrangement. "The autocratic isolation of the Secretariat in relation to the Engineering Department and the narrow and specialized meaning attached to the word 'Administrative' in respect to staff generally," stated the Bridgeman Committee, "prevent these two departments from taking an adequate part in the general scheme of control." Engineering experience is insufficiently brought into the consideration and formulation of general policy, and moreover the technical side has not been properly coordinated with the commercial management in actual operation.

It is obvious that great weight should be accorded engineering opinion in the formulation of policies relating to the electrical communication services. The need of collaboration is greater now than ever before. After a commercial enterprise has been securely established on a financial basis the engineer should be relied upon to improve the service and to keep it abreast of new developments. This observation is particularly applicable to the field of electricity, where developments take place so rapidly. For example, the Postmaster-General announced on October 21, 1932, that Post Office engineers had made remarkable progress in connection with the utilization of very short radio waves to ascertain whether they could be fitted into the telephone network and give a more direct and economic connection between such places as can at present, because of natural difficulties, only be connected by a circuitous route. The inclusion of the Engineer-in-Chief on the functional board should tend to make the Post Office management more progressive, and the establishment of a joint telegraph-telephone board should also produce salutary results.

The telegraph and telephone administrations would obtain considerably more autonomy and efficiency, concluded the Bridgeman Committee, if the executive officials were given authority to issue orders directly to the field representatives of the Engineering Department instead of acting through the higher engineering officials. This proposal raises a vexed question. Would not the logical application of the recommendation divide and subordinate the Engineering Department? It is argued that the engineering division should continue to be equal and parallel to the commercial branch, and that greater coordination of the two units has been and will be obtained. In April 1931 for example, only 45 per cent of the new telephone installation orders were completed by the London Engineering Department in less than a week; at the present time 90 per cent of the completions occur in less than a week. In the provinces the percentage is 10 to 20 per cent less, but rapid progress is being made. Greater coordination between the commercial and the engineering divisions appears essential, but it would seem possible to accomplish this without lessening the autonomy of the Engineering Department.

In recent years a considerable amount of devolution has been deliberately brought about by the Secretariat. Officials and staff are agreed on this point. In 1932 a deputation representing Post Office staff associations stated to the Postmaster-General that "the policy of decentralization has been considerably extended." In most cases the officials of the Secretariat desire to dispose of as much detail as possible. The general situation may be described by giving a typical instance from the experience of the telephone administration. Let us assume that a District Supervisor is presented with a new question on which no policy has ever been established. His problem is referred to the Secretariat for a decision. Then let us say that somewhat later a slightly different question is raised by another District Supervisor. If it appears that the problem will recur, the Secretariat then sends out an advice to all officials who might be confronted by the problem at some future time. Ordinarily this action completely ends the Secretariat's concern over the matter. This procedure is applied as widely and as frequently as possible. The charge that the Secretariat "usurps" powers is largely groundless.

One of the grounds of criticism of Secretariat centralization is to be found in the delegation of a great deal of authority to clerks and to minor officials of the Secretariat, with the result that important proposals of the chief operating officials are sometimes pigeon-holed when otherwise favorable action might have been expected. Of course it must be recognized that the delegation of responsibility is necessary in every large-scale enterprise. This might not be a serious matter if questions were settled more frequently by direct contacts between higher Post Office officials. In their official relations the British, like the Germans, seem to rely very largely upon the formality of written reports and memoranda, with the result that the meeting of minds in direct conference is not a frequent occurrence. Constant consultation is one of the chief desiderata of successful management. For example, in the offices of the American Bell companies the rooms of the principal functional officials are closely connected. Delay, jealousy, and red-tape are the inevitable results of reliance upon written communications. Centralization of office accommodation and frequency of personal conference would, it is believed, prove of inestimable benefit to the administration of the British Post Office. Furthermore, the establishment of deliberative boards would probably speed up the acceptance of practical proposals which originate in the manipulative services.

The question of organization is only one element of the problem of centralization, and not necessarily the most important The success of a centralized administration depends to a large extent upon the training, qualifications, and experience of the Headquarters Staff. "We have formed the impression," stated the Bridgeman Committee, "that individual members of the Secretariat possess considerable administrative ability but that the usurpation of executive functions by the Secretariat, as a body, has in some cases deflected this ability into channels for which it is less well suited." There then follows this extremely significant observation,

"The administrative staff of the Secretariat are recruited through the ordinary Civil Service Administrative Class Examination: on joining they are appointed to the Secretariat and although in the first years of their service they may be detached for a few months to the provinces for service under a Surveyor, they have had quite inadequate opportunity to acquire any thorough training in or experience of the actual work of the Post Office. Handicapped as they are by this absence of experience, they spend the remainder of their official career, not merely in administering, but to a considerable extent in controlling, the execution of services of which they may have considerable theoretical, but little practical knowledge."

The higher officials in the Secretariat are, with two or three exceptions, men who have gone into the Headquarters establishment almost directly after university graduation. With few exceptions they are Oxford or Cambridge products. University men have had an opportunity to acquire assets which "rankers" rarely attain, namely the ability to learn the "why" as well as the "how" which is the distinguishing mark of the coordinator. It may be said in passing that the same considerations account for the superiority of the Administrative Class of the Civil Service over British business leaders, who as a group discount theoretical knowledge and pin their faith on what they call "acumen."

At the present time only two or three out of twenty or more of the highest officials in the Secretariat came up from the ranks. The percentage of "rankers" has tended to diminish. On the other hand, the heads of the operating services are, almost without exception, men who have come up from the bottom. Some of the most successful higher officials in the operating services have spent a short period in the Secretariat and have then been transferred to an executive service. Too few have returned, after learning the problems of actual administration, to the Secretary's Office. This policy compares unfavorably with the sound Army rule, that a staff officer must first have proved himself a good regimental officer, and that service on the staff must be varied with tours of duty in the commands. Failure to observe this principle has led to a certain feeling of exclusiveness and distrust in the relations between the practical heads of services and the theoretical coordinators at Headquarters. This is the crux of so-called over-centralization.

It is a well-established principle of the British Civil Service that, having the necessary education, one learns to administer by administering. The Bridgeman Committee has recommended that the initial stage of the university-trained man's career should be spent in the provinces, where he will obtain practical knowledge and experience. The competition for Secretariat positions should be opened to technical and engineering candidates "while they are in their prime," and the more promising of these should receive especial encouragement. Secretariat officials have sometimes been too far removed from "flesh and blood" problems to learn the necessary practical details and points of view which would make them better administrators, and would result in more harmonious relations with those who are responsible for routine administration. Many of the above considerations, it will be observed, apply with equal force to the relations between the Secretariat and the provincial Post Office administrations.

Critics of Post Office administration contend that provincial areas are not given enough independence, particularly in matters relating to the staff. Suggested reforms range from a suggestion that local officials should be given more freedom over details to a proposal that each area should be controlled by a director who would be given a large degree of finality. Such proposals are usually found to be greatly influenced by the decentralized system of the American Bell companies. The analogy is not a fortunate one because the American practice is explained by the existence of State boundaries, whereas in Great Britain there is no equivalent consideration. The intrinsic merits of the case for decentralization may best be judged after the existing system has been explained.

The country outside of London and Scotland is divided for Post Office purposes into twenty-two Districts. The administration of each area is entrusted to either a Surveyor or a Postmaster-Surveyor, the latter being in charge of large towns and their immediately surrounding areas. The engineering organization is parallel to the commercial administration, but the Superintending Engineer in each district is responsible directly to the Engineer-in-Chief, with the result that there is no direct connection between the engineering and the commercial branches of the service. In actual practice the Surveyors and Postmaster-Surveyors confine their attention to the postal and the telegraph services, which have been securely coordinated as a result of long association, and because the same staff usually handles both classes of business. The telephone work of the district is managed by the Surveyor's chief assistant, the District Manager. The Secretary's Office communicates directly with the

District Manager so that increasingly the tendency has been to make the telephone administration independent of the older services. This division of responsibility, the general results of which are beneficial, has created a difficulty as the telegraph and telephone services have become more closely connected. Unlike the American Post Office, fortunately, none of the local Postmasters is a political appointee, but all are permanent officials subject to the authority of the Secretariat.

The powers of the Surveyor and of the Postmaster-Surveyor are, except in minor respects, the same. Within certain limits the provincial directors may exercise their own discretion and authority. For example, the number of letter deliveries and collections are prescribed by Headquarters, but the times and supplementary arrangements are determined by the regional officials according to local requirements. Any matter which requires authority beyond the powers delegated is referred to the proper division of the Secretariat.

Most proponents of devolution confine their suggestions to staff organization and personnel problems. The Royal Commission on the Civil Service, 1929-31, concluded with reference to Post Office centralization that "having regard to the extent of the undertaking, we should expect to find a greater degree of decentralization than appears to exist at present in matters of staff control and organization. Many minor points appear to us to be suitable for local settlement, despite the risk of some minor differences in practice between one part of the country and another." At present the Surveyor has a certain measure of disciplinary control but cannot dismiss or degrade established staff who have passed their probation. He has power to make promotions from the manipulative to the first supervisory grade. The regional officials can engage temporary staff for periods of pressure, and add to the permanent staff, subject in the latter case to subsequent statistical justi-

M

fication to the Accountant-General. Several years ago recognized associations of Post Office workers were given the right of appeal to Headquarters in case of dispute arising with provincial officials. As this right has been used, another important centralizing factor has appeared.

As a means of bringing about greater provincial autonomy, the Bridgeman Committee concluded that

"We regard it as of vital importance that the regional director should exercise jurisdiction over all the functions appertaining to the post, telegraph, and telephone services. He should be the coordinating authority for his region, and his organization would, in effect, be a reproduction in miniature of the Headquarters board. The regional director would be the chief executive of his region and would be assisted by a staff representing engineering, financial, and personnel functions, and within his region engineering, finance, and personnel would be under his jurisdiction. He would receive, direct, and execute all orders from Headquarters in consultation with his technical, financial, and personnel staff and would ensure that all interests involved were coordinated and brought into focus."

The Committee further suggested that constant contact should be maintained between the various regional directors, who should be encouraged to visit one another's regions and to exchange views and information. Similarly, close contact should exist between the regions and Headquarters, and members of the functional board should pay regular visits to regions and discuss matters of interest with regional directors.

In recent years the sum total of provincial autonomy has gradually increased. At the present time the reforms which are most needed consist of greater coordination between the commercial and the engineering divisions, a closer association between the telegraph and telephone services, and a constant interchange of higher directing officials between provincial centres and Post Office Headquarters. No alteration would be justifiable which involved the sacrifice of uniform standards of service throughout the country. The solution of controversies between workers and officials raises problems which can hardly be definitively settled by provincial directors. A sense of grievance among the staff due to arbitrary local differences in treatment would be a source of discontent harmful to the service.

## PERSONNEL PROBLEMS

"Staff cooperation can never be fully realized until the Staff is no longer governed by Civil Service regulations. Civil Service regulations were not framed with the object of industrial co-partnership," continued Lord Wolmer, "and cannot be effectively twisted in that direction." The Union of Post Office Workers, with a membership of 98,000 employees, replied to Lord Wolmer's assertions by admitting that "there should be greater facilities for staff cooperation," but that nevertheless the position of the postal worker is superior to the condition of labor under private management or under "the so-called public utility form of control." Which of these views should be accepted? The issue is an extremely vital one.

In order to understand the setting of Post Office personnel problems, it should be reemphasized that the Treasury controls the major conditions of employment in the Post Office as part of its responsibility over the entire Civil Service. Hence, although roughly two-thirds of the British Civil Service are found in the Post Office, only 14,000 Post Office employees out of a total staff of 230,000 are engaged in classes common to the Civil Service as a whole. The majority of the Post Office staff belong to manipulative classes, such as postman, sorter, telegraphist, telephonist, and the like, which have no close counterparts in other branches of the Civil Service.

A complete analysis of Post Office personnel matters would entail a thorough study of the British Civil Service. Fortunately, such materials are already available,[1] and hence

[1] Herman Finer, *The British Civil Service*, London, 1927; N. E. Mustoe, *The Law and Organization of the British Civil Service*, London, 1932.

we may be content with reference to the distinctive problems which have an especial bearing upon the objects of the present investigation. Questions of remuneration, promotion, morale, and employees' organizations and programs will most likely contribute to an understanding of the relative merits of employment in a Department of State.

### POST OFFICE REMUNERATION

In the British Civil Service the lower paid staff are—or at least have been until recent years—slightly better paid than in industry, but in the higher branches the remuneration of business and public utility executives is strikingly greater than in Civil Service positions of comparable responsibility. The same situation obtains in the American Civil Service. The Post Office is the second largest undertaking in the country; the L.M.S. railway alone employs a larger staff. Still, there are easily a score of corporations which pay their chief executives from three to ten times as much as the salary of the head of the Post Office. The Secretary to the Post Office receives £3,000 a year. The Engineer-in-Chief, who heads the largest engineering enterprise in the country, is paid less than £2,000 a year. Several engineers engaged in public utility undertakings receive two or three times as much. The Controller of the Post Office Savings Bank, which is one of the largest and admittedly the most efficient and progressive financial enterprise in the country, receives less than £1,200 a year, whereas some bankers with no greater responsibilities are given many times more. Judging solely on the basis of this evidence, one would almost certainly conclude that the Post Office could not hold its own in comparison with large-scale competitive enterprises.

Post Office salaries are merely the general level of salaries in the Civil Service as a whole. During the past ten years or more the general aim of the Government has been to keep the lower levels of Civil Service salaries as closely as possible in line with comparable wages in industry. The model employer theory has been cast aside. Recent economy committees have said that civil servants should not be regarded as a "privileged" class, and that they should not receive more than those from whose efforts they are sustained. The assumption underlying these statements is so old that it is familiar, but so false that it is vicious. Government work is usually presumed to be uneconomic. Those who work for the Government are presumed to be wards of the State or in a position analogous to the fighting forces. In point of fact, all activities which add to the social well-being are economic. Although it is frequently not realized, State services add to the wealth of the individual and frequently increase the permanent wealth of the community. The tax-payer has two pockets: in one he keeps the funds with which he purchases commodities from the tradesman; from the other pocket he buys the services which are provided by the State. This is true of all government activity, but nowhere is it so evident as in the facilities provided by the Post Office.

Civil Service emoluments cannot fairly be compared with average industrial employment because of the following considerations which attach to the merit system; the standard of recruitment is highly selective; the rate of successful to unsuccessful candidates is low; the average educational requirement is considerably higher; strict medical tests are imposed; age limits, often narrowly restricted, are prescribed for the various appointments; higher social and moral standards are demanded (for the higher grades); and it is often virtually impossible for the civil servant to transfer to some other employment, a possibility which may account for rapid promotion in the commercial field.

The assumptions relative to the principles of Civil Service remuneration which appear to operate today were set forth by the Anderson Committee in 1923. They were incorporated into two principles:

"On the one hand, the State should hold the scales even between its own servants and those through whose enterprise its servants are paid. On the other hand, employees of the Crown would have a real ground for complaint if their pay were related to wages in industry only in the time of low wages. If they do not get pay relative to the boom, they must be spared the full severity of the slump. The State as a model employer offers security, a pension, a dignified service, and a moderate wage in exchange for the excitement and possibilities of private employment."

Similar ideas have been incorporated into the cost-of-living index system of compensation which was put into operation in 1920. The wages of postal employees are subject to fluctuations in accordance with the movements of the Civil Service Cost-of-Living Sliding Scale. Under that scale the amount of bonus varies, the full percentage bonus being payable on "basic," i.e. 1914, wages of 35s. per week and under. On wages above that amount the percentage addition to wages diminishes as the wages increase. In December 1920 the bonus was calculated on the basis of a cost-of-living figure of 155. In December 1931 the corresponding figure was 50. The effect of this reduction in the wages of postal workers whose basic rates of pay were 25s., 35s., 45s., 55s., and 65s., per week, is as follows:[1]

| Basic Wages s. | Wages including Bonus at 155 s.  d. | Wages including Bonus at 50 s.  d. | Percentage Reduction |
|---|---|---|---|
| 25 | 63  9 | 37  6 | 41 |
| 35 | 89  3 | 52  6 | 41 |
| 45 | 106  5 | 64  10 | 39 |
| 55 | 123  7 | 77  2 | 38 |
| 65 | 140  9 | 89  6 | 36 |

These figures are indicative of the reductions which have taken place in the wages (including cost-of-living bonus) of postal employees since the end of 1920.

According to a statement made by the Postmaster-General in 1929, when the cost-of-living index number stood at 67, only 84,000 out of 180,000 full-time employees received the Rowntree Minimum Wage.

Post Office employees' organizations have striven to dis-

[1] (1932–33) *The Post Year Book*, 405.

pense with the sliding scale system, but the Treasury adamantly points to the fact that the employees gave their approval of the arrangement in 1920 and insists that the agreement must stand. The employees have replied that the 1920 agreement was a provisional and compromise agreement which has resulted in civil servants being unfairly treated as compared with wage tendencies in industry. Their argument is supported on several grounds. In the first place, the cost of living figure is based on a working-class budget, and is hence inapplicable to Civil Service employment. The pre-war standard of pay was inadequate. Finally the measure of compensation granted by the agreement of 1920 represented an inadequate measure of compensation for the rise in prices over the 1914 level. Inasmuch as the Royal Commission on the Civil Service, 1931, registered its disapproval of the sliding scale system, the adoption of a consolidated wage may be hoped for in 1934, at the expiration of a temporary agreement whereby the index number will remain at 50.

In conclusion, it may be said that employees in the lower grades are better paid than they were before the war, but that their remuneration then was very inadequate. At the present time, the Post Office staff within inner London is not as well off as employees in other parts of the country. Most of the recent complaints have come from the manipulative and clerical classes located in London. Because of the super-cut and the sliding scale system, higher officials are relatively worse off than they were before the war.

Governments which are determined to reduce income and other forms of taxation will, as experience amply proves, cut the salaries of government employees as much as they dare. The condition of Post Office workers has been made far more difficult in late years because of the rigors of chronic depression and because of the difficulties of balancing the national budget. Intrinsically, the complaint of the postal worker is justifiable, because the business of the Post

Office has continued to expand, but the remuneration of the employee has progressively shrunk. The ultimate solution of Post Office remuneration policies would seem to depend, in the writer's judgment, upon the acceptance of the principle advocated by Civil Service staff associations in their evidence before the Royal Commission on the Civil Service. "We claim," stated the employees, "that the State Service must once more lead, not follow, the world of business. The State as employer no less than the State as the provider of social services for those members of the community who need them, has a duty and an interest in providing its employees with the means of maintaining that comfort in their home lives which is an essential background to loyal and efficient service."

### PROMOTION POLICY AND MORALE

A sound system of staff promotion is one in which the devitalizing favoritism commonly found in industry and the deadening seniority often associated with the Civil Service have been eradicated. The British Post Office sets an enviable example in both these respects, and may justly claim to be a model for both industry and for other Civil Service systems. The record of the Post Office is particularly impressive because the size of the organization militates against the acquisition of first-hand knowledge concerning all the candidates for promotion. This difficulty is overcome by keeping service records, by consultation between the immediate supervising officers and higher officials, and by a highly developed committee system in which each member expresses his judgment concerning the candidates. By means of this system a wider knowledge of candidates is made possible, and the danger of personal prejudice is substantially less than under the one-man rule regime which is usually found in industry.

A successful promotion system should assure the rapid

advancement of young men of exceptional ability, and at the same time nourish the hope and ambition of the large number of faithful plodders whose claim to preference is based upon seniority. The several branches of the Post Office perform this difficult task with varying degrees of success, but the net result deserves commendation. Lord Haldane stated in 1919 that the constant willingness of the Post Office to promote the twentieth man on the eligibility list established a precedent which should be followed by government establishments everywhere. The practice of promoting promising postal employees, irrespective of seniority, appears to have increased steadily. For example, an instance came to the writer's attention in which an individual was promoted who was number 84 on the seniority list.

In most branches of the Post Office the choice between advancement according to seniority and promotion out of turn is decided as each case arises. The head of one of the most successful services has inaugurated a plan according to which a certain proportion of promotions are determined by seniority, and a definite proportion of openings are reserved for employees of unusual promise. Eventually these "A" men will fill executive positions requiring those rare qualities, leadership, imagination, and coordination. At the same time, the great group of "B" employees are assured that application and effort will be rewarded.

By means of the policies above described the Post Office has produced progressive leadership and a conviction on the part of the staff that advancement will depend upon merit rather than upon prejudice and favoritism. Even in recent years when salary conditions have been so depressing, the reassuring effect of Post Office promotion policies has helped to maintain the morale of the employees at a generally satisfactory level. Post Office promotions, although influenced by the depression, have been maintained far better than in industry. Employees are automatically pensioned at the age of sixty, and in the C.T.O. several employees who were slowing down were retired on pensions at the age of fifty-five in order to maintain the efficiency of the service and to provide more opportunity for promotions.

The above observations apply primarily to the higher grades of the Post Office service. In the manipulative class, promotion expectations have not been encouraging in recent years and immediate improvement is necessary. Among telegraphists and telephone operators, for example, there is a period between the ages of thirty and forty-five when promotions are negligible. The deadening effect of this situation is readily observable. Discouragement is particularly noticeable in the telegraph service. In recent years the situation has been thoroughly investigated by the National Institute of Industrial Pyschology, which has been engaged to study all departments of the Post Office. As a result of the Institute's findings and recommendations steps are now being taken to improve the promotion incentives of the manipulative workers.

Promotions and pensions are two important factors underlying the efficiency and atmosphere of the Post Office. Permanence of tenure, particularly in a period like the past twelve years, represents another advantage which government employment has over industrial or public utility employment, although in the latter case the differences are not quite as great. Low wages can be tolerated better when security and a pension are assured, and when promotion is within the realm of possibility.

The most important asset of any undertaking is "atmosphere," as Lord Haldane pointed out to the Coal Commission in 1919. This intangible quality is found among the higher officials of the Post Office to a more striking extent than in any enterprise within the writer's knowledge, and the influence is so important, and its extension in future years is so vital, that an attempt should be made to analyze the atmosphere which has been created in the Post Office services. A philosophy of administration has been evolved from the traditions and from the thinking of the academically inclined officials. The Civil Service philosophy has not solidified, nor are its details invariably interpreted in the same way, but the outlines may be learned by anyone who assiduously seeks them. Ruskin, Hobson, Shaw, Wells, Webb, Tawney, Cole, and Laski have had a great influence on the thinking and the conduct of Post Office leaders. Service is held to be the one incentive which transcends and regulates all others. Public service is the way and the end of a man's career. Wealth is not desired. Civil servants, as H. G. Wells says in *"Work, Wealth, and Happiness of Mankind,"* are the "priest" type. "Give me my work, a little house, a family, a garden, and simple recreation," stated the head of an important Post Office service, "and that is all I shall ask."

There are many practical ramifications of a philosophy of management which is posited on the public service ethic, but space permits reference only to one. Such an atmosphere is contagious, because an official who is imbued with motives such as those described will be fundamentally interested in his staff. A former employee of the National Telephone Company afforded an arresting comparison between staff relations under private management and under the existing control. "The manager was a dictator," he said. "We would be called in and upbraided without a chance to defend our actions. We soon learned to tell him what he would like and nothing else. Under the Post Office we say or suggest anything we believe, and so long as we tell the truth no one will suffer. We are absolutely free, and it makes a big difference in the enjoyment of our work. True, it takes a little longer to reach decisions, but when they are reached they are more likely to be right." There is a world of suggestion in this comparison. Civil servants need to be shaken up occasionally, but progress is sure, stable, and democratic.

### COOPERATIVE MANAGEMENT

In the administration of the Post Office there are several means by which the views of the staff are brought into the formulation and execution of policies. These methods consist of deputations representing employees' organizations which are received by the Postmaster-General or by the higher officials; the Local, Post Office departmental, and National Whitley Councils—the nearest approach to joint management; and arbitrations before the National Industrial Court. In all of these activities the staff is represented by officially recognized employees' organizations. There are in the neighborhood of thirty of these associations, representing every class and department of the Post Office. Prior to the Trade Disputes and Trade Unions Act of 1927, several Post Office unions were affiliated with the Trades Union Congress and the Labor party. Although formal collaboration was made illegal in 1927, informal cooperation remains very effective in several cases.

The Union of Post Office Workers, which was formed out of an amalgamation of several associations in 1920, is by far the largest of the unions. Its membership of 98,000 comprises the manipulative classes, as distinct from the supervising, engineering, and clerical classes. The main objectives of the Union of Post Office Workers are: "(1) Joint management of the Post Office in conjunction with the State and the development of the Service on lines of increased public usefulness; (2) Improvement of the conditions of pay and employment . . .; (3) The organization of Post Office workers into a comprehensive industrial union with a view to the Service being ultimately conducted and managed as a guild." It is obvious that a union which desires that the Post Office should be managed as a guild should consider the existing degree of cooperative management not entirely satisfactory.

Employees' organizations are almost ceaselessly engaged

in bringing large and small matters to the attention of the administration. Most of these questions concern claims which individual members wish to have presented, such as accident or compensation benefits. But the unions concentrate upon major policies as well, for they believe that theirs is the responsibility for making the Post Office progressive. For example, in recent years the Union of Post Office Workers has given particular attention to the desirability of introducing a Postal Cheque System and to the need for new Post Office buildings. The Union has had no success with the first proposal, but it may have had some influence in the latter case, judging from building operations. The importance of employees' representations before the Postmaster-General depends upon several factors, prominent among which are the complexion of the Government of the day, the approachability of the Postmaster-General, and his influence on the Cabinet, and the tact of the employees' representatives.

The Whitley Council system, which was instituted in 1919, affords the best opportunity for employee participation in Post Office management.[1] The hierarchy of Whitley Councils consists of local, departmental, and national boards, the latter serving the entire Civil Service. The National Whitley Council consists of fifty-four members, the official and the staff sides being equally represented. The Post Office unions are allotted ten out of the twenty-seven staff representatives.

The objects and functions of the Post Office Whitley Council are expressed as follows:

"The general objects of the Council shall be to secure the greatest measure of cooperation between the Administration, in its capacity as employer, and the general body of the staff in matters affecting the Department combined with the well-being of those employed; to provide machinery for dealing with grievances, and generally to bring

---

[1] Leonard D. White, *Whitley Councils in the British Civil Service*, 70–135, Chicago, 1933.

together the experience and different points of view respecting conditions of service within the Department."

The Council consists of not more than thirty-five members, of whom not more than ten are appointed by the official side and not more than twenty-five are selected by recognized staff associations. A member of the official side must be elected Chairman, and the Vice-Chairman is chosen from the employees' representatives.

The detailed functions of the Post Office Whitley Council are the same as those of the National Whitley Council. The jurisdiction of the Council will suggest the objects of the plan and the comprehensive character of the matters which are considered: (1) Provision of the best means for utilizing the ideas and experience of the staff; (2) Means for securing to the staff a greater share in and responsibility for the determination and observance of the conditions under which their duties are carried out; (3) Determination of the general principles governing conditions of service: e. g. recruitment, hours, tenure, and remuneration, in so far as these matters are peculiar to members of the staff of the Department; (4) The encouragement of the further education of the staff, and their training in higher administration and organization; (5) Improvement of office machinery and organization, and the provision of opportunities for the full consideration of suggestions by the staff on this subject; (6) The consideration of proposed legislation so far as it has a bearing upon the position of members of the staff in relation to their employment in the department; (7) The discussion of the general principles governing superannuation and their application to the members of the staff in the Department.

Two very important provisions regarding promotion and discipline are found in the constitution of the Post Office Whitley Council. "Without prejudice to the responsibility of the Postmaster-General for making promotions and maintaining discipline, it shall be within the competence of the

Council: (1) to discuss any promotion affecting the classes covered by the Council in regard to which it is represented by the staff side that the principles of promotion accepted by or with the sanction of the National Council have been violated; and (2) to discuss any case affecting the classes covered by the Council in which disciplinary action has been taken, if it is represented by the staff side that such a course is desirable."

Perhaps the most important provision of all is this one, which relates to decisions of the Council: "The decision of the Council shall be without prejudice to (a) the overriding authority of Parliament, and the responsibility of the Postmaster-General as such; (b) the responsibility of the staff side to its constituent bodies; (c) the authority of the National Council as the only Whitley Joint Body competent to deal with general questions. The decisions shall be arrived at by agreement between the two sides, shall be signed by the Chairman and the Vice-Chairman, shall be reported to the Postmaster-General, and thereupon shall become operative." The National Whitley Council will not hear appeals from departmental councils. In case of deadlock the matter may be referred to the Industrial Court if it is a matter which comes within the tribunal's jurisdiction.

The Whitley Council system has proved generally satisfactory, although it has not accomplished as much as was originally thought possible by some of its proponents. The Post Office and the Admiralty had already introduced a considerable degree of staff cooperation prior to the establishment of Whitleyism, so that there was a foundation upon which to build. In recent years the Whitley system has not accomplished spectacular feats like the reorganization scheme and the bonus agreement which were among the first fruits of the plan. During the period of financial stringency the Whitley Councils have produced very few cash results in response to the pleas presented by employees' associations. The principal benefit of Whitleyism is that staff organizations are able to get more closely in touch with the official side than could otherwise be the case. Whitleyism, one of the originators of the plan has stated,

"is a scheme for providing opportunities for workers to explain their ideas more intelligently and intelligibly than can be done by memorials or mass meeting resolutions and of affording employers equal opportunities of stating frankly what is their position and what are their difficulties. It gives chances and opens up avenues of information both as to fact and to the workings of the minds of both employers and workers which do not exist in any other scheme of industry. When the principle of Whitley is carried into effect, many things which seem harsh on the one side or unreasonable upon the other are shown to have some real foundation, and the harsher features can usually be improved even if the main trouble cannot be entirely eliminated, but this depends upon mutual frankness and in so far as either side refuses information on fact or successfully conceals the workings of its mind, Whitley is in danger of failure, for its whole success depends upon 'seeing what the other fellow thinks.' "

The principle of arbitration for the Civil Service was agreed upon in 1923, and in 1925 provision was made for appeals to the Industrial Court of certain disputes regarding remuneration and conditions of service. Proceedings may be instituted by government departments, by recognized associations of employees within the National Whitley Council system, and by Departmental Whitley Councils allied thereto on the application of either party. The court will consider claims involving the emoluments, weekly hours of work, and leave of classes of the Civil Service, but cases of individual officers are excluded. The court will not hear cases involving classes with salaries in excess of £700 a year, except by the consent of both parties concerned

The Industrial Court was established in 1919, and for the trial of cases affecting the Civil Service consists of an independent Chairman and two additional members, one of whom is drawn from the Government panel and one from the employees' panel. In substance, because the two other representatives usually disagree, the Chairman makes the decision.

Although it cannot be claimed that the Industrial Court has been of substantial benefit to Post Office workers, because it has rejected many claims, yet on the other hand it has handed down certain favorable decisions, notably one in 1927 which increased the basic wages of the manipulative classes by £570,000 a year (including cost-of-living bonus). Certain employees' organizations favor the extensive use of the Industrial Court, but the Union of Post Office Workers, although regarding the court as a very useful piece of machinery, prefers to try to secure agreement by direct negotiation and hence does not appeal to the Industrial Court as often as do some other Civil Service organizations.

Probably the most significant aspect of these limited forms of cooperation is that the employees are gradually being educated in the principles and the responsibilities of administration. As their knowledge and appreciation grow, a further extension of joint management may be expected. At any rate, the feeling of pride and proprietorship which cooperation engenders are unquestionably factors which produce good workmanship and permanent progress.

### SUMMARY

In conclusion, it should be repeated that the Post Office is by no means perfect, but that important improvements can be made. Chief among such reforms are more effective enlightenment of Parliament and of the public of actual Post Office accomplishments, greater freedom from Treasury domination, the creation of a functional board, more emphasis in general administration upon the financial and the engineering services, greater autonomy and coordination in the operating services, the prevention of too much centralization in the Secretariat, the granting of greater independence to provincial administration, and better standards of remuneration for employees generally.

N

When these suggestions are set forth apart from an accompanying explanation of the merits and accomplishments of the Post Office, the result is likely to appear more unfavorable than it really is. As a matter of fact, the efficiency of the Post Office has become so consistent that the public, having it permanently, mistakes minor dislocations and transitions in the continuous process of development for more serious complaints. The writer finds himself in agreement with a delegation of Post Office employees who, in answer to a proposal that the telephone service should be sold to a private company in order to raise revenue in the national emergency, stated to the Postmaster-General, "We submit that the critics will find it difficult, if not impossible, to point to any institution, or the staff of any institution, serving the public so well in the wide ramification of its services as the State-controlled British Post Office."

## CHAPTER VI

# NATIONAL ELECTRICITY PLANNING

## THE SIGNIFICANCE OF ELECTRICAL DEVELOPMENT

Post-war Britain, like most of the countries of the western world, has been conscious of the enormous social and industrial benefits to be obtained from a cheap and coordinated supply of electrical power. Like Germany, Austria, Italy, and other countries, Great Britain has concluded, as evidenced in the Electricity (Supply) Act of 1926, that the best means of modernizing industry and of keeping pace with world competition is to plan a coordinated scheme of electrical generation and transmission for the entire nation. The national electricity policy is impregnated with more industrial, social, and governmental potentialities than any public utility development yet undertaken in Great Britain.

Parliament decided upon rationalization in electricity production after a long and stubborn fight against vested interests and sheer complacency. If the Electricity (Supply) Act of 1919 had not been emasculated by the House of Lords, Great Britain would have led the countries which have given the State effective powers to unify the generation and distribution of super-power. Seven years later Parliament was forced to admit that urgent and courageous action must be taken if British industry were not to be outdistanced.

The principle underlying the Electricity (Supply) Act of 1926 provided that the country should be regarded as a single unit and that all the energy required for the nation should be generated in a series of stations of convenient size and situation, interconnected with one another; but the Act maintained the principle of separate distributing authorities as then existing.[1] The principal results to be expected from the plan, as viewed by the then Minister of Transport, were these: (1) the best existing stations would work at a higher load than is possible under localized conditions, while other selected stations would come in at peak periods to make up the requirements; (2) the less efficient stations would be closed down; (3) a considerable saving in fuel consumption; (4) the over-all reduction in capital expenditure by improving the load factor and the reduction of reserve plant; (5) the establishment of a uniform frequency for the entire country; and (6) the increased efficiency of industry: the adoption of labor-saving devices in the home: and the electrification of farms.

Great Britain has found it difficult to make advances in electrification because, to a greater extent than in any other country, industry has been naturally attached to coal and hence to the steam and gas engines. Many nations turned naturally to electrical power because coal was not plentiful. The transition from coal energy, consumed near the pit-head, to electrical power, to be made available throughout the country will probably bring about fundamental changes in the life of the nation. In recent years factories have sprung up by scores around the London area, bringing with the rapid redistribution of population stupendous problems of housing, traffic, and sanitation. The availability of electrical power has unquestionably played a significant part in the silent remoulding of the nation's fundamental alignments.

In 1926 Colonel Ashley pointed out that, compared with its principal competitors, Great Britain stood at the bottom of the list in the *per capita* consumption of

[1] Electricity (Supply) Act, 1926, 16 and 17 Geo. 5, ch. li; the best general treatments of the subject will be found in W. S. Kennedy, *The New Electricity Act*, London, 1927; Hugh Quigley, *Electrical Power and National Progress*, London, 1925; and Orren C. Hormell, "Electricity in Great Britain: a study in administration," (1928) Supplement, 17 *National Municipal Review*, 363–385.

electricity,[1] and this, he said, was an index of Britain's industrial decline in recent years.

In the period before the war coal had been the foundation of Britain's industrial structure. The export market for British coal had declined considerably by 1926. Countries which were formerly large users of coal, like Italy, had developed water power resources. Britain's industrial future, it was argued, depended upon the most effective use of the country's vast coal supplies as the means of intensive electrification. Moreover, a transition to electrified industry held out promise of remedying the serious smoke evil in the populous centers, of utilizing the by-products of coal, of reducing oil imports, and of reviving rural industries with the resultant improvement of social and health conditions in the country as a whole.[2]

Authorities on the subject believe that intensive electrification will play an important part in the efficient utilization of coal, formerly Britain's basic industry. This has been clearly illustrated by Mr. Hugh Quigley, a well-known authority on electricity development. At a time when France was rapidly expanding her generating plant, 1919–24, for example, her coal consumption rose from 45 million tons to more than 60 million tons. In 1924 Great Britain consumed 180 million tons of coal, and of this amount only 7 million tons went to produce electric power. In Great Britain the coal consumption per head of the population was 4·08 tons in 1914, 4·07 tons in 1920, and 3·52 tons in 1922, whereas countries which had speeded up their electrical development had either shown an increased consumption of coal or a less

---

[1] Consumption of electricity, unit per head of population (1926):

| | | | | | |
|---|---|---|---|---|---|
| Canada | .. | .. | 900 | Belgium .. .. | 230 |
| Switzerland | .. | .. | 700 | France and Germany | 140 |
| U.S.A. | .. | .. | 500 | Great Britain .. | 118 |
| Sweden and Norway | .. | 500 | | |

H.C. Debates, vol. 193, col. 1692, March 29, 1926.

[2] On these aspects of the subject, see particularly Liberal Party Enquiry, Coal and Power, London, 1924.

drastic decline. Mr. Quigley concludes that in the higher thermal efficiency of power stations a saving of 50 per cent in coal consumption might be effected, and this linked up with more exact study of fuel economy would save 18 million tons or one-third of the total national saving of 55 million tons mentioned as desirable by the Coal Conservation Report of 1917.[1] The same writer makes the following observation, which has a significant bearing upon the potentialities of the 1926 legislation:

"Twenty million tons of coal consumed under boilers generating steam for electric power purposes would supply energy equivalent to that already derived from fifty-three million tons. We are probably justified in stating that over sixty million tons of coal would be saved annually in this country through electrification of industry, transport, agriculture, and domestic heating and cooking methods."

The low average consumption of electrical power naturally contributes to higher prices than are found in more developed countries. The following comparison of the price of electricity, pence per unit sold, reveals the serious handicap borne by the British industry and indicates the urgency of the reform which was initiated in 1926:

|  | Year | Pence |
|---|---|---|
| Great Britain .. .. | 1922–23 | 2·07 |
| U.S.A. .. .. .. | 1923 | 1·05 |
| Canada .. .. | 1923 | ·72 |
| Switzerland .. .. | 1923 | ·60 |
| Italy[2] .. .. .. | 1924 | ·46 |

Although international experience had clearly revealed the uneconomic character of small generating units, Great Britain was covered by a maze of small, unconnected generating plants—presenting a striking contrast to any other leading nation. In 1926 there were 592 public generating stations, of which 494 belonged to authorized undertakers, mostly very small ones. Thirty-two stations were responsible for 50 per cent of the output, while no less than 462 small

[1] *Electrical Power and National Progress*, 28–44.
[2] Edison group of companies.

enterprises were required to produce the other half. The result was that the load factor was unreasonably low. Since electricity cannot be economically stored it must be generated as required. In the course of the 1926 debate the Minister of Transport stated,

"The demand of a station varies from hour to hour, rising from small loads to peak loads, and, as long as a station is working in isolation, it must have sufficient plant for the peak load, and for long periods most of the plant must be idle. The average load factor is no higher than 25 per cent, which means that only one-quarter of our plant is working at full capacity, and the other three-quarters of the plant is idle. To improve this load factor is really the great object of this Bill, and it should be the object of all electrical reform. In truth, it may be said that only about one-third of Great Britain is reasonably supplied with electricity. Over practically all the rest of the country there are small undertakings with territorial rights strong enough to prevent large enterprises being established in their areas, but incapable themselves of generating electricity on a sufficiently large scale and at a price low enough to encourage large-scale consumption. In our rural areas only about one-tenth are afforded even the semblance of a supply."

Because of the small units in which commercial power was supplied and the high prices charged by public supply companies, industrialists were virtually compelled to establish their own generating plants. In 1932 there were more than 4,400 privately operated generating stations in use by industry, coal mines, public utilities, and other forms of enterprise. This development aggravated the uneconomic character of the country's electrical development. The change to public supply will take several years, but the transition has begun. In 1924 public supply undertakings were responsible for about 58·6 per cent of all generating plant in great Britain, but in 1931 this figure had risen to 65·4 per cent, while private generating plant in industry, as apart from the railways, declined from 37·4 per cent to 30·2 per cent.

The Government estimated that by means of the national electricity plan inaugurated in 1926, the saving to the public would amount to £44,000,000 a year by 1940. Critics of the bill were justified in saying that this sanguine expectation will not be carried out automatically. If substantial savings are to be passed on to commercial and domestic users, the plan of development alone will not only need to prove successful, but adequate provision must be made to lower rates whenever the economies of large-scale operation make it possible. Whether the existing machinery of control may be expected to pass on the expected benefits to the community will require careful examination.

The new electricity scheme has had an important bearing upon the development of governmental and social policy. A precedent (so potent in British life) has been established for national planning in other fields of economic enterprise, and the fact that the Act was the creation of a Conservative Government makes its significance all the more striking. Moreover, the C.E.B., a public utility trust which the Act created to put the plan into operation, has since been considered the model example of the public board type of development. This is particularly evident in the debates regarding the B.B.C. and the London Passenger Transport Board. It is not too much to say that the popularity of the public utility trust in recent years owes its origin primarily to the satisfaction which has attended the creation of the C.E.B. The extension or restriction of the public utility trust will undoubtedly depend, therefore, upon the ultimate judgment regarding the success or failure of the present form of control over national electricity planning.

PUBLIC POLICY PRIOR TO 1926

Only three periods of Parliamentary policy relative to electricity development need to be distinguished. In the early stage, 1882–1919, Parliament treated public and private electricity undertakings in much the same way as it did water and gas supply: maximum rates were established and general provisions concerning service were laid down in General and Special Acts, but effective control was negligible. Municipalities obtained an early lead in the field. In 1919 the Electricity (Supply) Act was passed which established Electricity Commissioners who were instructed to draw up plans for the regional generation and transmission of electrical energy; but when the bill emerged from the House of Lords all provision of compulsory powers whereby the scheme might be made effective had been eliminated, and as a result very little was accomplished. The current era began with the passing of the Electricity (Supply) Act, 1926. The Electricity Commission was preserved as the planning and controlling agency, while the C.E.B. was created as the operating agency which would carry the scheme into effect. Profiting by experience, compulsory power has been provided in order that coercion may be used if negotiation fails.

In the early stages of electrical development in Great Britain there were many obstacles to encounter which were not found in new countries like Canada and the United States. Concerning the modest beginnings of the electrical industry in Great Britain C. R. Fay has written,

"Great Britain entered the age of electricity through the telegraph and submarine cable. She already had cheap power in the form of steam power generated by coal. Towards the end of the nineteenth century electricity was applied to lighting and local communications. During the last twenty years electricity has risen to be the rival of the steam engine as the motive power of the workshop. In 1905 in engineering workshops there was an electrically driven tool only here and there. Now they are in the majority; and the trend is towards ever smaller units of electrically driven machines."

The Minister of Transport said, during the course of the 1926 debate, "It is doubtful whether more than 34 per cent of the industrial equipment engaged in production in this country, and supplied from public systems, is operated by electricity." However, it will be generally agreed that only in comparatively recent times has electricity come to be regarded predominantly in terms of industrial power, rather than merely for lighting purposes. A statement made by

Colonel Ashley in 1926 throws a great deal of light on the situation:

"When electricity was first discovered, it could only be transmitted a few miles and it could only be used for lighting in congested or thickly populated urban areas, because that was the only place where it would pay. Therefore, any undertaking, whether municipal or that of a private company, normally took the municipal area as the jurisdiction over .which it was to range. Consequently, there sprung up, under legislative sanction, up and down this country, hundreds of these generating stations, and, as the radius for transmitting energy became greater, as it is today, these stations did not disappear as they naturally would have done, because, again, of our conservative nature, and also, as the House will understand, because of the very obvious difficulty of overstepping the municipal boundaries."

The municipalities obtained an early lead in the supply of local electricity, with the result that by 1926 public bodies owned and operated 335 supply undertakings and 248 generating stations, representing a capital investment of £103,480,000, while private companies accounted for only 209 supply services and 190 generating stations, with a total investment of £58,270,000.[1] There were several reasons for the greater number of municipal undertakings. In the first place, private capital was not willing to take the risks at certain times and places, particularly, so it is said, when the municipalities were guaranteed the right to expropriate the companies at fixed periods. Municipalities were guaranteed the right to purchase private supply companies in their areas —a right which was frequently exercised. Moreover, the municipalities frequently demanded the electricity concession in their areas in order to protect their investments in gas undertakings. Electricity supply companies were confined to corporate limits, with the result that when large-scale operations had been proved the most economical form of electricity supply, the parochial limitations forestalled the interconnection and consolidation of generating plants. The contrasting result, a small number of super-power zones, has

[1] *Report of the Weir Committee on National Electricity Supply*, 4 Stationery Office, 1927.

occurred in France and the United States, where companies are free from geographical restrictions. But perhaps the principal reason for municipal enterprise in the electricity field is that other forms of municipal service had established public confidence, and electricity undertakings themselves have proved conspicuously successful.[1] Cities like Birmingham, Leeds, Sheffield, and Manchester have for years operated some of the most progressive public services in the country, and eminent Conservatives, such as the Chamberlain family, have played a prominent part in extending the commercial services of the local authorities.

The most important Acts regulating electricity, prior to 1926, were the Electric Lighting Acts of 1882, 1888, and 1909, the Electricity Clauses Act of 1899, and the Electricity (Supply) Acts of 1919 and 1922. Many of the provisions of these early Acts have been superseded, but others are of great importance today. Prior to the legislation of 1919, the licensing and issuing of Provisional Orders to both private companies and local authorities was exercised by the Board of Trade, subject of course to a confirming Act of Parliament. In 1919 all electricity powers were transferred either to the Ministry of Transport or to the Electricity Commission.

The original Act of 1882 gave the Board of Trade power to require annual accounts from electricity undertakings, but the only other provision with reference to efficiency and profits stipulated that the companies and the municipalities might make "such charges for the supply of electricity as may be agreed upon, not exceeding the limits of price imposed by or in pursuance of their license, order, or special Act." The system of maximum prices has not worked well, and electricity is no exception. The maximum price plan encourages inefficiency. There is little wonder that the Minister of Transport stated in 1926, "The bill is necessary because only a small percentage of stations of this country are in an efficient state."

[1] Hormell, op. cit., (1928) 17 *National Municipal Review*, 368.

With reference to the revision of prices, Section 22 of the Electricity (Supply) Act of 1922 provided that the prices or methods of charge of both private and public undertakings may be reviewed every three years in case of complaint to the Minister of Transport by not less than twenty consumers, a private company, a municipality, or the L.C.C. This power, as we shall see, is exercised in conjunction with the Electricity Commissioners.

Two provisions in earlier laws afford an explanation of the parochial character of British electricity development prior to 1926—the vice that national planning primarily aims to cure. Parliament provided in the Electric Lighting Clauses Act of 1899 that companies shall not purchase or acquire the undertaking of, or associate themselves with, any company or person supplying energy unless authorized by Parliament to do so, and in case of contravention of this provision the Board of Trade might revoke the offender's license. In the Act of 1909, however, Parliament made lawful the taking of a supply of electricity in bulk. Not only was freedom of consolidation denied to private companies, but the municipalities' powers were, as it later appeared, uneconomically circumscribed.[1] In the Clauses Act (Sect. 4) Parliament prohibited the giving of supply and the laying of electric lines and works outside the prescribed area of the undertakers in the absence of express authorization. This provision has had a particularly adverse affect upon municipalities, who were often forbidden to sell power to "fringe" areas.[2]

[1] The fault was partly the municipalities', as William A. Robson has pointed out. "It was, no doubt, the reluctance of local authorities to combine voluntarily on a large scale for electrical supply purposes—despite notable exceptions such as the Manchester City Council—which led to the far-reaching measures for joint action introduced by the coercive legislation of 1919 and 1926." *Development of Local Government*, 117, London, 1931.

[2] Sir Charles Wilson, referring to the experience of Leeds, stated: "We could have supplied large areas by including them within our city boundary, but this House threw out the bill after the Department had reported in favor of our having the power to extend our boundary. Having spent £4,000,000 on our electricity enterprise, we were not allowed to sell the product of our great station to people about us, as we were desirous of doing." *H.C. Debates*, col. 1733, March 29, 1926.

The Member of Parliament who referred to this policy as "the dead hand of the State" really had reference to the parochialism and conservatism which have been the characteristics of governments dominated by the landed gentry. However, the 1909 Electricity Act permitted two adjacent municipalities to give a bulk supply from one to the other; and under the 1919 Act, any two local authorities—wherever situated within a power company's area—may be authorized to give a bulk supply one to another.

Joint electricity authorities are one of the most important aspects of national electricity planning. The Electric Lighting Act of 1909 first provided for the creation of joint committees or boards composed of two or more local authorities as regards any area of supply consisting of the whole or parts of the districts concerned. Here at last Parliament showed an inclination to permit coordination. This power, which was originally entrusted to the Local Government Board (later the Ministry of Health), is now a prerogative of the Electricity Commissioners. Although only three joint electricity authorities are now in existence, and only one had been created prior to 1926, some observers believe that this movement is the most promising aspect of future development.

The eventual planning of electricity supply was facilitated by Parliamentary provision for electric power companies in 1898 and 1899. These companies were vested with authority to supply large areas, generally as large as counties and sometimes larger. Their powers were strictly circumscribed, but most of the limitations were removed when large generating stations were made the central feature of the Electricity (Supply) Act of 1926.

In short, the period of regulation prior to 1919 was characterized by parochialism in distribution and very small beginnings toward large units of generation and transmission. Parliament's policy aimed at protecting vested interests and historical regions rather than at the greatest efficiency to be obtained from the coordination of regional power zones into a national plan. The maximum price system failed to stimulate efficiency, to lower prices to the consumer, or to prevent greatly variant prices in closely contiguous sections. The machinery of inspection and control was negligible and impotent. "In the past," stated the Minister of Transport in 1926, "legislation affecting electricity supply has had all the defects of State interference without effective control." The existence of varying frequencies in different sections of the country or even in the same city, worked a hardship on industry and on domestic users, and militated against interconnection. On the other hand, after 1909 a few large generating stations had been established; the way had been cleared for the development of joint electricity boards; and, in a few cases, interlocking directorates and the amalgamation of generating and distributing companies had already emerged amid the welter of private enterprise. Although rationalization and coordination were not really effective before 1926, the Electricity (Supply) Act of 1919 inaugurated a new era by the creation of a permanent planning body, the Electricity Commissioners.

THE ELECTRICITY COMMISSION

The Electricity (Supply) Act of 1919[1] was based upon the Report of the Williamson Committee,[2] which sought a method of reorganizing the electricity supply industry. Although the Act as passed by the House of Commons substantially incorporated the recommendations of the Committee, the opposition of the private companies in the House of Lords succeeded in eliminating the most vital aspect to the Bill, namely the Electricity Commissioners' compulsory powers. This fatal omission was rectified by the 1926 Act. Although not a single plan was put into operation in six

---

[1] 9 and 10 Geo. 5, ch. c; Keen, op. cit., 257–282; Hormell, 17 *National Municipal Review*, op. cit., 373–375.
[2] Cmd. 9062, Stationery Office, 1918.

years, it should not be concluded that the Act of 1919 was wholly unavailing: the Electricity Commission began to operate and to gain experience and a wealth of information.

The 1919 Act provided that Electricity Commissioners, not more than five in number, were to be appointed by the Minister of Transport, with the concurrence of the Board of Trade. Three were to be full-time officers, and three also were to be selected for practical, commercial, and scientific knowledge, including that of electrical supply. No member may be personally interested in any undertaking for the supply of electricity. The personnel of the Commission is generally admitted to be creditable. Sir John Snell, an engineer, is Chairman, and Sir John Brooke, formerly permanent Secretary to the Ministry of Transport, was recently appointed Vice-Chairman of the Commission. The remaining members are engineers. The term of members is seven years, but provision is made for reappointment.

On March 31, 1932, the staff of the Electricity Commission numbered eighty-one in all and consisted of thirty-seven established officers and forty-six unestablished and temporary officers. The Commission retains the professional services of certain consulting electrical engineers and employs chartered accountants whenever the necessity arises.

The Act made the Commission solely responsible to the Minister of Transport. Most of the electricity powers previously exercised by government departments were vested in the Electricity Commissioners. Yet, prior to 1926, the Commission had only a shadow of real power. W. S. Kennedy did not exaggerate when he wrote, following the passage of the 1926 Act,

"If the Act of 1919 had not been emasculated in its passage through Parliament, or if the wolves of the municipalities and the lambs of the private companies had fed together amicably under the aegis of the Commissioners in 1920 and the following years, the present Act would in all probability never have been introduced. It would still have been necessary to remove many of the legislative restrictions which have too long hampered electrical development in this country, but there would have been much less need to recast the whole system, as has now been done."

The Commission conducted some valuable studies during the first six years of its existence and issued several illuminating Reports, but prior to 1926 the work of the Commissioners never got beyond the stage of paper plans. The formation of electricity districts was undertaken immediately by the Commissioners, but it is conclusive evidence of the insufficient powers possessed by the Commission that, after six years, only seven of the sixteen areas originally contemplated had been tentatively delimited. This meant that only four of the great industrial centers of the country had been incorporated in potential electricity districts. Some competent observers believe that the Commission could have accomplished a great deal more if there had been a strong enough incentive to do so.

The difference between what was originally contemplated by the 1919 Bill and what finally became law may be shown by comparison. The Bill proposed to create Electricity Districts with District Boards composed of representatives of the supply companies, local authorities, and large power consumers in the districts delimited. They were to have powers to fix maximum prices, to compel service and extensions of electrical facilities to new territory, to take over generating stations in the area, to build generating stations if required, and to centralize the supply and distribution of electricity in large stations feeding out to small undertakers who would abandon generation of electricity and undertake distribution only. In other words, the Act of 1919 proposed to substitute effective regional control under a central body of Electricity Commissioners for the complexity then existing and to create a system by which the large generating station might come into existence and the work of effective interconnection be carried out. The Act of 1919, as originally drafted, really went further than the law of 1926, because it made more adequate provision for coordinated distribution and made obstructionist tactics less likely. Instead of this, Electricity Districts with Central Advisory Boards or Joint Electricity Authorities, and the Electricity Commission were created, but with no powers to compel any fundamental changes. The Commission had power to fix maximum prices and to arrange the generation and distribution of electricity in the Electricity Districts finally determined (but only in agreement with representatives of the undertakings in the several areas), to determine additions to generating plant, to approve of new power stations and extensions, to collect statistics, and to examine new projects dealing with electrical development. The Commission had no powers to overcome the system of local self-sufficiency, to effect interconnection of existing systems, to compel an undertaking generating electricity in a small station at excessive cost to obtain its power requirement in bulk from a more efficient station, and it had no effective sanctions in the matter of maximum prices or of service. "The situation was, therefore, scarcely affected by the Supply Act of 1919 and the additional financial clauses which allowed the Joint Electricity Authority as constituted to borrow money for the establishment of new capital stations became inoperative owing to the fact that no Joint Electricity Authority had yet entered into operation."

In certain sections of the country, however, large power companies and interlocking directorates began to assume dominant positions. The power companies then occupied and continue to hold the most advantageous position in the entire electrical field. They were created for the purpose of generating electricity and of selling it either to distributing companies or directly to great industrial concerns.[1] From

[1] If established industries (except railways, tramways, canals, and water companies) are located in the area served by distributing companies, the power company must secure permission from the latter before a supply may be furnished. Power companies are also prohibited from selling a supply for lighting purposes, except to authorized undertakers or when purely incidental, as in the case of a factory buying bulk power. Quigley, op. cit., 127; Keen, op. cit., 253, 254.

the very outset the franchises of power companies have been perpetual in tenure; they were not subject to the purchase clause of the Act of 1888. Another great advantage power companies possess is that they are protected from loss due to unprofitable extensions. This is made possible by a binding contract relative to the minimum period of supply, and a minimum return on the actual investment incurred in the extension. For example, the power companies require authorized undertakers before receiving a supply in bulk to agree to continue the supply for a period of at least seven years and to pay annually for the energy an amount equalling not less than 20 per cent on the outlay incurred by the company in making provision for the supply. Finally, through stock ownership and interlocking directorates some of the large power companies have been able to control not only the supply of power in bulk but also the distributing side of the industry as well. The most familiar example of this is the North-Eastern Electric Supply Company (formerly known as the Newcastle-upon-Tyne Electric Supply Company), which through stock ownership of a large number of distributing companies controls and actually operates the generation and distribution "throughout an area of over 2,400 square miles embracing practically the whole of the industrial area of the north-east coast." By the end of the war there were about thirty power companies in operation, but they were definitely limited by the retention of local monopolies in most of the large towns.

By 1926 the concentration of control was assuming a national complexion, as illustrated by the fact that a single Member of Parliament, Mr. George Balfour, was said to be a director of not less than thirty-three electricity companies. It is interesting to note that he was one of the principal opponents of the 1919 and 1926 Acts.

This was the situation which obtained at the time the Electricity (Supply) Act of 1926 was passed and when a second administrative agency, the C.E.B., was created. The complication of the administrative machinery caused a good deal of comment and criticism in the House of Commons, and it is still a debated subject today. "I am by no means satisfied that the relationship of the Central Board and the Commissioners are the right relationships," was the gist of several speakers' criticisms in 1926. Naturally, the multiplication of bureaucracy brought forth sharp protests. Opposite views were held regarding the likely result of the relationship between the Commission and the Board: either they would form a close partnership, removing all criticism and protection of the public interest, or else, so some said, the two bodies would disagree and cause obstructions and embarrassment. It must be admitted that in several instances the Act of 1926 left the division of functions and authority quite vague and confused. The administrative juxtaposition leaves a great deal to be desired, but the general outlines of control may be distinguished with a fair degree of definiteness.

### THE PLANNING POWERS

The functions of the Electricity Commission may conveniently be divided into the planning, judicial, and regulatory aspects of its work, whereas the C.E.B. is primarily the executive agency by means of which the scheme of interconnection and bulk transmission will be carried into effect.

Under the terms of the Electricity (Supply) Act of 1926 (Sect. 4) the Electricity Commissioners were instructed to prepare and transmit to the Board, as soon as practicable, a scheme relating to each of the electricity zones into which the country has been divided. The plans to be determined by the Commission dealt with three chief matters:

(a) to determine what generating stations (whether existing stations or new stations) shall be the "selected" stations at which electricity shall be generated for the purposes of the Board;

(b) to provide for the interconnection of selected stations and also for the connections with the systems of authorized undertakers. The main transmission connecting lines are to be constructed or, if they exist in any cases, and are suitable, are to be acquired by the Board;

(c) to provide (subject to the conditions explained later) for such standardization of frequency as is necessary for carrying out the interconnection referred to in (b).

Obviously these technical matters are the proper concern of electrical engineers—and that is what four of the five members of the Commission actually are. The members of the C.E.B., on the other hand, were not chosen for their professional proficiency, but for their practical experience in a variety of pursuits.

The Commission has decided upon ten electricity areas, instead of the sixteen originally contemplated in 1919. Nine of these units have been finally delimited and cover more than nine-tenths of the country. A small section in the north of Scotland will be further investigated and development is meantime deferred. The details of the several plans and the progress that has been made in carrying out the actual work of establishing selected stations, constructing the high-tension lines, effecting interconnections, and standardizing frequencies may best be discussed in the next chapter. At this point it will be desirable to consider the principles which have influenced the Commission in planning the several power zones.

The consensus of professional opinion in Great Britain has favored the view that centralization is wholly justified in a densely populated industrial area, while interconnection applies with equal force to a widely scattered area. World experience has demonstrated that the scientific development of electricity supply can take place in one large generating station or through interconnection of a number of fairly large stations in order to pool the demand for power over a wider area and hence relieve the pressure on any one station. Prior to 1926 the super-power station and the super-power zone could scarcely be said to exist in Great Britain since the largest power station did not exceed 150,000 h.p. and the largest power zone had an output of not more than 800 million units.

The most remarkable example of the advantages of inter-connection has been supplied by Germany, and the British have been primarily influenced by this experience. For example, three super-power stations now feed into a net-work supplying Berlin. In 1924 these stations had an output of 1,770 million units compared with 400 million units in 1918, an increase of 340 per cent.

The super-power zone has presented the British with a more difficult and a more urgent problem than the super-power station. Investigations which have been made make it "fairly obvious that the heart of the problem of electricity supply on a national scale lies in transmission, and the future of the super-power zone is tied up with it." Mr. Quigley has pointed out that of the capital cost of generation and transmission in twenty British undertakings, 1922–23, genera-tion accounted for 23·4 per cent of the average cost, while transmission and distribution represented 27·6 per cent of the total capital outlay. He therefore concluded that in almost every case the capital cost of transmission and dis-tribution is greater than the cost of generating plant, and that it is only in exceptional cases, where overhead trans-mission can be carried out, that this item is definitely less. On the basis of the 1922–23 figures, an addition of seven million kilowatts of generating plant would cost £163,800,000, but the transmission and distribution to correspond to this would amount to a charge of £193,200,000; in other words, out of a total of £357,000,000, transmission and dis-tribution would account for 54 per cent. At the end of 1930, out of a total capital expenditure of £354,000,000, £218,000,000 or 61·6 per cent was devoted to transmission and distribution.

In the determination of the proper electricity areas the Commissioners have been influenced by many factors, among which are the recognition of existing groupings, the supply of industrial and populous areas, the avoidance of trans-mission beyond the point at which it becomes uneconomical, equalization of the load on generating stations, ease of technical administration, and population and industrial trends. As the Electricity Commissioners stated in their First Annual Report,

"it is not a question of starting *ab initio,* to develop a comprehensive and standardized system of generation, transmission, and distribution on the basis of present-day knowledge and technical practice, as there already exists an extensive and heterogeneous development representing the uncoordinated growth of many years. It is obvious that, in many circumstances, the problem of reorganization resolves itself into the determination of the best method of adapting, modifying, and expanding the existing development with the view of ensuring as speedily as possible an improvement in the supply of electricity for the numerous and growing needs of the community."

The choosing of "selected" generating stations is fraught with difficulties, because vested interests must be placated and suspicions arising from political differences cannot be completely obviated. So far as concerns the technical criteria whereby generating stations are selected, the factors to be considered are quite clear, but the application of these standards in given instances is a subject of some difficulty. The basis of selection of generating stations, stated the C.E.B. in their First (1928) Annual Report, involves consideration of the cost of coal delivered to the station, the abundance of water for condensing purposes, technical characteristics of the station such as type and size of the plant units, steam pressure, etc., proximity to the load, and the possibilities of the site for the further expansion of the station. All electricity generated at selected stations is to be sold by the owners to the Board. The price at which it is to be sold is specified by the Second Schedule of the 1926 Act. Owners of selected stations must run them as regards total output, times, and rate of output, and with due regard to economy and efficiency, under the direction of the Board. Owners of other stations in the area may, subject to the provisions according to which generating stations may be closed, continue to manage their plants as they think best.

Certain selected stations will naturally have to be altered and extended as the scheme develops, and the Commission, on the application of the Board, has power to deal with these cases. In such circumstances the judicial as well as the technical competence of the Commission is involved. These extensions and alterations are divided into two categories: (a) such as are required by the scheme, and (b) additional extensions and alterations required from time to time by the Board with the Commission's approval.[1] The two cases are subject to different procedures. The former will be dealt with at this point, but the latter is a proper question for consideration under the judicial powers arising under the Act.

An effective refusal to enter into agreement with the Board as regards the original selection of stations and their operation under the Board's direction would soon make the Act a dead letter. Consequently Section 5 of the 1926 Act provides that in case the Board, subject to the Commission's oversight, fails to reach an agreement with the owners of a selected station, the station in question may be purchased by the Board and "transferred to a Joint Authority, if there be one in the district, or, failing the Joint Authority, to any authorized undertaker or company approved by the Board." As a last resort, the Board itself may acquire and operate the station. The same principles apply to main transmission lines.

In the case of disagreement with a municipality as a result of which its generating station or transmission line may be taken over or transferred, a great injustice is possible. Acquisition in the case of a power company will involve payment of the total capital expenditure on the generating station or main transmission line less depreciation on a scale to be fixed by the Electricity Commission; in the case of a local authority or joint electricity authority it means merely the transfer to the Board of the responsibility for meeting annual interest and sinking fund charges on the capital

[1] Electricity (Supply) Act of 1926, Sects. 5, 6, 7. Kennedy, op. cit., 19, 20.

borrowed, without repayment of those sums. The only proviso against this lies in the possibility of the C.E.B.'s refunding any capital expenditure raised directly by the municipality without recourse to loans. The writer agrees that "In any case, such a discrimination against the local authority is scarcely justified since the latter has been forced to expend considerable sums on development in the early stages without return, and the value of the electricity department as an asset in the accounts of any municipality for general purposes is very great indeed."[1] If these provisions should be used against the municipalities, and in some cases they are certain to be, the resulting resentment would undoubtedly be very great. Parliament assiduously protects private property in the case of compulsory purchase, but this recent instance and the provisions regarding municipal tramways in the London Transport Bill, prove that the rights of community property (the ratepayer's asset) are treated with little respect when they can be used to increase the earnings of the investing public.

The provisions of the 1926 Act relating to the closing down of generating stations are of great potential importance. In case the owners of a generating station, not being a selected station, are notified by the Board that the latter can supply the same quantity of electricity as then required at a lower rate, the generating station will be given a period of three months in which to accept or reject the Board's offer. If during the subsequent year the cost of generation remains higher than the rate offered by the Board, the Commission is empowered to close down the station within a period of not less than six months and to order the undertaker to receive his supply from the Board for a period of not less than seven years, on specified terms ascertained in accordance with the provisions of the 1926 Act. If the owners of the generating station are not satisfied with the decision regarding the relative costs of production, the matter may be referred to an

[1] "Financial aspects of the Electricity Bill," (1926) 102 *Economist*, 671.

arbitrator and assessors appointed by the Minister of Transport from a panel set up under the Act. "In calculating for the purposes of this section the cost of production of electricity generated by the authorized undertakers," reads an important provision of Section 14 of the 1926 Act, "no account shall be taken of the capital charges in respect of capital expended on the generating station."

The Act contemplates, as the normal procedure in the future, the erection of new generating stations under the auspices of the Board. Here again the Board may neither erect nor operate the new station unless the Commissioners are satisfied that no existing body can be found with whom satisfactory arrangements can be made. This is the only case in which the Joint Authority is not given preference. In case no other arrangement seems possible, the Commissioners may authorize the Board itself to provide the station by a Special Order under Section 26 of the Act of 1919.

The remaining technical powers of the Electricity Commission may be dismissed with brief reference. The only other planning power of importance is the establishment of a standard frequency. At the end of the year 1926 no less than 77 per cent of the total installed capacity in the generating stations of authorized undertakers was 50-cycle plant and most of it was designed for 3-phase working. Furthermore, the systems adopted throughout Europe, with the exception of Italy, are uniformly 3-phase 50 cycles. This is the frequency that has been adopted by the Electricity Commission.

The provisions of the 1926 Act (Sect. 9) relative to "Standardization of Frequency" are of such great importance that the exact wording should be given. The establishment of a standardized frequency, it will be observed, is a necessary concomitant of interconnection, and hence the Act provides that

"The Board may require any authorized undertakers or owners of any selected station to amend or alter the frequency employed in their undertaking or station, if and so far as such amendment or alteration is required to effect the standardization of frequency as the Board with the approval of the Electricity Commissioners may think expedient, subject to the payment to the authorized undertakers or owners of any expenses which they may properly incur in carrying into effect (including the cost of altering or replacing plant belonging to consumers), and the Board shall if required advance free of interest such sums as may be necessary to enable the said authorized undertakers or owners to comply with such requirements and they are hereby authorized to do so notwithstanding anything in any special Act or Order relating to their undertaking."

If the Board and the undertakers do not agree as to the sum necessary to carry out the work, the matter is to be determined by reference to the Commissioners, or at the option of the owners, by arbitration before a barrister selected by the Minister of Transport.

The Weir Committee estimated that the net cost of converting the stations of selected and authorized undertakers alone would amount to £8,000,000, but the Commission has stated that the net cost for the country as a whole will be double this amount. One of the aims of the Commission is to establish alternating current (A.C.) instead of direct current (D.C.) and common voltages throughout the country. In 1929–30, 145 undertakings were supplying D.C. only, while many were giving both A.C. and D.C. Most of the enterprises were operating within a field of about nine different voltages, but there were still forty-six declared voltages in operation between 100 and 480. The Act of 1926 provides that the cost will eventually be repaid by the electricity industry as a whole. The Electricity Commissioners act as the collecting agency through which the money is turned over to the Board. The necessary annual charges for interest and sinking fund are spread over the whole of the revenue received from the sale of electricity and apportioned between the suppliers in proportion to the revenue from all sales. The Commission has determined that forty years will be required to liquidate the necessary outlay for standardization.

The powers granted to the Electricity Commission and to the C.E.B. should be sufficient to guarantee national uniformity of frequency as expeditiously as possible. Standardization affects utilization as well as generation, and the inducement to the industrial firm to carry out conversion through the substitution of new motors must be sufficient to break down a feeling of natural reluctance and opposition. A policy of regionalism and of gradualness would have proved impotent, whereas a national policy vigorously pursued will make of Britain "one scientifically coordinated power zone."

THE COMMISSION'S JUDICIAL FUNCTIONS

The Electricity Commission combines the power to issue orders and establish policies with the duty to hold hearings and to decide controversies. At one time it acts as a planning body, at another it serves in a judicial capacity. True, no words of any Act refer to the Commission as a "court," but the powers provided by legislation, the attitude of the Commissioners themselves, and the nature and method of their procedure on certain occasions definitely establish the judicial character of an important part of the Commission's work. Whether hearings held before the Commissioners, and open to the public, are "judicial" or "quasi-judicial" is sheer sophistry.

The Electricity Commission does not by any means possess a monopoly of the judicial functions which arise under the provisions of the several electricity Acts. It was a matter of common comment at the time the Electricity (Supply) Act of 1926 was passed that no matter what else happened, the legal profession had been well taken care of and, if many disputes should arise, stood to profit generously. This is due to the fact that the principle of arbitration, as one writer has stated, "is sunk right into the Bill." In several cases an authorized undertaker may appeal against the findings of the C.E.B. or the Electricity Commissioners, or both, to the arbitration of a barrister appointed by the Minister of Transport. This barrister may call in the aid of one or more qualified assessors in the consideration of the appeal, and his decision, with certain modifications, is final. In several cases the Commission and the barrister have supplementary or alternative jurisdictions.

The principal cases in which the Commission may be called upon to act judicially are these: disagreement regarding the price to be paid for the acquisition of generating stations and main transmission lines; any dispute relative to the obligations and rights of owners of selected stations except those involving the cost of production, in which case the matter is referred to an arbitrator; questions regarding the cost, etc., of altering frequency; the relative cost of electricity in cases where an owner objects to the requirement that his station should take an exclusive supply from the Board; disputes regarding the closing of generating stations; applications for Special Orders by gas companies supplying electricity under the Act of 1925; and whether, in an application for wage compensation, a given station shall be deemed closed or restricted within the meaning of the 1926 Act.

At these hearings the parties concerned are frequently represented by counsel and the whole proceeding is similar to that of the Railway Rates Tribunal or the Traffic Commissioners. The procedure is more informal than in the case of the other two bodies, however, because the Commissioners are not legally trained and members of the public rarely attend the hearings.

The provision for appeals to the Electricity Commission received unfavorable criticism when the Electricity Bill of 1926 was before the House of Commons. Sir Charles Wilson stated that the Electricity Commissioners had been given powers of dictators and that appeals from the Board to the

Commission would never be properly heard.[1] Mr. Lloyd George said, "I hope there will not be these appeals to the Electricity Commissioners"; and Mr. Trevelyan Thomas concluded that "It is not much good saying that one can appeal to the Electricity Commissioners because the Board is the child of the Commissioners, and one does not get the independent judgment necessary when appeals are made. I hope that something may be done to establish a judicial authority to which appeals can be made from the judgment of the Board."

The suggestion that a special judicial tribunal should be created to hear disputes regarding the electricity plan is very interesting, but on balance it appears that the existing method of appeals to the Electricity Commission is preferable. Appeals to a court would involve delay, invite litigation, and transfer questions which are primarily technical into the legal domain. Moreover, as a result of seven years' experience with the Electricity Commission, it is the consensus of informed opinion that the Commission has discharged its judicial functions with scrupulous fairness and good judgment. However, it must be observed that the "argumentative" or coercive stage of the development has just arrived, so that the Commission has never been severely tested. So long as men like Sir John Brooke, who has had many years of experience hearing appeals as the former chief administrative official of the Ministry of Transport, are members of the Commission, it is doubtful if any strictly judicial body could command the confidence enjoyed by the skilled Electricity Commissioners. It is significant that the electricity industry and the municipalities have shown a preference for appeals to the Electricity Commission, rather than the alternative method of arbitrations before barristers

[1] *H.C. Debates*, vol. 193, col. 1731, March 29, 1926. "Then as to appeals," said the same speaker, "will anyone tell me the difference between the new Board and the Electricity Commissioners? It is true that they are different in name, but I say unhesitatingly that appeals from one to the other will never be considered satisfactory by anyone."

and assessors. Since 1926 many quasi-judicial hearings have been held by the Electricity Commission, but not a single arbitration has taken place. This situation may possibly be altered when additional generating stations have been closed or restricted.

The 1926 Act provides for several cases in which arbitrations by barristers are allowed. These relate to the scheme for interconnection, the selection, extension, and closing of generating stations, the cost of supply to main transmission lines and generating stations, the determination of expenses incurred through standardization of frequency and alteration of transmission lines, the price to be paid for generating stations and main transmission lines, and the adjustment of wage compensation when stations are closed or restricted. These are important powers, but it will be observed that in several instances the Commissioners possess an alternative, original, or complementary jurisdiction.

The law relating to the compulsory alteration and extension of selected stations may be taken as an example of the important duties imposed upon the arbitrator. It is provided under Section 5 of the 1926 Act that a selected station may be made the principal source of energy for a much larger area than was originally supplied, or it may be required to deal with a greatly increased load in the same area. The owners may feel in such cases that they are not in a position to accept the financial burdens made necessary by the Board's requirements, and they may then appeal to an arbitrator appointed by the Minister of Transport on the ground that to carry out the extensions and alterations would impose an "unreasonable financial burden" on them.

In the view of W. S. Kennedy, an authority on electricity law, the Act is not clear as to the result of the arbitrator's inquiry, and consequently a complete deadlock may occur.[1] If the arbitrator should find in favor of the owners, concludes Mr. Kennedy, "the appeal to the arbitrator in this case is of

[1] *The New Electricity Act*, 21, 22.

very little use," because the Board is empowered to take over the station or authorize some other undertaker to acquire and operate it. On the other hand, if the arbitrator finds in favor of the Board, it will be impossible to compel the complainant to carry out the extensions. No provision has been made in the Act whereby the Board may render financial assistance to the owners when extensions have been found necessary. It appears, therefore, that the provisions regarding compulsory extensions provide no real protection to owners, but fortunately these stipulations, like the utilization of the services of an arbitrator, are not likely to be employed in many instances.

If we add up all the cases in which arbitration machinery may be set up, the *Economist* has pointed out[1] that there is little of fundamental importance left apart, and the business of coordinating electricity supply depends almost entirely upon the ability of the Board to preserve "the goodwill of the authorized undertakers, or failing that, a barrister assisted by one or more assessors will virtually take over their duties." Moreover, in two important cases special orders made by the Minister of Transport must lie before each House of Parliament for thirty days, during which time there is opportunity for either House to take steps to prevent the orders coming into operation. In the first case, the right of the Board to acquire a generating station owned by an authorized undertaker where the latter is unwilling to carry out the arrangements considered necessary by the Board, and in the second case the determination of the tariff to be paid for the supply to and by the Board are at stake. Hence, on careful examination it appears that

"practically every feature of real importance for the successful realization of a nationally coordinated scheme of electricity supply lies at the mercy of a barrister or of a party sufficiently strong to carry either House of Parliament with it against the provisions, in certain instances, of the bill. It is obvious that, in the desire to avoid victimization the

[1] "The Electricity Bill in Committee," (1926) 103 *Economist*, 456.

Government has gone to the opposite extreme and placed the bill in danger of obstructionist tactics as adopted by an authorized undertaker determined to reduce the bill to nullity. The opposition to the bill in 1926 shows this probability is by no means an impossibility."

The real test of the compulsory powers of the Act appears to lie immediately ahead. The grid has been practically completed, and many additional generating stations must be closed. Objectors and obstructors have made their presence known. How will the Commission and the arbitral system withstand the baptism of fire? Litigation in the law courts would be unfortunate, but this is the ultimate sanction, as early experience has already demonstrated.[1] In the long run, however, the statesmanship and aggressiveness of the C.E.B. must be relied upon primarily if obstacles are to be successfully surmounted.

### LABOR POLICIES

The closing down of generating plants and the concentration of production in selected stations will ultimately mean the dislocation of a considerable number of employees. Rationalization always throws men out of work. Realizing that national benefits would involve inevitable personal hardships,

[1] In the course of correspondence between the Commissioners and the Corporation of Ealing during 1923 it transpired that the municipality had removed from its generating station certain obsolete units having a total capacity of 300 kw., and had substituted therefor a unit having a capacity of 2,000 kw., and that it was proposed to defray the cost of the alterations out of the accumulated profits of the undertaking. The Corporation contended that the alterations did not constitute an extension of an existing generating station within the meaning of the Act of 1919, and that the proposed manner of payment was expressly sanctioned by Section 52 of the Ealing Electric Lighting Order of 1891. The Electricity Commission held otherwise, and the case was referred to the High Court by the Attorney-General. The court decided that the expression "generating station" where used in the Act of 1919 means any buildings and plant used for generating electricity as well as the site of such buildings, and that the prohibition of Section 11 of the Act against extending the plant used for generating electricity covered an extension of the plant's capacity, and that the cost of providing an entirely new generating set was an expense properly chargeable to capital. Liberty was granted to the Attorney-General to apply for an injunction in the event of its being considered necessary. Attorney-General v. Ealing Corporation, (1924) 131 L.T. 467; 88 J.P. 153; Fourth Annual Report of the Electricity Commissioners, 44.

the framers of the 1926 Act adopted the policy of assisting employees who will be adversely affected by the national plan to adjust themselves after their employment has been automatically taken away.

Compensation is guaranteed to regularly employed officers and employees of electricity enterprises when, in consequence of the changes in the electricity industry brought about by the Act, they have been deprived of their employment or have suffered diminution in salary and have not been given "equivalent employment under like conditions." The guarantee extends over a period of five years from the date when a generating station has been closed or a main transmission line has been acquired. The employees affected are required to prove to a referee appointed by the Minister of Labor that their loss of employment or diminution of salary has not been on the grounds of misconduct, incapacity, or superannuation, and that the case otherwise comes within the law granting compensation. The amount of compensation is to be paid by the owners of the station or the main transmission line. These are policies which should have been more widely followed in recent years.

The Whitley Council system has been adopted in the electrical industry. The problems of fixing wages and of settling disputes relating to hours and conditions of service are handled almost entirely in the electrical industry by a framework of regional conciliation boards leading to a national council.

District Councils have been established in the principal industrial areas, approximately coterminous with the power areas. For example, District Council No. 1 has jurisdiction within the North-East Coast area. The board is composed of twenty-eight members, employers and employees having fourteen members each. In this area eight of the employers' representatives are appointed by company undertakings and six are chosen by municipal services. The employees' representatives are chosen by the trade unions in the several branches of the industry. These unions are strongly organized and are national in scope.

Appeals may be taken from the district councils to the Joint Industrial Council for the Electrical Supply Industry—the national tribunal in the Whitley system. Here again representation is equal, and practical results depend upon reason, goodwill, and patience rather than upon a decision having coercive force. Questions affecting the industry as a whole are also considered by the national council.

The relations between employers and employees in the electrical industry appear to be satisfactory, due largely no doubt to the beneficial effect of the Whitley regime. Collective bargaining seems to have proved successful in settling the wage disputes and in creating more uniform standards of service throughout the country. However, the electrical unions have not succeeded in preventing wage cuts as well as have the railway unions. Like the railway unions, though, the official policy of the electrical unions favors State management of the electrical industry and workers' cooperation in management.

SUMMARY

Great Britain has begun to plan. The first step in the direction of planned basic industries has been auspiciously taken because throughout the world it is generally recognized that intensive electrical development is the key to almost limitless industrial and social advantages. The first serious effort to coordinate national electricity generation was made in 1919 and if the bill had been passed without alteration the electricity scheme would have been superior in some respects to the compromise Act of 1926. The 1919 Act made room for local initiative and provided for the problem of distribution as well as for the organization of power production. The present Act is only the first step in a thoroughly integrated electrical network, but it is an important one.

Electricity Commissioners, created by the Act of 1919,

have powers to plan the generation scheme and to decide important controversies arising from the carrying out of the actual work by the C.E.B. The Commission also has certain regulatory powers which will be considered in the next chapter.

The entire country has been divided into ten electricity areas, but only nine of these will be intensively developed for the time being. All areas will, by means of interconnections and the construction of high-tension transmission lines, form a single network from which power will be sold to authorized distributors by the C.E.B. Selected generating stations, which will supply most of the bulk power, have been chosen. The Commission has established a standard frequency of A.C. 50 cycles for the entire country.

The time has just arrived when the judicial powers of the Commission may be put to a severe test, but experience to date has indicated that this function has been well administered. The Act of 1926 also made provision for the determination of disputes by means of arbitrations before a barrister selected by the Minister of Transport, but it is thought that these provisions were mere gestures and that they will prove to be of little importance.

In order to safeguard the interests of the workers who will be displaced as a result of the national plan, a policy of financial compensation has been devised. This provision, combined with the Whitley Council system for settling wage and employment disputes, has created a foundation for amicable labor relations.

The real test of any plan is what transpires in actual practice. In the case of the national electricity development this result may be learned by studying the record of the C.E.B.

## CHAPTER VII

# ELECTRICAL PROGRESS AND THE NATIONAL ECONOMY

## THE CENTRAL ELECTRICITY BOARD

The dynamics of national electricity planning are represented by the Central Electricity Board or the C.E.B. as it is usually called. During the first five years of its existence the Board has evidenced definite objectives, aggressive action, and highly satisfactory results. Progress on the national electricity scheme has surpassed the expectations even of its most ardent supporters. Those who prophesied that the Board would be merely the "child" of the Electricity Commission have been proved mistaken, or at any rate the precocious youngster bears no close resemblance to the older generation.

The Act of 1926 provided for the creation of a national organization, the C.E.B. The primary duty of this body was to carry out the work of concentrating energy in certain selected power stations and to erect a high-tension main transmission line which would interconnect these stations and link up the existing regional systems into a national "Grid." The Board does not own the generating stations and has no control over distribution. Its function is to make production more efficient through concentration and coordination, the instrument of coordination being represented by the main transmission system. It has power to obtain land compulsorily for wayleave purposes in common with any other public authority.

The C.E.B. is a new type of public coordinating board with distinct differences from organizations like the Port of London Authority and the Metropolitan Water Board. As has been stated, it is generally regarded as the model type

of public utility trust. Parliamentary control over the activities of the Board is not much greater than it is in the case
of the ordinary electricity supply undertaking, which, under
present legislation, must obtain the approval of the Electricity Commission for raising capital for the construction of
generating stations and for the erection of transmission
lines. The C.E.B. is a public body created by statute,
financed by the issue of stock which bears with it no voting
rights. Therefore the stockholders exercise no control over
policy. Principal and interest on the stock may be, but have
not been, guaranteed by the Treasury; but such guarantee
does not carry with it any additional supervision of the
work carried out by the Central Board. The C.E.B. is forbidden to earn profits. The Board can make its own arrangements with supply undertakings, fix its own tariffs, and control
absolutely its own administrative organization. It is, consequently, a singular type which combines public control and
the elimination of profit-making with a very large measure
of independence in operation.

The Board itself is nominated by the Minister of Transport, who, in selection, has paid attention to special qualities such as knowledge of industrial organization, finance, and
the control of large manufacturing establishments. Some
attention has been given to interests involved in or affected by
the national power scheme, such as the railways, labor,
local authorities, and electrical supply companies, but ability
has been considered the principal test of selection. The
membership of the Board has been criticized because it
is not as representative as the Act of 1926 contemplated.
Following the appointment of the Board in 1927, a writer
in the *Economist* observed that "The success of the new
legislation depends above all on the strength of the executive ability of the Board, since the latter has before it the
difficult task of conciliating many interests and pushing
through at the same time the national coordination of
electricity supply. At first sight the Board would promise

such ability since its members are well known in industry and trade; but closer examination does much to weaken the first impression. In the first place, it cannot be considered as genuinely representative within the meaning of Clause 1 of the Act," since electricity supply with three members bears too high a proportion, while shipbuilding with two members, including the Chairman, Sir Andrew Duncan, is also too heavily weighted. Local government, commerce, industry, transport, and labor are crowded into the two remaining positions.[1] The members of the Board have been appointed for terms varying between five and ten years. The above criticism undoubtedly possesses merit, because it is important for many reasons that the unequivocal policy of broad representation should be respected. Nevertheless, the auspicious launching of the plan seems to have justified the original selections, and now that five years have elapsed opportunities to broaden the personnel of the Board will arise.

The Board has made considerable use of the committee system, the most important ones being those which deal with the authorization of all acquisitions of land required for sub-station sites and other purposes of the Board, and to deal with all questions in relation to the obtaining of wayleaves not coming within certain guiding principles laid down by the Board. The organization at Headquarters consists of the Engineering Department, the Accounting Department, and the Secretariat, including the Solicitor's Branch. The Engineering Department is subdivided into the construction, the operating, the research, and the supply sections. Each district has its engineering and wayleave officials, who are responsible to the appropriate Headquarters Department. The coordination of the organization as a whole is performed by the Chairman and the General Manager. Most of the costs incurred by the Board are paid to consultants, manufacturers, and contractors, the latter of whom do

[1] "The Central Electricity Board," (1927) 104 *Economist*, 317.

the actual construction work. The Board's expenses will eventually be absorbed by the sale of power from the grid.

A special branch of the Central Board carries on a very intensive but unobtrusive campaign of education and publicity. The popular interest manifested in national electricity planning and the conciliation of diverse interests have been primarily attributable to the remarkable success of this department. Several tomes of signed articles have been produced since 1931, educational motion pictures are being circulated, and the active support of the highly organized electrical manufacturing industry has been enlisted. This liaison has had a great deal to do with the fact that since the depression there has been greater activity in the British electrical industry as a whole than in any other country in the world.

The work of the C.E.B. may be conveniently considered under three main heads: the establishment of the main transmission system, the standardization of frequency, and the development of power areas.

THE NATIONAL GRID

The principal accomplishment of the C.E.B. has been the virtual completion of the 4,000 miles of transmission lines which are required for the national electricity scheme.[1] The progress of the work has been attended by more popular interest than any construction program since the war. Broadcasts have been arranged on the spot and films have been taken when important units of the transmission system were completed. Some of these engineering feats have been truly inspiring, and naturally appeal to national pride. For example, the Roding Tower near Barking reaches a height of 362 feet, and the Thames Crossing Tower

[1] A large part of the information in this section was supplied by Mr. Hugh Quigley in the form of a special memorandum. The present development of the grid has been described in (1932) *Fifth Annual Report of the C.E.B.*

further east a height of 487 feet. The latter tower is the highest erection in England, exceeding Salisbury Cathedral, the tallest building, by 84 feet.

The completion of the high-tension transmission lines has been carried out a year in advance of original expectations. When the C.E.B. began to function in 1927 it was confronted by the following main problems:

(1) To concentrate the output of electricity into a number of generating stations selected for their efficiency and low operating costs, to construct a transmission system which would interconnect these stations and in this way improve the load factor and general operating conditions.

(2) To standardize frequency of generation at A.C. 50 cycles throughout the whole of Great Britain so that interconnection could be carried out and a national power system be created capable of functioning smoothly from one district to another.

(3) To take over the entire output of selected generating stations and sell the power to authorized distributors, the selling price to be composed of a fixed charge based on the kilowatts of maximum load and a running charge covering the costs of production.

In the preliminary discussion of the grid itself it was generally agreed that the scheme could not be expected to be in full operation much before 1934. The program for the grid's construction was not drawn up in absolute detail, as provision had to be made for changes and modifications dependent upon local conditions and unexpected difficulties. The Act of 1926 provided that after the Commission had prepared a plan for each area the Board should publish the scheme and give an opportunity to all interested parties to place objections to it before the Board. As a result of these representations some considerable modifications have been made in the plans originally drawn up by the Commission. In certain cases the routes have been shortened to link up more directly main grid points and in other cases, largely owing to wayleave negotiations, alternative methods of approach have been developed.

The first scheme prepared by the Electricity Commissioners was adopted by the Board in June 1927, and other plans followed at the rate of two each year. The last one was adopted for Southern Scotland in August 1931. The Commissioners listed the stations to be selected and to a certain extent planned the interconnecting transmission system for each area, leaving the construction to the Board.

In legal matters, negotiations have been protracted in connection with certain wayleaves where local opposition developed. The Board has been very successful, however, in avoiding expensive and protracted government inquiries and litigation. Only 2·36 per cent of all wayleaves secured in 1931, for example, were obtained compulsorily, although 10,000 wayleaves were obtained in that year. There appears to be no question that alterations of plan made necessary by wayleave difficulties have been, in some cases at least, a factor accounting for the fact that the grid has cost slightly more than anticipated.

The technical details regarding the transmission system are inappropriate in this discussion, but a few of the facts may be of interest. The transmission lines are steel-cored aluminium, capable of taking 50,000 kw. These lines are borne principally on transmission towers ranging in height from 70 feet to 487 feet. The largest river towers weigh as much as 290 tons, and the Thames Crossing towers near Dagenham have a span length of 3,060 feet. For primary lines operating at 132,000 volts, about six towers are required per mile and for secondary lines operating at 33,000 volts about eight towers. Thus for the purpose of the national scheme about 17,275 towers are required for primary lines and about 9,000 towers for secondary lines, making a grand total of 26,275. The total estimated tonnage of steel which has gone into the construction of the grid, inclusive of sub-stations and river crossing towers, is about 150,000 tons, while aluminium required for the complete system will probably be in excess of 12,000 tons.

The relation between overhead transmission and the

amenity question has raised local agitations which have occupied a good deal of space in the press, but which have not seriously retarded the progress of the plan. The Board has followed the policy of working in close contact with bodies interested in these matters, such as the local rural preservation societies, and has preferred to use the method of negotiation in preference to the method of compulsion. The areas in which agitation has been most marked have been the Lake District, the South Downs, Oxford, the New Forest, and parts of the line from Malton to Whitby. Certain negotiations have not been entirely completed, and, as has been said, in other instances some deviation of the proposed line has been necessary. For the most part, however, the country has been educated to the fact that the whole weight of engineering knowledge and experience in the United States, Germany, France, Italy, and Switzerland has been on the side of overhead transmission over large areas, and that the cost of underground transmission is from twice to ten times as great, depending upon the character of the country.

In practically every case the grid, either through primary or secondary lines, has established points of contact and supply, and wide areas are served by authorized undertakers with existing transmission and distribution systems, so that immediate advantage can be taken of the national power supply when it is available. The Board commenced trading in two areas, Central Scotland and Mid-East England, in January 1933, when 1,360 miles of primary transmission lines, 596 miles of secondary lines, and 94 miles of underground cables had been energized. In the completed scheme there will be more than 273 grid points from which authorized distributors will be able to obtain supplies of electricity. Switching stations are intended to link up different areas without transformation of electricity. At each selected generating station a transforming station will raise the voltage of generation to the transmission voltage of

132,000 volts, while at the other end of the circuit a second transforming station will reduce it to 33,000 volts, or lower pressures, to make it available to authorized distributors. A further stage in the process will be represented by distribution sub-stations transforming from 33,000 volts to the voltage required for supply direct to the consumer. The grid, therefore, carries out about half of the process from the production of electricity to its consumption by the public, the remaining half being performed by distributing companies, local authorities, and municipalities.

The national transmission system may at the outset prove in excess of existing requirements, but in the view of the C.E.B. it is certain to be fully loaded in a few years' time. In 1924 the total capacity of all generating plant in Great Britain (inclusive of private industry) was about 6,351,800 kw., whereas in 1931 it had risen to 10,744,200 kw. This means that the country had "increased its industrial capacity over the seven years by as much as the total increment from the beginning of industrial electrification to the end of 1914." The Board's plans have predicated a volume of electricity equivalent to about 500 units per head of population, this figure to be reached, it is hoped, about 1940. At that point the whole transmission line will be fully loaded; but the entire power scheme will not be completed much before 1935, when it is assumed that the output of electricity will not be less than 17,000,000 units compared with the estimated figure of 25,000,000 in 1940. The grid should be loaded, even in 1935, to the extent of 70 per cent, which is regarded as an economic load. The areas in which there is already standard frequency may be expected to develop more rapidly than those in which large-scale conversion of frequency must be brought about.

In making grid calculations for future electrification, the Electricity Commissioners and the Board have carefully avoided any supposition that railway electrification would take place. Railway electrification would undoubtedly be advantageous to the supply industry, however, because the railway load factor is very high, between 40 and 50 per cent. Financially it would make little difference to the Board, because the price quoted to the railways has been cut close to cost. The Southern Railway has already electrified its suburban lines, and judging from its increased passenger traffic and superior financial showing since that time, it will be difficult for the other railways to resist electrification on parts of their lines at least. As a matter of fact, it seems almost certain that the electrification of suburban services will take place as a result of the adoption of the London transport scheme.

### THE STANDARDIZATION OF FREQUENCY

The second function of the C.E.B. is to establish a standard frequency for the national electricity scheme. The Weir Committee advocated this policy very strongly, since they believed that without it, interconnection on a national scale would not be entirely effective. The Commission and the Board have accepted the same view and are determined to carry through the necessary reforms. On the other hand, the policy has met with strenuous opposition in certain quarters because the cost, roughly £19,000,000, will be spread over the supply industry as a whole for a number of years, and because the incidence of the transformation falls mostly upon certain areas rather than upon all districts equally. About £9,000,000 of the expense has been incurred in the North-East England area alone. The national view and the long look ahead justify the program of standardization which has been promulgated. Moreover, the advantages of uniformity to the manufacturers of electrical equipment and the resulting benefit to the export trade are important factors properly deserving consideration. The convenience to the retail buyer will also be a great advantage.

The Weir Committee expressed the opinion that the change-over to standardized frequency could be completed by 1929, but in this they were badly mistaken. The conversion of the North-East England area alone will probably not be completed much before 1935. In the meantime, the policy has made work for large numbers of electrical workers at a time when employment was very much needed. In every case of conversion to a standardized frequency the owner must obtain the authorization of the Board, and the actual work is carefully supervised by engineers and auditors employed by the Board.

The areas most affected by the standardization of frequency are North-East England, Central England, and Central Scotland. The consequent installation of new or altered electrical plant in consumers' premises will contribute to the work of modernization and reequipment of many of the most important industrial establishments in the country. It is hoped that the reduction in price of electricity supplied from the grid will more than offset the capital charges incurred by standardization of frequency. If all elements of the national plan are properly administered there is every reason to suppose that this expectation will be fulfilled.

### THE FINANCE OF NATIONAL ELECTRICITY DEVELOPMENT

When the Electricity Bill was before Parliament in 1926 more attention was given to the financial powers of the C.E.B. than to any other feature of the legislation. Since the passage of the Act criticism of the financial provisions of the electricity scheme has continued, but in decreasing volume.

The Weir Committee estimated that £25,000,000 would be needed to construct the transmission system and that the cost of standardization of frequency would be about £8,000,000. Parliament provided that the "maximum" sum which the Board might borrow is £33,500,000, but that this amount might be increased by the Board obtaining a Special Order under the Act of 1919. The Special Order must be approved by the Electricity Commissioners and by the Minister of Transport. Experience has demonstrated that the "maximum" is not a maximum at. all, because a stock issue of £50,000,000 has already been authorized. The engineering computations of the Weir Committee did not take into account all factors and were therefore not wholly reliable.

The Board may borrow specifically for the following purposes: (a) the construction or acquisition of main transmission lines or generating stations; (b) any other payment or any permanent work which the Board is authorized to assume and which the Commissioners decide should be spread over a term of years.[1] The cost of standardizing frequency, amounting to £19,000,000 instead of £8,000,000 in the Commission's judgment, falls within the latter category. The Board may borrow to pay interest on capital for the period during which it remains unremunerative. What that period is, the Commissioners, after consulting the Treasury, are to determine. An elastic clause further stipulates that the Board may borrow to provide working capital and for any other purpose which the Act provides that they may borrow.

In the last analysis, the Treasury exercises a fairly complete control over the general purposes for which borrowing may take place. A blanket provision, of very great importance, expressly stipulates that any borrowing must receive the consent of the Commissioners and that it is to be carried out subject only to regulations as to repayment and the like laid down by the Minister of Transport and approved by the Treasury. All sums are to be repaid within such period as the Commissioners may determine, and that period is not to exceed sixty years. Here again the Treasury must be consulted. Treasury supervision is a fitting and necessary

[1] Electricity (Supply) Act of 1926, Sects. 26–30; Kennedy, op. cit., 54–59.

form of control over public utility trusts so long as the impetus to free initiative is not stifled. These conditions appear to be fulfilled.

The money borrowed by the Board is to be raised by the issue of stock to the public. Section 29 of the 1926 Act provides for a Treasury guarantee to the Board. It is in form permissive, the words of the section being, "Subject to the provisions of this section, the Treasury may guarantee— the payment of the interest and principal of any loan proposed to be raised by the Board, or of either the interest or the principal." This provision raised a storm of protest from the individualists, but its inclusion was undoubtedly salutary. The mere possibility of a Treasury guarantee unquestionably makes it possible to raise money at a lower rate of interest, and it recognizes a *prima facie* right of public oversight of the finances of the Board. The Treasury guarantee has never been used and it seems unlikely that it will be. The outstanding stock of the C.E.B. bears interest at the rate of 4, 4½, and 5 per cent. Inasmuch as recent issues of stock have not been as readily subscribed as some earlier ones and have hence borne a higher rate of interest, the criticism may properly be made that the Board might have used the Treasury guarantee provision to the advantage of all except the investing public, naturally desirous of higher rates of interest. With money as cheap as it has been, and with the synchronous lowering of Treasury interest rates, it appears unwarranted to pay 5 per cent on stock invested in an enterprise of the character of the C.E.B.

In keeping with the usual provision, the Board may suspend interest and sinking fund payments for a period not exceeding five years, subject to the consent of the Commissioners, who must consult the Treasury before deciding. The latter part of this provision was utilized in 1931.

All sums received by the Board must be paid into a separate account with the Bank of England. The Act of 1926 expressly states the current expenses which must be paid out of receipts. These include: salaries and fees to members, officers, and employees of the Board; pensions and gratuities; repayment to the Commissioners of expenses incurred in preparing schemes under the Act; and repayment to the Minister of Transport of any expenses—roughly £30,000—incurred before the Act came into operation. The Board's accounts must be audited and published once a year and offered for sale at a price not exceeding one shilling.

Thus far, the Board's stock has, on the whole, had a favorable reception by the investing public. Out of £36,000,000 nominal capital raised in the market to July 31, 1932, £16,000,000 was definitely oversubscribed, £3,000,000 was raised privately, and about £17,000,000 was not fully subscribed. Every issue of the Board was standing at a high premium at the end of 1932.

The Electricity Commissioners have established regulations prescribing the period within which provision must be made for repayment. In respect of money borrowed for the purpose of standardization of frequency the period stipulated is 40 years; in respect of borrowings for other purposes various periods have been fixed for the respective classes of expenditure, e.g. freehold land, 60 years; buildings, 30 years; overhead lines, 25 years; underground mains, 40 years; plant and machinery, 20 years.[1]

Preliminary figures indicating the total cost of the national grid as apart from standardization of frequency, are now available, and it appears that both the estimates of the Weir Committee and also the original estimates of the Electricity Commission have been exceeded. The Weir Committee's computations applied to the year 1924 and did not visualize so comprehensive a program as has actually been undertaken. The Commission's analysis of the total expenditure required for the purposes of the scheme lay between £45,000,000 and £50,000,000, standardization of frequency, according to the latest estimates, accounting

[1] (1929) *Second Annual Report of the C.E.B.*, 24.

for about £19,000,000 and the construction of the main transmission system for roughly £25,000,000. Capitalization of interest on the latter during the first five years, and the cost of carrying out and operating the national power scheme account for the remaining sum.

In the *Fifth Annual Report of the C.E.B.* a significant statement was made relative to grid cost. It reads as follows:

"The cost of constructing the grid is now ascertainable within narrow limits, although some small degree of estimation is still necessary. . . . The cost will amount to about £26,700,000. In comparing this figure with the estimates made by the Electricity Commissioners in formulating the Schemes, it is necessary to note that the Schemes, as adopted by the Board, differed in some important respects from those prepared by the Commissioners; putting the two sets of figures on a comparable basis, the cost will come out within 2½ per cent in excess of the Commissioners' estimates, despite substantial expenditure on experimental lengths of 132,000-volt cable and on the undergrounding of some sections of secondary lines for the preservation of the amenities."

Criticisms of the cost of the national electricity development have been heard, but it is impossible to tell how much importance should be attached to them. Critics frequently base their suppositions on the Weir Committee estimates, an unwarranted procedure. The price paid for wayleaves is also mentioned, and it is alleged that in its haste the Board has been extravagant. This argument cannot be answered with certainty, but it may be observed that in the long run higher prices for land are probably more economical than long delays which would tie up capital and impede the progress of the national plan.

The criticism which does deserve frank consideration, because it is capable of constructive treatment, is the privileged position which the electrical manufacturing industry holds in relation to the contracts and construction work of the C.E.B. The British electrical manufacturing industry has one of the most closely organized and highly developed associations in the country. Moreover, the principal costs incurred by the Board involve wants which are filled by this and allied trade associations. Although Continental firms have been able to supply a small percentage of the Board's contracts, the time is not distant when the British manufacturers may (and many would say should) have a monopoly of the Board's business. That point has practically arrived now. Under such circumstances it has been suggested that Parliament should, by some means never definitely analyzed, take action to regulate the electric manufacturing industry, in order that the capital costs of the national electricity scheme may be properly safeguarded in the public interest. Tariff policies are bound to make the question of public utility status arise more frequently and acutely.

The interest and sinking fund charges represented by capital expenditure on the national transmission scheme will be recovered from the sales of electricity in bulk from selected generating stations to authorized undertakers. According to the Act of 1926, the Board was empowered to purchase from the owners of selected generating stations the total output of such stations and sell back to them what is required for their own purposes plus a certain charge to meet the Board's expenses. In a few years the Board will become the largest wholesaler of power in the country, and when that time comes the financial responsibilities of the Board should be considerably lightened. However, the Board is prevented by law from making a profit. The real problem lies in the proper integration and the maintenance at high efficiency of the generating stations and supply undertakings forming the backbone of the power areas.

## POWER AREAS

Nine of the schemes which will eventually form the national power system have been completely planned, while actual development of the tenth, Northern Scotland, will probably be deferred for several years due to the sparsely developed nature of the country. The nine schemes comprising the present network, and the dates of their adoption, are as follows: Central Scotland, 1927; South-East England, 1927; Central England, 1928; North-West England and North Wales, 1928; North-East England, 1929; Mid-East England, 1929; South Scotland, 1931; East England, 1930; and South-West England and South Wales, 1930. The smallest schemes, East England and South Scotland, cover areas which are predominantly agricultural and may really be considered part of the neighboring schemes—South-East England in the one case and Central Scotland in the other.

The importance of the other areas arises predominantly from their industrial character, which played an important part in the basis of selection. An economic analysis of the several zones may be of interest. "North-East England covers the shipbuilding, iron and steel, chemical and coal-mining industries of the North-East coast and hinterland. The North-West England scheme covers Lancashire with its textile industries, its coal mines, iron and steel plants, and engineering works in the vicinity of Manchester, as well as Cheshire, with its great chemical works concentrated round Runcorn and Widnes, while the Mersey estuary with its grain-milling and seed-crushing industries, shipbuilding and soap works also is included. Mid-East England covers the three main industries of woollen textiles, coal-mining, iron and steel; Central England, great engineering and electrical manufacturing industries, metal-working generally and automobile construction. The South-West England and South Wales scheme covers the coal mines, iron and steel plants of South Wales, confectionery, tobacco, and paper-making works in and around Bristol and wide stretches of agricultural territory. It covers also the great port of Southampton and runs as far north as Oxford with its automobile industries. South-East England, which has been one of the most recently industrialized sections of Great Britain, is

notable for an enormous number of small industries supplying articles in general consumption or materials required
for building construction of all kinds. It has, however,
three important industries, notably paper, cement, and electrical cable manufacture, as well as the Port of London.
Scotland as a whole has very large shipbuilding yards,
iron and steel plants, coal mines, while it has a number of
less important industries devoted to chemicals, oil-refining,
cotton and woollen textiles, paper, and printing."

A power map, contained in the Board's reports, will
indicate the exact division of the country. Reference to the
map will suggest the strategic importance of the Central
England area. As one writer has stated, "The Central
Midlands will probably be the most important section in
the whole national scheme, owing to territorial considerations, and the power center located in Birmingham may well
become one of the most active and economically operated
of any such centers in the country."

Each area should be ultimately in a position to meet
costs of operation and capital charges without subsidy
from other areas. In the meantime, agricultural areas lying
between industrial centers will be assured of a supply sufficiently cheap and available to develop their resources.
The main transmission lines are connected at certain points
in each scheme area with the trunk lines which run north
and south throughout the country. From those points
radiation rings radiate to link up a series of towns which
are distributing points.

In the selection of the most efficient generating stations
to supply each area the Board has departed from the Weir
Committee proposals on finding that the best results would
be obtained by a rather broader selection and greater
number of stations than the Weir Committee contemplated.
The total number of selected stations under the nine schemes
adopted is 135, new stations to the number of 16 being built.
Some of these stations, notably Clarence Dock and Iron-

bridge, are in operation, while, in the London area, two of the principal new stations, at Battersea and Fulham, have, in the one case, been completed, and in the other been placed on contract.

The total number of generating stations closed down between 1927 and 1933 was 146. Of this total, 39 stations can be traced to the operations of the Board. It is interesting to note that the grid as constructed links up twelve water power stations in North Scotland, Central Scotland, South Scotland, and North Wales—these being the only sections with effective water power resources.

Objections are sure to be heard when further generating stations are closed, but little opposition may be expected from the owners of selected stations. They have a great deal to gain and seemingly little to lose except complete freedom of action. In the Act of 1926 there is a proviso that where the owner of a selected generating station can prove that his cost of production would be less under independent operation than the price charged him by the Board, he can obtain from the Board his energy requirements at his own cost of production with no addition to cover the expenses of the Board. In practice, however, the fact that the national production of electricity will be concentrated in 135 stations instead of spread over 474 and that the demand for electricity is still increasing rapidly in Great Britain, will mean that each selected station will have a much greater output as part of the national system than it would have independent of it, and it will be almost impossible for the supply undertaking to prove conclusively that its costs would be less under independent operation.

The development of the grid and the unification of power areas have reached the stage where the results will soon be apparent. It is only natural, therefore, that attention should begin to be focussed upon the complementary aspects of national electricity planning, namely the improvement of distribution and the price regulation reforms which are

necessary if the advantages of cheap power are to be passed
on to the users. Both of these vital questions require careful
and candid examination. A great deal of study will be required. Our efforts can only scratch the surface and stress
the importance of the next steps.

The price of electricity in Great Britain is high and varies
greatly within neighboring districts. Although the average
price of electricity for all purposes has fallen from 2·047d.
in 1924 to 1·38d. in 1931, there must be a further reduction
of domestic and commercial charges before electrical power
will be widely used for household purposes. There is, therefore, a close and inescapable relation between the lowering
of retail and commercial electricity rates and the economic
use of the national grid. This fact is clearly recognized by
the Electricity Commission, the C.E.B., the electrical manufacturing industry, and Chambers of Commerce, from whom
the impetus to reform electricity rates may be chiefly
expected. The private distributing companies, on the other
hand, seem to be content in many cases to supply a low
density of consumers at high prices and with correspondingly
high profits. As a matter of fact, the view seems to
be quite generally taken that the result of the 1926 Act
will be to reduce consumers' rates only slightly but to
increase profits considerably. If this course of events is
permitted to transpire, the electricity scheme will be at
best but a partial success, and may create dissatisfaction
more serious than that found among consumers prior to
1926. It is only as trustees for the community of users
that public utility trusts should continue to receive
support.

The present status of price regulation cannot be considered satisfactory, because the official policy is passive,
public complaints are not easy to register, and corrective

action is usually slow and disappointing. The regulatory powers of the Electricity Commission are, from the consumer's standpoint, the most important of all; but under existing circumstances they are the least effective part of the Commission's functions. Although the announced object of the 1926 Act was to give a cheap electricity supply to the consumer, Professor Hormell has properly concluded that the present provisions are "hardly stringent enough to bring about a reduction of price in the absence of a will in that direction on the part of the distributor. The · machinery for readjusting prices to the consumer was not thoroughly overhauled and brought down to date in 1926. The provisions of the Act do something for the consumer, but it is questionable if they do enough."[1]

The existing situation relative to the general control over prices and profits may best be explained by an analysis of the historical evolution which accounts for the relation of the Electricity Commission to the Minister of Transport. Prior to the establishment of the Ministry of Transport in 1919 the electricity powers arising under early Acts, including the regulation of prices, were vested in the Board of Trade. The only important exception to the unified control exercised by the Board of Trade was in the matter of authorizing electricity loans by municipalities, which was originally the responsibility of the Local Government Board and later of the Ministry of Health. In 1919 all powers relating to electricity supply were transferred to the Ministry of Transport, and later when the Electricity Commission was established certain powers were granted to it, subject to the Commission's responsibility to the Minister of Transport. Because of this relationship, the Minister of Transport has chosen to delegate to the Commission all reserved powers relating to electricity except those which directly affect his responsibility to Parliament and to the consumers. The regulation of electricity prices is the most important of the

[1] (1928) 17 *National Municipal Review*, op. cit., 380.

three or four matters in which the Minister has retained the ultimate decision and responsibility. The exercise of the compulsory wayleave powers, the obtaining of consents for overhead lines, and the revocation of electricity licenses are the other reserved powers of great importance.

In the matter of regulating the price of electricity to the consumer, therefore, the Electricity Commission acts in merely an investigatory and advisory capacity to the Minister of Transport. He need not follow their advice, nor that of the electricity inspectors in his own Department. In matters which affect the ballot-box the Minister alone must assume the responsibility. Nevertheless, through their express powers and their advisory powers, the Electricity Commissioners have more practical influence over price regulation than the Minister himself.

When the national electricity scheme has entered into complete operation the C.E.B. will act as a middleman, buying power from generating stations and selling it without profit to the distributing enterprises. The price to be paid for the supply received from selected stations has been defined by the second schedule of the 1926 Act, and the Commission has general responsibility for seeing that there is a compliance with these provisions. The cost of production of electricity, as furnished to the Board by the undertakers owning a station selected under the scheme, is based on the following factors: (a) generating costs, (b) rents, rates and taxes, (c) management and general charges, (d) allowance for depreciation, (e) interest. The accounts of all authorized undertakers are subject to the periodic scrutiny of the Electricity Commission, and special audits will be made whenever ground for such action arises. In determining financial standards for the factors of cost referred to above, the Commissioners exercise a very broad discretion and their word is final. For example, the Act refers to "the proper proportion of management and general establishment charges attributable to the station," and in the case of depreciation to "charges properly attributable" and "such amount as the Electricity Commissioners think just."

The provisions relative to interest charges are of vital importance, and have received more criticism than any other item entering into the price of the bulk supply. Where the owners of the selected station are a joint electricity authority or a municipal body, the rate of interest shall be the average rate payable on the money raised for electricity purposes, and where the owners are a company the allowance shall consist of the average rate of dividends and interest paid on their share and loan capital during the preceding year, so, however, that the rate shall in no case be less than 5 nor more than 6½ per cent per annum. The stipulation regarding the maximum charge for interest has given rise to the most severe criticism, especially in the case of the power companies which have paid more than 6½ per cent on their capital during recent years. However, an impartial consideration of the whole financial picture reveals that the provision in question is just.[1]

Although the rates charged by municipalities and local authorities have been on the whole substantially lower than the tariffs of private companies, the law has narrowly limited the amount of the public undertakings' surplus which may be applied in aid of local taxation and provides that the major portion of the surplus shall go to reducing charges and toward paying off capital loans. To the writer this provision appears to be another case of unfair discrimination against the municipal services. Why should the directors of a municipality be limited to an infinitesimal dividend declaration, divisible among all the ratepayers, so long as directors of private companies may distribute dividends amounting, in the case of some companies, to ten or fifteen per cent? It is entirely just and proper that municipalities should provide additional public services and improvements from the earnings derived from vital supply undertakings. The

[1] "Financial aspects of the Electricity Bill," (1926) 102 *Economist*, 670.

writer hazards the view that Parliament's policy relative to municipal services will meet with wide-spread objection within a relatively short time and that the equal claims of public authorities will have to be recognized. The revolt will be hastened by the fact that since 1926 it has become infinitely more difficult for local authorities to purchase private companies when dissatisfaction has arisen because of the company's service, prices, or profits.

As a result of changes in the law since 1919, municipalities will find it much more difficult to control the price of electricity in their areas by exercising the right of purchase at stated intervals, as provided in the 1888 Act. The original provisions of the purchase clause making it possible for the local authority to take over a private company at the end of forty-two years and at intervals thereafter, were altered by the Act of 1919. This legislation provided that the purchase of a private company's holdings by a local authority, except in the district of a joint authority, was conditioned upon the consent of the Electricity Commissioners. The Act of 1922 further modified the purchase provisions by a stipulation that the power of purchase might be suspended for such period and on such conditions as the Company and the Municipality agreed upon, subject to the approval of the Electricity Commission. In 1924 the Weir Committee proposed that the municipalities' right of purchase should be completely withdrawn, but an amendment to this effect failed to pass in 1926.

The Act of 1926 made significant changes in the purchase clause. In the case of companies formed after 1926 and whose area extends over the districts of two or more local authorities, only a joint electricity authority or a joint committee of local governments can exercise a right of purchase. Companies have been given a tenure of fifty years. Notice of intent to purchase may be given six months after the expiration of each subsequent ten-year period. The price shall be "a sum equal to the capital properly expended for the provision of the land, buildings, works, materials, and plant in use or available for use at the time of purchase for the purposes of the undertaking, less depreciation according to a scale as may be determined by special order." Finally, the Act of 1926 provided that local authorities and private companies might, with the permission of the Electricity Commission, amend, vary, or alter the terms of purchase at any time within ten years of the date of purchase. As Professor Hormell has stated, "Under the conditions produced by the new Act probably few occasions will arise where it will seem expedient or advisable for a single municipality to purchase the plant of a private company."

The Electricity Commission has been given a very extensive control over the electricity departments of municipalities. The Commissioners must approve all borrowing by municipal electricity undertakings, and their accounts are subject to the Commission's audit. Furthermore, the amount that may be applied in aid of local rates in any year shall not exceed $\frac{1}{2}$ per cent of the outstanding debt of the undertaking, and since March 31, 1931, "no sum shall be paid in aid of the local rates unless the reserve fund amounts to more than one-twentieth of the aggregate capital expenditure on the undertaking."

One of the most important questions arising from national electricity planning is the ultimate effect of the 1926 Act upon the low prices heretofore found in municipal undertakings and the survival of the electricity undertakings of local authorities. Several speakers in the course of the 1926 debate expressed the view that "in the long run this series of checks and counter-checks will make it extremely difficult for a successful municipality to develop to a still more successful degree the industry for which it is responsible." Was the electricity scheme intended as a blow to municipal electricity undertakings? Municipalities will be well-advised to form joint committees and joint electricity authorities if they wish to protect and extend their interests.

The possibilities of what may be done in this direction may be seen in the development around Manchester. The Ontario (Canada) power scheme may also be studied with great profit.

The Weir Committee found that the average price charged to the consumers for all purposes in 1924 was 2·047d. but at the same time many municipalities, like Leeds, Birmingham, and Huddersfield, had reduced their prices to 1d. or less, while private companies charged as much as 7d. per unit in some cases. The writer has come across a recent instance in which a family living in a section of Greater London served by a large holding company decided to move to a contiguous section in order to come within the area of a municipal electricity service. The price for lighting was 7d. in the first instance and only 3½d. in the latter, while the comparison between power rates was 1¾ and 1. This situation is duplicated in many cases throughout the country. Not long ago the rates charged by a private company near London were investigated by the Electricity Commission. It was found that the company was earning a profit of 16 per cent, so the price of electricity was reduced. The company now earns 11 per cent. These are not isolated instances.

A recent analysis by the financial editor of a London paper reveals the profits which are permitted in electricity supply undertakings. "Electricity shares," he said, "maintain a strong hold on the investors' fancy owing to the good records of the various companies and the increased stability of the industry." He then gave as illustrations two companies that "have maintained their present rates of dividend (15 per cent and 10 per cent) for many years," and another which had just paid the same as last year, 10½ per cent, on a larger capital. The whole situation requires investigation and reform. Public service enterprises should not be permitted to earn profits like these; seven or eight per cent is quite sufficient.

As far back as 1926 Sir John Snell, the Chairman of the Electricity Commission, stated that in a few years the average price of electricity should be ·9d. per unit and that the average lighting cost should be 9d. Most consumers will find a considerable discrepancy between this engineering verdict and their present electricity bills.

One factor complicating price regulation is the extension of holding company operations in recent years. The development has not proceeded nearly so far as in the United States and it is not expected that anywhere near the same difficulty will be experienced in dealing with the question of control. There are four centers of the holding company development at the present time, namely London, Central England, North Wales, and Scotland. Fortunately for themselves, the British have no problems of federalism or of judicial review. Hence if it should appear from the accounts of an operating company that a holding company was charging fees or in some other way "skimming the cream off the profits," the Commissioners could simply reduce the prices which the operating company is permitted to charge and automatically eliminate the objectionable features. In British law electricity holding companies have no guaranteed charging powers, because unlike the ordinary distributing companies they are not "statutory undertakers" but simply commercial organizations formed under the Companies Acts. As such they are not subject to direct regulation. However, the problem of regulating large power companies which own distributing companies as well as generating undertakings presents a much more difficult problem of regulation.

The alleged speculation with electricity stocks is another factor complicating the future control of prices and profits. According to the *Economist's* electricity correspondent, "speculation of a dangerous type has entered, and economic values are being shaken. The supply undertakings find their shares quoted at almost fantastic rates on the Stock

Exchange, where returns on such a valuation with dividends paid as at present are not much more than 3 to 4 per cent, and in one case 2½ per cent."[1] This is unquestionably another evidence of the widely held view that the profits of electricity undertakings will soar as a result of the national power scheme.

Complaints by consumers to the Ministry of Transport should be facilitated. Although the Act of 1922 provides that the Minister may commence an investigation of electricity tariffs where twenty consumers complain, in practice many more than this are usually required. The policy adopted in recent years has had the effect of dicouraging unorganized users who might have a very good case. Despite this attitude, judging from newspaper accounts, dissatisfaction with retail electricity prices evidences a tendency to become more wide-spread. In conversation with various sections of the population one finds a deep-rooted conviction that electricity prices require a thorough overhauling. Such a reform is not likely to be effected until steps have been taken to get at the root of the problem, the distribution system. This is the next step in national electricity planning.

### THE PROBLEM OF DISTRIBUTION

Generation is only one side of the electricity supply industry, and not necessarily the more important. During the period since 1926 the number of distributing companies has actually increased. On March 31, 1932, there were 661 authorized undertakers in Great Britain—a net gain of 126 since 1921. Of the 661 enterprises 378 were owned by municipalities, 275 by companies and persons, 3 by Joint Electricity Authorities (combinations of companies and local authorities), and 5 were operated by Joint Boards (representative of

[1] "Electricity supply—the influence of speculation," (1928) 106 *Economist*, 1173.

local authorities). During the interval since 1926, unlike the earlier stages, the number of new company undertakings has rapidly outstripped the municipal expansion.

In their Twelfth Annual Report the Electricity Commissioners dealt primarily with the problems of distribution— an augur of the attention the question is likely to receive in the near future. "It has become increasingly evident," stated the Report, "that centralization of generation will require to be supplemented by improvement in and coordination of distribution if the opportunities for expansion presenting themselves to the supply industry are to be utilized to the fullest possible extent."[1]

Provision has been made to standardize frequency in the generating side of the industry, but conditions among distributors remain chaotic. The official statistics for 1930–31 showed that 253 undertakings were distributing alternating current only; that 288 enterprises were utilizing both alternating and direct current; that 121 supply services were distributing direct current only; and that there were as many as 45 different declared voltages between the range of 100 to 480 volts at which supplies were being given to consumers in various parts of the country. Standardization of voltage in the distributing side of the industry will require nation-wide action and enforcement machinery to carry it out.

The Commissioners also referred to the fact that there are "considerable differences in various parts of the country in the degree of development attained and in the nature and extent of the facilities and service offered to existing and potential consumers." An aggressive policy was counselled because "In no case, even among the best developed areas, can it yet be said that the saturation point of economic electrical development is in sight of attainment."

The lowering of prices for domestic and industrial power depends very largely, as has been said, upon the reorganization

[1] (1932) *Twelfth Annual Report of the Electricity Commissioners*, 8.

of the distribution system. A former Minister of Transport, Herbert Morrison, pointed out recently that "The significant fact stands out that while generation costs are falling and will continue to fall as the grid system develops, distribution costs are practically standing still; in some instances there is actually a tendency for distribution costs to advance." Compulsion on a wide scale must be used if any effective relief is to be obtained.

Finally, certain sections of the country are deprived of a satisfactory electricity supply even where there is an effective demand. Engineering authorities stated in 1928 that only one-fifth of England and Wales could be regarded as "within the range of effective development at that time."[1] This is due to the fact that some areas have not attracted financial development and in others undertakers are content to make a large profit on a small number of consumers, when the potential number of consumers is known to be much greater. At present the owners of concessions cannot be forced to develop their monopolies. The policy of many distributors is inclined to be unprogressive relative to the conditions imposed upon prospective customers in the matter of service connections. Guarantees and installation charges imposed are frequently so heavy that large sections of the population, particularly in rural and suburban communities, cannot afford the service. In addition, concession hunting, speculation in distribution rights, and territorial expansion of electrical service must be dealt with, it is claimed, if the national plan is to be effective.

The whole position may be summarized by the following analysis:

"The danger of the electricity supply industry falling out of balance —between manufacture and sales—is a danger which must be considered. It would be absurd if the C.E.B. were to reduce the national cost of electricity to less than ·4d. per unit to find the ultimate consumer paying to the distributor an average of 1¼d. per unit or even

[1] "Electricity supply—the distribution problem," (1928) 106 *Economist*, 1068. This article contains many significant statistical observations.

more. Distribution cannot be left to the play of natural economic forces if generation and transmission have already been organized on a scientific basis: the existence of an enormous number of distributors supplying small areas cannot make for efficiency or reduction of waste. Each of these undertakings must obtain a margin of profit on expenditure and a return on capital which through its limited range of application becomes special in character and excessively high when related to total sales."[1]

The case for organizing the distributing side of the power industry is convincing, but its accomplishment far more difficult than in the case of generation and transmission. Several possibilities suggest themselves: (a) the extension of power companies over wide areas; (b) the widespread development of Joint Electricity Authorities and Joint Boards; (c) the creation of a National Distribution Board on the order of the C.E.B. The respective suggestions are not exclusive, but complementary. The Electricity (Supply) Act of 1919, as originally drafted, incorporated all of the general principles contained in the above analysis.

Power companies alone are not likely to be a satisfactory solution of the problem, due to the natural resistance of municipal undertakings and the difficulties of regulating them effectively—as illustrated by the experience of the United States. They may well be an important element in a larger scheme, however. Joint Boards and Joint Electricity Authorities are a particularly satisfactory means of integration. The municipalities must act: if they stand still their position is likely to become extremely hazardous. Municipal purchase suffers from the drawback that such action, except through Joint Boards, tends to retard the development of large distributing systems.

The National Distribution Board would be primarily a coordinating agency, although it should be given power to purchase. It would work in conjunction with the C.E.B. The functions of the latter might conceivably be extended

[1] 106 *Economist*, 1068; see also "Electrical supply—capital cost of distribution," (1928) 106 Ibid., 1120.

to cover distribution in addition to generation and transmission. Such a plan would have to be based upon regional foundations and local responsibility if it were to succeed. The success of a national distribution scheme would depend upon "service, on active enterprise, and on selling efficiency; and a national board would not furnish these things and be able to create a scheme capable of dealing with every type of consumer which would be elastic in operation and consistent in principle." National planning, joined to local initiative and responsibility, is likely to produce the formula most congenial to British temperament and tradition.

ELECTRICITY PROGRESS AND FUTURE POTENTIALITIES

The national electricity scheme is merely a means to an end—the development of the resources of the country—and an ultimate judgment regarding the soundness of the plan must therefore be suspended until it has been shown that cheap power available to consumers in every part of the country is a reality. The potentialities of national electricity planning, assuming a corresponding overhauling of distribution, are truly inspiring. The strengthening of British industry, the revival of economic activity in the rural township or village, the industrialization of agriculture, and the location of new industries destined to meet the requirements of the consumer in those self-contained power areas, the elimination of the smoke evil, and the provision of labor-saving devices for the housewife, are all benefits which can reasonably be expected if the power resources of the country are completely developed and controlled in the public interest.

Great Britain's world economic position has been considerably bettered as a result of the electricity program of recent years. In 1933 Great Britain ranked third in power production for the first time. Ever since 1927 Great Britain has been making up some part of the deficiency in electrical consumption which weakened her relative position in world electrical development; and over the first five years, 1927–31, the expansion in the output of electricity from public supply undertakings has been 34·9 per cent in Great Britain compared with 16·3 in the United States of America, 14·6 in Germany, 12·6 in Canada, and 21 per cent in Italy.[1] Great Britain's relative position has improved even more in the past two years, and now that the grid has commenced operation even more gratifying progress should be made.

The benefits of a national plan may be observed in the improvement of the British electrical manufacturing industry in recent years. Although the grid was not erected for the purpose of electrical experimentation, a prominent leader of the electrical industry stated recently, "it has provided a good example of that cooperation which is essential to national economic planning of any kind." He described as follows the tangible gains to the British electrical industry as a whole:

"The competitive strength of the manufacturing industry must have been considerably increased largely through the knowledge gained in fine modifications of plant and equipment to ensure greater reliability of service and more exact operation. In the early years a great part of this experience had to be derived from export contracts and it is notorious that defects in plant shipped overseas are much more widely advertised and used by competitors than defects in plant supplied for the home market. In many ways, therefore, the grid has proved a valuable center of development and experiment, much greater than the most spectacular research organizations could create in the United States or elsewhere."[1]

The national electricity plan has proved a constructive way of dealing with unemployment. An official statement issued in 1933 revealed that including the electrical engineering, cable-making, structural engineering, building and contracting, iron and steel, coal-mining, cement and pottery industries, the total number of workers employed

[1] (1931) *Fourth Annual Report of the C.E.B.*, 3.

directly or indirectly on the construction of the grid and on standardization of frequency, as far as it had progressed, was between 100,000 and 120,000 for one year. In these estimates no allowance was made for employment in industries feeding into those main supplying industries or of the labor used in railway and road transport.

Cheap electricity is a method of speeding up the "back to the farm" movement, a social transition which is likely to take place in many countries during the course of the next few years. The grid renders it possible for the supply undertaking to open up areas with a low density of population because it is in a position to supply electricity in bulk at a price which, joined to the highly simplified distribution networks designed now for rural electrification purposes, can justify the extension of supplies to small villages, townships, farms, hamlets, and even country houses.

Cheap rural power has already encouraged agriculture, local artisanship, and small manufactures in the rural regions of several European countries; it can do the same thing in Great Britain. Examples of what can be done may be seen in the rural industrial centers near London, such as Welwyn Garden City.

In conclusion, the relation of electrical progress to the national economy of Great Britain cannot be better expressed than in the words of Sir John Snell, Chairman of the Electricity Commission, who said in his presidential address to the British Association,

"As Great Britain is essentially dependent on imported foodstuffs to a large degree and on other raw materials for the feeding of her essential industries, it is clear that the most efficient and economic systems of industrial power and transport are necessary parts of the future equipment of the country. If we add to this work of increased power application a notable improvement in the conditions of rural life, we shall help to improve the physical conditions of our people in both urban and rural districts, in addition to providing those engaged in industrial pursuits with better means of competing and holding their own with manufacturers in other countries. In this, electricity must necessarily play a great part."

The national grid has commenced operation a year in advance of original expectations. During the five years of its life the C.E.B. has been characterized by initiative and foresight. Now that construction work on the grid has been completed the functions of the Board will be to perfect interconnections, to build additional secondary transmission lines if and as the need arises, to carry through the standardization of frequency schemes, and to act as the national manufacturer of bulk power—the principal purpose for which the Board was created.

It is too soon to form a final judgment concerning the merits and defects of the type of public utility development represented by the C.E.B. The organization and functioning of the Board have not settled down into any hard and fast lines—no doubt to its advantage in many respects. Aggressive action and freedom from burdensome restrictions—the chief virtues which are claimed for the public utility trust—have undoubtedly characterized the work of the Board so far. On the other hand, it may be found that a public utility organization of this sort is less able to protect itself from the demands and pressures of various and sundry interest groups than a public service which is more closely integrated with the machinery of the central government.

The powers and activities of the C.E.B. are subject to more regulation and control by agencies representing the larger interests of the public than many Members of Parliament seemed to think in 1926, or than most people seem to think today. The threads of control running to the Electricity Commission, the Minister of Transport, and the Treasury are not so tightly drawn that they interfere with the initiative and the detailed administration of the Board, but they guarantee the public's representatives a controlling voice in questions relating to major policies such as finance, equal treatment of regional sections, electricity tariffs, and the amenities of the countryside. However, the responsibility for the actions of the Board itself is so diffused (being divided among eight members), and the agencies of public control are so many and complex that direct responsibility through Parliament to the people is impossible. Press criticism of the Board's policies and practices, except in isolated and unimportant instances, is now virtually out of the question. This situation may be compared with the steady and effective criticism directed through Parliament at the Post Office. Opinions differ widely as to the effect of democratic criticism on monopolies entrusted with important powers and privileges, but it may be suggested that the virtual immunity of the C.E.B. from criticism has gone as far in the opposite direction as critics of Post Office administration complain that it has gone in the direction of Parliamentary interference.

The planning of generation and transmission must be regarded as only the first step in national reform if the real industrial and social benefits of power potentialities are to be obtained. The questions of high electricity prices and of the chaos of distribution require a great deal of study, followed by effective action from Parliament. The Electricity Commission and the C.E.B. are already keenly aware of the direct bearing of effective distribution on the economic use of the national grid. The solution of the distribution problem raises more difficult and important questions than have been dealt with in the planning of generation and transmission. The existing method of regulating electricity prices leaves a great deal to be desired. If cheap power, available equally in all parts of the country, is to revitalize British industry, electrify agriculture, redistribute the population over the countryside, eradicate the smoke curse, and make the latest inventions of science available to all classes of the population, national planning of electricity must be applied to the problem of distribution as well.

## CHAPTER VIII

# THE BROADCASTING MONOPOLY

## BROADCASTING—NATION BUILDER

The young giant of the air, broadcasting, has almost completed its eleventh year of life in the British environment.
On May 4, 1922, the Postmaster-General announced in the
House of Commons that it had been decided to authorize
regular broadcasting in Great Britain, but operation was not
officially commenced until November of that year. From the
very outset the new service has been recognized as a public
service undertaking, operating within the limits of the Post
Office's monopoly of all forms of communication. The
British Broadcasting Company, organized by agreement
between the Postmaster-General and the principal radio
manufacturers, began its official existence in December, 1922.
The service has been carried on since January 1927 by the
same staff, but under a new form of control. The successor
to the company, the British Broadcasting Corporation, was
formed by Royal Charter, and in organization and control
is a public utility trust, in general character like, but with
distinct differences in detail from, the Central Electricity
Board.

The B.B.C. is one of the newest and most important of
the national public service undertakings now in existence. Its
possibilities in the framework of national development are
seemingly limitless. Our first task must be to analyze the
influence and potentialities of broadcasting and the various
ways in which it has been developed throughout the world.
After providing a setting for the British system we may deal
in greater detail with the problems of control, organization,
finance, management, policies, and public relations.

When broadcasting was commenced in the United States during 1920, the world paid very little attention to the popularity of the radio, and the few persons who stated that broadcasting's possibilities were comparable to the revolution brought about by the printing press were thought to be "balmy." The radio was merely a toy. The owner of a set usually spent most of his time attempting to get distance: the serious uses of broadcasting were to be discovered later. The radio mania did not seize the British as it did the Americans, which is undoubtedly one of the reasons accounting for the different emphasis in the two countries.

It would be superfluous to enter into a lengthy disquisition on the revolutionary character of broadcasting, because years of experience have clearly established its strategic and manifold uses in modern life. A word, however, concerning radio's possibilities should be said in passing, because even the intimate is frequently not fully assessed, and it is important that this should be done in the present case. The possibility of employing broadcasting for one or another of its possible emphases underlies the most important questions of policy and control.

The first point that should be observed is the universality of broadcasting's scope, and the intimate and subtle nature of its appeal. Newspapers and cinemas reach only limited audiences, but the radio can be made the possession of the masses—witness the largely fulfilled ambition of Russia. William Randolph Hearst, the American newspaper king, is reported to have said that of the three organs of opinion—newspapers, cinemas, and broadcasting—the last-mentioned will soon become the one of paramount importance. Its appeal is subtle, ingratiating, inescapable. No other instrument possesses greater possibilities of good or evil, of bondage or of emancipation.

The scope of broadcasting's influence is as broad as human interests, but the alternative emphases or uses to which the ether has been put may be divided conveniently into commercial (i.e. advertising), political, and cultural. The last-named may be subdivided into intellectual, social, ethical, and religious. But where, it is asked, does entertainment come in? Is not this the principal desire of the public? Entertainment, in the broad sense, is what everyone desires. But if by entertainment is meant relaxation from humdrum duties, and mental and emotional stimulation, the term is broad enough to include all three of the emphases suggested above. The reason that commercial, political, and cultural uses have been taken as a convenient classification is that most of the broadcasting systems of the world manifest a predominance in one of the three respects. In several countries broadcasting serves two purposes, commercial and cultural, but in some, notably in Great Britain, the cultural objective (including entertainment) stands alone. A brief analysis of the international situation will explain the possible varieties of emphasis and control.

Since the United States was first to exploit the radio and since it is the principal example of the commercial incentive in broadcasting, the American system may be examined first. Prior to the creation of the Federal Radio Commission in 1927 there was virtually no control over radio development in the United States, with the result that broadcasting stations sprang up like mushrooms, the ether currents became overcrowded, and uninterrupted reception was virtually impossible. Broadcasting was and still is financed primarily by selling time to advertisers. No license of any kind is required of the owners of listening sets. Over half of the receiving sets in the world are found in the United States, but the absence of a licensing system and the nature of the broadcasting development do not necessarily have a great deal to do with the fact. Under the present control a commission of five members, appointed by the President with the consent of the Senate for terms of six years, has power to license stations, fix wave lengths and technical requirements, and under certain conditions put a station off the air. There are still over 600 independent stations in the United States. However, two national chains, the National and the Columbia, have increased their influence and the quality of their programs very rapidly in recent years. Largely through the influence of the Department of Commerce, the amount of educational and cultural material entering into programs has been considerably increased. The most popular hours are still reserved to advertisers, however, and this must continue so long as this is the only means of financial support. In France and Canada broadcasting is still predominantly under private management and control, but for several years both of these countries have been considering a change to a system similar to the British.

In Europe organized systems under a unified control now exist in most countries, among which the most prominent are Austria, Germany, Italy, Russia, Switzerland, Sweden, Poland, Hungary, and the Irish Free State.[1] Generally speaking, broadcasting has been considered a monopoly to be granted and controlled by the Post Office, and hence in most countries it becomes a source of government revenue. Licenses are required on receiving sets in most of the countries of the world.

Broadcasting is controlled for political and propaganda purposes in Russia, Italy, and Germany. It is interesting to note that the system in the Irish Free State is operated directly by the Post Office.

The B.B.C. is unlike any of the systems mentioned: it is neither a private company supported by advertising, nor a department of State, subject to the will of the Government in power. True, the public corporation was established under the aegis of the State, and it is ultimately subject to public control. In ordinary matters of policy and management,

[1] For further information regarding the varieties of control, see (1928) *B.B.C. Handbook*, 301; (1929) Ibid., 104; (1930) *Yearbook*, 125, 131; (1932) Ibid., 35; (1933) Ibid., 313, 318.

however, the B.B.C. is autonomous. Legally, the corporation consists of the Board of Governors, the members of which are appointed for fixed terms by the Crown. The undertaking is not organized for profit and hence attention can be entirely focussed on producing the best possible programs for listeners. With no stockholders and no government which must be served, the permanent staff, under the leadership of the Director-General, are actuated solely by their membership in the broadcasting profession, in which traditions of impartiality like those found in the Civil Service have had an opportunity to develop. The officials of the B.B.C. have been prominent in the Union Internationale de Radiophonie, the world organization which settles wave-length disputes and disseminates information of interest to the broadcasting profession.

Some writers have argued that the emphasis, subject-matter, and control of broadcasting in the several countries of the world is merely a reflection of national characteristics and desires. This view sounds plausible enough, but it is over-simplified in many cases. Broadcasting may be a means of raising the standard of what the average citizen would choose. It may be argued that high standards of broadcasting content produce higher demands from the hypothetical average man. This is clearly the cultural foundation of the British broadcasting system.

Under a type of control which is neither private nor governmental, the B.B.C. is enabled to concentrate upon the dissemination of culture, upon nation building. This has become a definite objective. It is an enormous responsibility, and those in control fully appreciate the fact. Positive policies of enlightenment and uplift have been followed, instead of catering to what might be thought a cross-section or a general level of individual desire and culture. "I do not know of any responsibility entrusted to any man or body of men more immense or more inspiring," an official of the B.B.C. has stated. "I know of none fraught with so many dangers nor with so many potential benefits." The same writer has said, "Can democratic principle and democratic purpose best be served—can they, in the long run, be served at all—by democratic means as we understand them?" This is his answer. "The problems of today are not of subdivision but of integration. We are concerned with the unity of the nervous system of the body politic. That it is imperfect few will deny. I suggest that broadcasting is the integrating element, and that rightly understood and applied a national broadcasting service will supply the integrator for democracy."

Sir John Reith, Director-General of the B.B.C., whose views have been quoted, has been at the helm since organized broadcasting started in Great Britain. His philosophy has largely moulded the B.B.C. Concerning the principles of national broadcasting development he has written that (1) broadcasting should be conducted as a public service and nothing else; (2) there should be a central unified control; (3) the service should be established under the auspices of the State but certainly not be conducted by the State; (4) there must be adequate finance, because "the ether should not be put at the power of money"; (5) there should be a conscious social purpose in its development; (6) the stewardship should be interpreted as carrying the responsibility of contributing constantly and cumulatively to the intellectual and moral well-being of the community; and (7) the officials must not be afraid to postulate "a policy in which idealism plays a part, perhaps a determining part."

"Institutions in themselves," it has been truly observed, "are little apart from the personalities who control and operate them."

### CONSTITUTIONAL STATUS AND PUBLIC CONTROL

The public utility status of the B.B.C. may be more clearly understood by considering briefly the growth of broadcasting prior to 1927, the year in which the present form of control came into existence.[1] In 1922 negotiations were completed between the Postmaster-General (having authority over all forms of communication) and a committee representative of radio manufacturers, as a result of which the British Broadcasting Company was created. The company was constituted with a capital of £100,000, of which £60,000 was contributed in equal parts by six great wireless firms, all of which were represented on the board. The remaining manufacturers were given a very small proportion of the control. From the very first it was held that broadcasting should be a limited monopoly under unified control, and that competition would be impracticable and unwise. The company's public service character was signalized by the limitation of profits to 7½ per cent and by the prohibition of radio advertising except by consent of the Postmaster-General. The license system, which had been introduced in the early days with the wireless experimenter's license, was extended. By the time the company had been in existence a year eight main stations had been opened, these being located in London, Birmingham, Manchester, Newcastle, Cardiff, Glasgow, Aberdeen, and Bournemouth. At the end of 1923 over half a million licenses were in force.

Before the company was a year old difficulties had arisen which resulted in the creation of a Parliamentary Committee of inquiry, the Sykes Committee. The principal criticism arose because of the alleged monopolistic control of the "big six." No receivers could be made without the consent of the Marconi Company. Certain newspapers accused the broadcasting monopoly of being a "ramp." Furthermore, a royalty was charged on all sets manufactured outside of the country. This mode of raising revenue proved unworkable and undesirable, and the company therefore decided to abolish the royalty system voluntarily. The principal con-

---

[1] J. C. W. Reith, "Business management of the public services," (1930) 8 *Pub. Admin.*, 16; (1928) *B.B.C. Handbook*, 37; (1933) *B.B.C. Yearbook*, 9.

clusions of the Sykes Committee were that (1) the company should become less dependent upon the wireless trade for revenue, and reliance should entirely cease at a given date; (2) the company's share of the listeners' license fees should be 75 per cent instead of 50 per cent; (3) a uniform fee should be established, and restrictions as to the origin and nature of the receiving set should be abolished. There were other recommendations, but they did not prove particularly important in the evolution of broadcasting's constitutional position.[1] The acceptance of the report made it possible to adopt "a complete national system accessible to the owner of the cheapest form of set, wherever he might happen to live."

By the time of the second Parliamentary inquiry, in 1925–26, it was almost a foregone conclusion that the last vestiges of the wireless trade's influence would be removed. This was accomplished as a result of the acceptance of the Crawford Committee Report.[2] When on January 1, 1927, the "Corporation" replaced the "Company," the change did not greatly affect the undertaking, because it meant taking over the staff, system, and plant as a going concern. The shareholders were eliminated by being repaid at par. The assets of the company were transferred to the Postmaster-General and by him to the new B.B.C.

From this point onwards we may disregard chronological factors and confine ourselves to the powers and limitations of the B.B.C. as at present constituted. The Corporation was created under Royal Charter,[3] as from January 1, 1927, for a period of ten years. This means that an opportunity to reconsider the question of control will be presented in 1936. Although in early years there had been sporadic criticisms of the monopolistic character of broadcasting, the results obtained from four years of experience had convinced most

[1] *Sykes Committee Report*, Cmd. 1951, Stationery Office, 1923.

[2] Cmd. 2599, Stationery Office, 1926.

[3] Cmd. 2756, Stationery Office, 1926.

critics that unified control was desirable, and hence the possibility of creating several competing companies was not even considered.

The public corporation consists of a Board of Governors, five in number, the members of which are appointed by the Crown. Actually the appointments are made on the joint recommendation of the Prime Minister and the Postmaster-General. The first Governors were appointed for terms of five years, but subsequent appointees will remain in office as directed by the Postmaster-General, in no case exceeding five years. If a Governor should disqualify himself, the vacancy will be filled by the Government. The personnel of the Board has been composed of public-spirited citizens, chosen because of their broad interests and abilities. The three major parties have been represented at all times. The present Chairman was formerly Speaker of the House of Commons—a position requiring impartiality and tact. The Governors may retain as their annual remuneration sums not exceeding £3,000 for Chairman, £1,000 for Vice-Chairman, and £700 for other Governors. No other sums may be divided by way of profit or otherwise among the Governors of the Corporation. The Board appoints all officers and staff and may remove any officer (other than a Governor) however appointed. The Corporation also fixes rates of remuneration. Sir John Reith was designated in the Charter as first Director-General.

Under the new organization the licensing system has been continued, and the percentage allotted to the B.B.C. was increased. The Corporation was prohibited from earning distributable profits by the stipulation that all surpluses from licenses must flow into the Treasury. Borrowing powers were limited to £500,000 at any one time. However, profits derived from the Corporation's publishing business may be used as capital assets.

The duties of the B.B.C., as provided in the Charter, help to explain its constitutional position and the control exercised over it as a public service undertaking. It is granted in order that the broadcasting service should be conducted "by a public corporation acting as trustees for the national interest." In view of the "widespread interest" taken in, and the "great value" of, the service "as a means of education and entertainment," it is "deemed desirable that the service should be developed and exploited to the best advantage and in the national interest." The Corporation is therefore given the power to "do all matters and things incidental or pertaining to a body corporate, but the Corporation shall apply the whole of its surplus revenue (if any) and other income solely in promoting its objects."

The responsibility of the Corporation is to "carry on a broadcasting service" for Great Britain, Northern Ireland, the Channel Islands and the Isle of Man, "as a public utility service," and for that purpose it (*a*) is licensed by the Postmaster-General to operate stations under conditions presented by him, (*b*) may make agreements with governments (subject to Post Office consent) or municipal authorities, (*c*) may develop and exploit its service in any other direction and by means other than wireless telephony, if the Postmaster-General permits, (*d*) may broadcast any matter which for the time being may be permitted by or be within the scope or ambit of the Postmaster-General's "license," (*e*) may itself collect news or subscribe to news agencies, (*f*) is empowered to receive and employ the funds "annually or otherwise granted by the legislature" and, further, may raise money by way of loan, (*g*) may publish books, journals, etc. In addition it has the necessary power to develop and sell its property, to acquire and hold copyrights and patents, to establish pension funds and so forth. In other words, in its management, business dealings, and policy formulation the B.B.C. enjoys almost complete autonomy. On the other hand, several important provisions have been made for the supervision and control.

There is general agreement that an undertaking which

exercises such enormous responsibilities as those possessed by the B.B.C. should be subject to public safeguards. These are provided in the license and are exercised by the Postmaster-General, who stands in a general supervisory capacity to the B.B.C. For example, Members of Parliament may and have addressed questions to the Postmaster-General relating to some policy or action of the B.B.C. However, it is important to note that if the clerk at the table or the Postmaster-General considers that the question is petty or that it goes beyond the latter's responsibility in connection with the B.B.C., a refusal to print the question in the Orders of the Day is the course taken. The clerk has rejected a great many questions, and some which he has let through the Postmaster-General has rejected.

The license accompanying the Charter contains many technical requirements relating to non-interference with existing communication services, but these provisions are not particularly interesting. Public control is exercised through the Postmaster-General, who acts as Parliament's agent. The most important of the Postmaster-General's powers of control are those which relate to subject-matter, service, dissolution, and finance. These should be examined rather carefully.

The provision in the B.B.C.'s license which has given rise to most speculation and remark is the one providing that the Postmaster-General may, by giving notice, require the Corporation to refrain from broadcasting any matter, either particular or general. This safeguard was probably included because of the possibility of the Corporation's involving the Government in a misunderstanding with a foreign Power. On the other hand, the Government does not and has no reason to assume responsibility for any statement made over the radio, except where announcements are officially supplied. In any case, the stipulation is important solely because of what it suggests or authorizes. The power has not been used to date. Another provision, really the reverse of the one just mentioned, states that the B.B.C. is to broadcast, at its own

s

expense, anything which any government department may require. Concerning this clause Sir John Reith has written, "no improper advantage has been taken of this clause, and I imagine the Corporation would not be forced to broadcast contentious matter against its own judgment." Government departments do not apply to the Postmaster-General to have material broadcast; they go directly to the B.B.C. The Corporation encourages them to do so, but has indicated that it will use discriminatory power if necessary.

Amongst the numerous provisions governing actual broadcasting is one to the effect that the B.B.C. is to broadcast every day including Sunday during the hours specified from time to time by the Postmaster-General, but he has never felt called upon to regulate hours. Another proviso relating to service stipulates that if interference takes place with any other form of signalling, the B.B.C. may be required to close down the station responsible.

The most drastic reserved powers are those relating to expropriation in case of emergency or for breach of agreements. In the first case (an emergency resulting from war, let us say), the Government has reserved the right to occupy and use all stations without being liable to any claim of compensation except as provided in the license. Furthermore, if it appears to the Postmaster-General that the provisions of the Charter are not being carried out, and if the Corporation fails to comply within a specified period, he may certify this to the Crown and the Charter may be revoked. In case of voluntary or compulsory dissolution, the property and assets of the Corporation are to be applied in satisfaction of the liabilities, and thereafter as the Postmaster-General may direct.

The financial control also provides public safeguards of great practical and potential significance. The general provision to the effect that the Corporation shall give the Postmaster-General an annual general report and statement of accounts duly audited and certified, and that he is entitled

to have the accounts examined, is merely the usual requirement imposed upon a public undertaking. The Postmaster-
General also has the right to have his Comptroller and
Accountant-General audit the accounts. This has not been
done for several years. With reference to the powers of control
which are held in reserve, Sir John Reith has written,

"There are provisions, the exercise of which would be not only unfair
but even incredible. The Postmaster-General may, if he choose, decline
to take action to enforce the licensing regulations, and can abolish or
reduce the listener's license fee. In some respects the Corporation's
license from the Postmaster-General is distinctly a one-way document.
This is the natural outcome, on paper, of the statutory principle that
the right to transmit wireless signals is a State prerogative, and is only
exercised by other parties in the capacity of concessionaires. . . . In
practice relations with the Post Office have been very satisfactory, and
both Company and Corporation have met with sympathy, encouragement, and support."

So far our discussion of the control over broadcasting has
been confined to the variety of duties and restrictions placed
upon the Corporation by Parliament. This is undoubtedly
what is meant by public control. But an analysis of the
subject would be incomplete if we did not refer to the
importance of inner control, i.e. the determination of policy
and the selection of materials to be broadcast. After all is
said and done, this is the aspect of control that really matters
most: those who determine what shall go over the ether
have the power to influence public policy, national tastes,
and the outlook of the younger generation. Consideration
of the actual determination of policy may best be deferred
until we have discussed the finances and the organization
of the B.B.C., but one aspect of what may be called "selective" control should be emphasized before proceeding further.
In the words of the Director-General of the B.B.C., "Broadcasting is an integral: no part of its service is wholly distinct
from the rest. This singular, and hitherto unparalleled unity
has led some over-hasty thinkers to regard it as no more than
the technical engine for collecting and distributing the output
of many fields of culture, themselves separate. So it is, but it

is more. Integration is a process not of gross summation, but of ordering and valuation. And broadcasting is, and in its nature must be, not only the collector but the selector of material. And therein lies the supreme responsibility."

In the managerial aspects of its operation the B.B.C. enjoys a considerable degree of autonomy. This, however, is not as true with respect to finance as in many other ways. When the Crawford Committee reported in 1926 several financial principles were laid down which have gone a long way to assure the independence and elasticity of administration which are necessary to an undertaking of this nature. The committee concluded that the B.B.C. should be guaranteed ample funds to provide a first-class service; secondly, that under no circumstances should broadcasting be supported from public funds; and finally, that the receipts from broadcasting should not be regarded by the Treasury as a source of general revenue. On the other hand, it was impliedly recognized that the B.B.C. was not entitled to the total receipts of the 10s. license fee levied on receiving sets. Although the reduction of the license fee was considered at the time, it was not thought advisable to do so.

The arrangement which was finally made between the Post Office and the B.B.C. relative to the division of the revenue from listeners' licenses was that the former should take 12½ per cent (now 10 per cent) for administering the licensing system. Of the balance, 10 per cent on the first million licenses, 20 per cent on the second, 30 per cent on the third, and 40 per cent on the fourth million are retained by the Treasury. This graduated system is based upon the assumption that costs do not increase in direct proportion to the revenue. Hence, although the B.B.C. does not receive the entire revenue, at least its income is definitely fixed in advance and is subject to increase as the service becomes more popular. Furthermore, once the receipts are turned over to the B.B.C. the spending of these sums is free from outside interference.

The division of revenue has been criticized as unsound in principle. It was revealed in 1932, for example, that of the 10s. subscribed by the listener, only 5s. is used for the purpose he has in mind, since that amount is all that reaches the B.B.C. On the other hand, it has been replied that so long as the Corporation has sufficient resources with which to produce good programs, the best plan is either to reduce the license fee (a plan which meets with enthusiastic approval from the public), or to assist the hard-pressed Exchequer as at present. Although the existing plan does not leave a relatively large surplus from licenses for capital reserve and development, the Corporation's borrowing has been arranged without difficulty and the receipts from publishing activities provide a handsome revenue with which to defray sinking fund obligations. In 1931, for instance, publications produced a net revenue of more than a quarter of a million pounds. In the same year the Treasury's portion of broadcasting receipts was over a million pounds. The B.B.C. has nearly completed capital schemes of over £2,000,000 with only half a million borrowed, and in the balance sheet at December 1932 there were reserves in the bank to clear off the whole of this debt. The B.B.C. is giving a voluntary contribution to the Treasury of £250,000 in 1933–34, and gave £150,000 in the financial year 1932–33.

The popularity of broadcasting has increased so rapidly that the B.B.C. would not seem to have any ground for financial concern.

*Growth in Number of Licensed Listeners*

| 1923[1] | .. | .. | 580,380 | 1928 .. | .. | 2,628,392 |
|------|------|------|------|------|------|------|
| 1924 | .. | .. | 1,140,119 | 1929 .. | .. | 2,956,736 |
| 1925 | .. | .. | 1,645,207 | 1930 .. | .. | 3,411,910 |
| 1926 | .. | .. | 2,178,447 | 1931 .. | .. | 4,330,735 |
| 1927 | .. | .. | 2,395,174 | 1932 .. | .. | 5,262,953 |

[1] Figures for December 31st in each year.

Moreover, licenses have increased with greater rapidity in recent months than ever before. Relative to the significance of this expansion we read in the 1933 *B.B.C. Yearbook* that,

"Only one country employing a license system can show a higher percentage of listeners to population—namely, Denmark, and there the problems are simpler. Even in America, though broadcast listening is 'free' there, the census of sets disclosed a percentage not much greater than the British. It would not be claimed that this numerical prosperity alone and by itself proves the success of the service, . . . but at least it proves the acceptableness of the service."

Provision has been made to reconsider the income terms of the 1927 agreement at any time after the initial period of two years. Several financial issues still appear to be open questions. The first one is whether the 10s. licensing fee should not be reduced as expeditiously as possible. Is it not only fair that the benefit resulting from doubling the number of licenses since 1927 should be passed on to the present and potential subscribers? Another problem is whether the B.B.C.'s proportion of the license should not be increased and whether it should not have greater control over license income generally. The principal objection to the existing arrangement is said to arise in connection with funds from licenses representing the unexpired period of the year. The Corporation's income for any year to March is based on the number of licenses issued at the end of the previous year, and even so is only handed over monthly. Had the B.B.C. been empowered to receive and administer the net license income after deducting Post Office costs, additional reserves by the end of 1928 would have totalled over £1,000,000.

Although the spirit of the Crawford Committee's principles relative to broadcasting finance has been carried out, the payment of over £1,000,000 to the Treasury appears to vitiate a strict interpretation of the doctrine relative to the undesirability of using broadcasting receipts for general governmental purposes. The future of that issue still appears to be in the balance. Broadcasting licenses have increased far more rapidly than anyone thought they would. A general opinion exists that the B.B.C. is financially one of the most favorably situated institutions in the country. But unless the balancing of the national budget becomes less arduous, it will probably take more than a pious hope to bring about either a reduction in license fees or an increased proportion of the revenue to the B.B.C.

## MANAGEMENT OF THE B.B.C.

Formal constitutional provisions are merely a general framework within which the machinery and the spirit of an organization develop; and it will usually be found that the objectives and the personalities of the management are the ultimate forces creating policy and practice. This will be found to be true to a special degree of broadcasting generally, and of the B.B.C. in particular. The management of the B.B.C. has possessed two notable advantages—that of continuity of purpose and practical continuity of constitution, and that of continuity of direction in the person of the Director-General. His immediate subordinates too, with few exeptions, have had from seven to nine years' experience in the organization.

The evolution of the B.B.C.'s leadership may be compared to the relationship which has come to exist between the political head and the permanent officials of government departments. Constitutionally the Board of Governors is the Corporation; practically the full-time officials, with a modicum of suggestions, run the show. This division of responsibility—not in the least paradoxical but perfectly natural—has caused Herbert Morrison to state in his recent book that "It is a matter of some doubt as to who is the more powerful, the Board of Governors or the strong-willed Director-General ——." Personality is the final arbiter of questions of this nature. The relations between the lay and the professional officials of any organization depend upon the personalities of the several parties at any particular time. Directors

with so-called "strong" personalities usually concern themselves more with policies and problems than do other members.
So it is in the conduct of the B.B.C. However, it may be said
with greater definiteness that the Chairman of the Board of
Governors is the individual who naturally assumes a more
active oversight of the affairs of the Corporation. He is paid
three times as much as any other member. The Chairman
has an office at Headquarters and comes in whenever his
presence is required, actually an hour or so three or four
mornings a week.

The general responsibility of the Board of Governors is
primarily over policy and results, not over the actual carrying out of that policy. At the fortnightly meetings of the
Governors, comments are usually made on some aspects of
the past programs, but the sanction of forthcoming programs
is not required. At times future events are discussed, when
the particular broadcast involves some new or controversial
features. The list of forthcoming talks is usually presented.
The Governors naturally reflect public views and criticisms,
but this is not the main object of the Board. Its rôle is to
assume responsibility to Parliament and to the public for
what takes place; and hence to keep a general oversight and
to make suggestions. The initiative in matters of policy,
program, and administration comes from the officials.
Governors sometimes make program suggestions. The exact
relationship between the Governors and the Director-
General has never been precisely defined, and it will not
need to be, so long as they work together harmoniously.

The evolution of the formal organization—the "genea-
logical tree" need not detain us. We are more interested in
seeing how the machinery works than in the details of its
construction. Moreover, the administrative organization is
in the process of adjustment so that existing details might
not apply in every case. However, the fundamental principles
remain unchanged.

The chief executive of the B.B.C. is the Director-General,

who controls and directs all aspects of the management, in addition to being the liaison official between the Board of Governors, the Postmaster-General, and the public. His deputy is the Controller, who is concerned with the two major divisions of the work, administration and programs. In other words, the administration of the B.B.C. consists of developing programs and of then seeing that they are performed. These two stages, or functions, have been increasingly distinguished. They are not placed in watertight compartments, however, because the underlying theory of B.B.C. management is functional; in actual working the system depends on "horizontal" liaisons almost as much as on "vertical." When present plans are fully carried out there will be two Controllers, one in charge of administration and another in charge of program output. Instead of there being eight branch chiefs reporting to the Director-General and the Controller, there will be four to each Controller.

The practical or detailed stage at which policy formulation occurs is in the Control Board, which has met weekly since the earliest days of the B.B.C. This important body is composed of the heads of the six principal branches—Administration, Engineering, Information, Programs, Finance, and Talks, in addition to the Controller and the Director-General. It may be compared to the Bridgeman Committee's proposed functional board in the Post Office. The principal difference is that the B.B.C. functional board consists entirely of administrative officials.

Most of the divisions of the B.B.C. organization are self-explanatory, but a brief analysis may make certain functions better understood in relation to the whole.

The department of the Assistant Controller, which deals with administrative work, is concerned with formal and official relationships with outside organizations, with staff, premises, office matters, and "particularly with the review of organization in the light of rapidly changing needs." The total personnel of the B.B.C., exclusive of artists, exceeds

1,700, of whom over 1,000 are located in London.. The remaining employees are engaged primarily in the four regional offices, but the B.B.C. maintains almost fifty premises altogether.

The engineering branch has undergone very little change in comparison with other departments. Its main functions may be classified under the heading of "Maintenance" (i.e. the day-to-day running of the technical service), "Research" or "Development," "Stores," and "Buildings." One of the most interesting aspects of the Chief Engineer's department is the research station which is conducted outside of London. Here the research engineer works on new ideas, new applications of old ideas, and improvement of material. The principal emphasis is laid on acoustics in connection with studios and microphones. Outside London there is also a central receiving station for foreign relays and for checking purposes.

The departments dealing with programs and talks are naturally the largest units in the Head Office organization. Originally the two branches were one, but by 1932 the work of the original "Programme" division became so heavy that "Talks" was made a separate branch. Under the existing arrangement the old program branch deals with music, drama, entertainment, and the common service relating to the building-up, fitting-in, and execution of the programs considered as a whole. The "Talks" division has responsibility for the spoken word—news, education, lectures, and so forth.

The information department is more than its name suggests: it deals with publications and with public relations, other than those of a business nature, as well. The publishing activities of the B.B.C. have grown to immense proportions. *The Radio Times*, which was founded in 1923, reaches one in every two listeners. *World-Radio* and *The Listener* have also developed rapidly. In addition to the *B.B.C. Yearbook*, the Corporation publishes a large number of pamphlets and reprints connected with broadcasts, giving it a virtual monopoly over printed matter dealing with broadcasting.

The same officials are responsible for relations with the press and for public contacts and publicity generally. In order to keep in touch with all sections of the country and with the principal interests affected "a fairly complete but quite fluid and personal system of relationships" has been developed by the headquarters and the regional officials. Advisory committees dealing with music and religion have been set up in local, regional, and national areas. The most important advisory committees are those employed at Head Office in connection with adult education and school broadcasts. So far the activities of the public relations branch appear to have been directed primarily at interpreting public opinion rather than at controlling it. The B.B.C. never advertises, but an immense number of communications go on between the publicity people and the newspaper men.

We shall return to certain problems connected with personnel administration, program management, and public relations, growing out of the framework of organization described above. Consideration of the structure and general features of management will be completed by reference to the regional stations of the B.B.C.

During 1924 the system of relay stations was brought into effect, but for several years it was the London station that provided the bulk of the output of these stations. In 1925 Daventry, with its long wave, assumed a national rôle, and the idea gradually emerged of presenting listeners with a choice of "national" or "regional" programs. The present organization of regional stations is built around the Regional Director in each of the five regions. Hence the complete B.B.C. network consists of Head Office (London), Midland Region, North Region, Scottish Region, Welsh and Western, and Belfast. Besides the main studios and offices in each region, certain studios formerly served by local stations have been retained. In a few cases where technical considerations make it difficult to give the standard service from the regional transmitters, local stations have been maintained as such. These local stations have certain program powers of their own. They are, nevertheless, within the control of the Regional Directors. Although each station as a unit is in the charge of the Station Director, the Engineer-in-Charge of each station is independent within his technical sphere. He conforms to the Station Director's policy, but performs his work under the direct control of the Superintendent Engineer. It will be recalled that a corresponding feature of organization was objected to by the Bridgeman Committee in the case of the Post Office.

Centralization has frankly been the policy of the B.B.C. management. The Regional Director, who controls the regional programs, is the agent of the Corporation in his area for most purposes, but is responsible to the Director-General, through whom most of his business is conducted with officials at the Head Office. The progress of centralization has naturally been attended by controversy between those in favor of unity and those who advocate a greater degree of regional autonomy. One result appears indisputable: the general consensus of opinion throughout the country approves of the opportunity to choose between the national and the regional programs.

In the latter part of 1931, although financial arrangements had not been fully completed, the B.B.C. decided to develop an Empire broadcasting service. A permanent short-wave station has been built at Daventry, and the service is in successful operation. The saving resulting from the use of directional aerials is such that the transmitter is able to work on a sixteenth of the power that would be required for omnidirectional broadcasting. The new service is under the supervision of the Empire and Foreign branch of the B.B.C.

Having analyzed the principal outlines of the organization, the remainder of the discussion relating to management may be considered under the general heading of personnel. It should be said in the first place that the staff of the B.B.C. would be much larger than 1,700 persons if the artists under contract were included. The figure mentioned takes account only of the permanent staff of the B.B.C., including of course a large number who manufacture and supervise the actual programs. The program branch is responsible for dealing with the detailed program communications to all stations, the heaviest expenditures of the entire organization, the settlement of copyright claims, and the program correspondence with thousands of listeners. However, most features that are sent over the air are supplied by persons or by organizations under contracts of varying length, rather than by permanent employees of the B.B.C. Large-scale negotiations with variety managers, the legitimate stage, concert promoters, lecture organizers, and news editors supply the foundation of the B.B.C.'s extra-mural talent. However, the B.B.C. has to adapt many of these programs to the form required by a new medium and subject to the interests of a cosmopolitan audience. Adaptation is therefore one of the principal staff duties.

The permanent employees of the B.B.C., unlike those of the other public service undertakings we have considered, are unorganized. Their status does not differ materially from that of persons employed by an ordinary private business. The reasons for non-organization are probably explained by the wide variety of duties involved in the work of the B.B.C. Moreover, the staff policies of the management have been so progressive that no strong incentive to unionize has arisen. For example, the Corporation has voluntarily adopted a retirement system for its employees. Salaries and wages compare favorably with those of other professional, technical, and clerical workers. The Corporation has expanded so rapidly that initiative and ability have been able to find their reward in promotions. This is not meant to suggest that personnel administration has reached the acme of perfection. However, it is true that the *esprit de corps* and the initiative of the B.B.C. staff are immediately discernible by those who have dealings with the organization.

The only serious personnel difficulties have arisen in connection with the professional unions of entertainers. In these disputes the B.B.C. has sometimes refused to accept the conditions specified by the organized actors and the variety amalgamations, and has announced that it would, if necessary, build up an independent galaxy of its own stars. The present relationship existing between the B.B.C. and the organized artists may best be described as a truce. The issue involved is an important one affecting public policy, and it does not appear to be permanently settled at the present time.

It may be said that structurally the B.B.C. has not settled down into hard and fast lines. After ten years it is still experimenting and evolving. This is perfectly natural and entirely desirable. By the avoidance of water-tight compartments and the incorporation of the functional principle, a large degree of interaction and collaboration has been secured in the going concern. These factors, combined with an experienced and progressive leadership, have made it possible for the B.B.C. to expand in consonance with the requirements imposed by a rapidly growing business.

Centralization relative to personnel and policy is an outstanding characteristic of the undertaking. Regionalism and devolution, two of the principal desiderata advocated in Parliament by proponents of "business management of the public services," are lacking in this enterprise. Responsibility has been concentrated as in the Post Office, and for much the same reason: someone must be accountable to Parliament or to the public when the policies or the activities of the management are questioned. There is also the "strong-willed" leadership which has been referred to above. The result is that the B.B.C. has evoked considerably more accusations of "dictatorship" in recent years than has the Post Office. Should centralization be regarded as an accusatory matter? The question is usually treated emotionally rather than rationally. Can management be divorced from policy? Is this possible in the case of the B.B.C. at any rate? It may be said that policy and management are more inseparable in broadcasting than in any other public service. If the centralization of responsibility for policy and management is considered objectionable, what practicable alternative is there?

The primary purpose of British broadcasting, as we have already stated, is cultural. There has been "a conscious social purpose in its development, but not to the prejudice of wholesome and satisfying entertainment." The foundation of broadcasting policy, Sir John Reith has written, "should be the endeavor of the broadcasting authority to bring into the maximum possible number of homes in the country an appreciation of all that is best in every sphere of human endeavor and achievement." At the same time he reminds us that in a business which covers so many different lines of activity it is impossible to enunciate one comprehensive policy. There may be, in fact, as many policies as there are lines of activity, and with every policy subsidiary and derivative ones as well. It is important that the difficulties of studying program policy should be completely recognized at the outset. All we can hope to do is to explain the relative emphasis given to various types and classes of subject-matter and attempt to supply the materials for an objective appraisal of the general policy. These matters will be approached from another angle in the following section, which deals with criticisms of the B.B.C. and its policies.

An analysis of the 1932 program of the B.B.C. reveals that in the national service, originating from Daventry National and London Regional, the greatest amount of time was given to light music, which occupied approximately 22 per cent, while serious music accounted for 19 per cent of the total time. The balance was made up principally as follows: news and running commentaries, 10 per cent; school and adult education, 8 per cent; talks, 8 per cent; children's hour, 6 per cent; and religious services 5½ per cent. The percentages from regional broadcasts gave a slightly different result. Light music occupied almost 40 per cent of the time, serious music 16 per cent, news and running commentaries 8 per cent, religious services 4 per cent, variety 3 per cent, and talks and educational features about 4 per cent.

Concerning program policy as a whole the B.B.C. has stated officially that "Program-building is still (perhaps always will be) far more of an art than an exact science." Experience has, nevertheless, declared some fixed points and these may be briefly set forth here:

"(1) There is no such thing as the 'mean listener'; the public falls into many different groups, each consisting at any given moment of persons of like taste and mood. Therefore (a) the day's program should contain 'something for everyone,' and (b) in the scheme for a week or longer each genre should be represented proportionately to its intrinsic importance and the strength of its following.

"(2) Alternatives imply, hour for hour, contrasted matter. But this idea of contrast has itself evolved with experience. Extremes do not contrast well; an extreme should be balanced by a mean."

In the actual presentation of the broadcast the B.B.C. has adopted the impersonal type of announcing. The American "master of ceremonies," with his expansive personality, is unknown to British broadcasting. However, the announcing personnel is not all of one type, and persons other than announcers (for example, drama directors) may, and do in varying degree, participate directly in the presentation. The British method of impersonal presentation is necessarily more formal than that in certain other countries, notably the United States.

Not long ago, during a debate in the House of Commons, the Postmaster-General stated that probably every listener has his own idea about what is desirable in wireless broadcasts. Some people, he said, want the B.B.C. "to be gay"; others say "Too much uplift." As a matter of fact it is almost impossible to discover exactly what listeners want, but the B.B.C. attempts to tap diverse channels of opinion as best it can by inviting suggestions and by sending out inquiries. However, a policy of not offering as much frivolity as the average person might desire has been consciously adopted. The B.B.C. has agreed to develop the nation's appreciation of good music and of education. Sir John Reith has stated candidly that "The best way to give the public what it wants is to reject the express policy of giving the public what it wants. Or simpler still, if you set out to give the public what it wants, you won't do it." This policy is not meant to be "autocratic or arbitrary in attitude or procedure," the Director-General has emphasized, but it is based on the experience that "a supply of good things creates a demand." Although the utterance caused criticism from the press at the time, Sir John Reith has reiterated his belief that

"to set out to 'give the public what it wants' is a dangerous and fallacious policy, involving almost always an underestimate of the public's intelligence and continual lowering of standard. Thus, paradoxically, it turns out to be not the monopoly system that is obliged to play for safety. On the contrary, it is not insistent autocracy but wisdom that suggests the policy of prosecuting carefully and persistently a basis of giving people what you believe they should like and will come to like, granting, of course, discretion and human understanding on the part of those who carry out the policy—and resolution."

The B.B.C.'s policy regarding educational broadcasts deserves special consideration, because it is at one and the same time so important and yet fraught with so many difficulties. A Member of Parliament recently referred to the B.B.C. as "the university of the common man," and Mr. Lloyd George concluded that because of the changes which have taken place in the journalistic world, he knew of no other agency which could "present the vast issues upon which the life of the country depended except the British

T

Broadcasting Corporation." In the same debate, however, the Member representing London University pointed out that "it was forgotten that the Charter of the B.B.C. was granted on the specific promise that there should be a widely spread education broadcast." The speaker stated that out of 300 or 400 broadcasts in ten months, "only four of those contributions could, in any sense, be described as promoting education in a wide and liberal sense." He therefore pleaded for a wider use of educational opportunities in the programs. On the other hand, many people may be found who state that the B.B.C. devotes too much time to "uplift."

The B.B.C. management appears to be aware of the difficulties accompanying the use of the wireless as an educational medium. For example, the Director-General of the B.B.C. stated to a group of educators in New York City that "The attachment of the adjective 'educational' to any matter is apt to weigh heavily against its acceptance. People object to any open proposal to educate them. A pontifical attitude, or still more the suspicion in ordinary people's minds that it exists, is perhaps the greatest danger that Radio Education has to face. It is not normal indifference that has to be overcome, but definite aversion in those very educable elements that you wish to reach."

The broadcasting of religion is one of the outstanding policies of the B.B.C., and one that creates controversy and criticism. This is to be expected. The emphasis placed on religious subject-matter may be measured by the fact that it receives four-fifths as much time as talks. Some critics state that religion is given altogether too much time, others object to the necessity of turning to Continental stations for diversity on Sundays, and others find the broadcasts either too fundamental or too liberal. Needless to say, many people consider them just right.

The B.B.C.'s policy regarding religious broadcasting was explained in the 1933 *Yearbook*. The policy began in the first months of the Company's existence. The evolution has been described as follows:

"The simple religious address of those first days soon developed into the Studio Service; this again was supplemented by the outside broadcasts of services from churches. To these were added in the course of time, first a mid-week service and then a short daily morning service; other services and religious programs, occasional or regular, find their places in the schedule; and lastly, there is the Epilogue, a form rather of meditation than of service, by which the Sunday evening's program is closed on a note in harmony with the day."

Concerning the control of religious broadcasting, it has been stated, "Each of the Christian churches (subject of course to the condition that it possesses a large membership) now has, and welcomes, its opportunities of conducting services and preaching to the nation—and the Religious Advisory Committees have reached a considerable measure of practical agreement as to what constitutes non-sectarian Christianity that can be preached to a Christian country of many confessions." Because of the regional nature of the B.B.C. network , allowance has been made for religious solidarities existing in certain sections of the country, particularly in Scotland.

The basis of the "Sunday policy" of the B.B.C. has been officially explained as follows: (a) dedication of certain Sunday hours to religious broadcasts, (b) abstention from broadcasting, religious or other, during normal church hours, and (c) the preservation of the character of the "British Sunday," so far as broadcasting can operate to preserve it. Concerning the place of religion in broadcasting and the general results of the policy, Sir John Reith stated in 1930,

"Religion is certainly a controversial subject, at any rate as the term is commonly understood. On analysis, however, one finds that there are large numbers of people who, while owning no allegiance to any recognizable church or sect, regard themselves, and often with every justification, as religious people. One is well aware that the alienation of great numbers from the church can be mistaken for an alienation from religion, whereas in fact it is nothing of the sort. The popularity of the Sunday services, the Bible readings, the daily morning service, and the Epilogue, would be astonishing had it not been anticipated. It leads to the conclusion that there is still a place of priority for religion in this country, a response to it and a need for it, that the country is religious at heart, or capable of being so, and this in spite of seeming indifference, diminishing attendance at church, and the growth of materialism and irresponsibility."

On the other hand, it is a well-known fact that British advertisers find that Sunday is the best time to advertise in English from Continental stations.

When policies are based upon convictions it is inevitable that strong objections and strong approval should be found in opposition. It is a short step from the consideration of B.B.C. policies to the criticisms that are levelled at the organization from various and sundry quarters.

### THE B.B.C. AND ITS CRITICS

The life of a broadcasting official is not designed to increase his popularity. Even a seemingly innocent field like music arouses sharp differences of opinion. All broadcasting involves either taste or opinion, and hence no one may be expected to be pleased all of the time. It is quite natural, therefore, that at one time or another the B.B.C. should have many critics. Vested interests become alarmed, minorities and reactionaries protest, Liberals demand more controversy, indiscretions are bound to occur, and the management's power is inevitably regarded with suspicion if not with dislike. Despite these circumstances, the Postmaster-General stated recently that there are "10,000 satisfied but silent listeners" for every critic. So far as the future of the B.B.C. is concerned it is only the final judgment of the individual and the general effect of all criticisms that really count; but each of these factors is influenced by the various sorts of criticism levelled at the B.B.C.

The most persistent and powerful critics of the B.B.C. are those whose interests are—or are thought to be—adversely affected by the development of broadcasting. Other old-established interests and operations have feared that broadcasting would "queer the pitch" for them in one way or another. These fears were particularly strong and actively expressed in the early years of the wireless. The newspaper interests formed a solid phalanx of opposition, apprehensive lest their circulation might be adversely affected. Attempts were made to charge for newspaper space occupied by program announcements. News broadcasts were openly opposed and in early years satisfactory arrangements were difficult to make. Moreover, the publishing activities of the B.B.C. have always been regarded with disapproval by the newspaper fraternity. Suspicion and enmity have by no means disappeared, but relations have become increasingly more satisfactory. In the 1930 *Yearbook* of the B.B.C. the attitude of the press toward broadcasting was characterized thus, "It cannot be described as ever having been cordial, although it has fluctuated between definite hostility and mere watchfulness." In recent months the attitude of the newspaper interests has tended to change from "hostility on its own behalf to active, but by no means invariably informed and responsible, criticism on behalf of the listener's interests as it sees them."

Many of the fears held by vested interests in the early years of broadcasting have tended to disappear. Concert promoters and theatrical managers no longer regard the radio as destructive, although the full result of the competition may not yet have appeared. Owners of musical and literary copyrights have discovered that the value of their property has not been depreciated; in fact, the reverse is usually the case. The churches, which were said in some cases to be disturbed about religious broadcasting, now in most cases regard it as a valuable ally.

The principal criticisms of the B.B.C. arise from minorities who contend that they are not given a fair opportunity to use the facilities of broadcasting. This is the point at which unified control pinches tightly. In a House of Commons debate centering around this point, the Postmaster-General stated that there is no foundation to the criticism, because it comes from the right as well as from the left, and hence the criticisms "cancel each other out." This is not a satisfactory answer. It has a bearing upon the question of alleged bias on the part of the B.B.C., but it does not afford a satisfactory reply to the charge that minorities are denied a fair opportunity to be heard. It might as well be admitted that the problem could probably never be solved in a way that would satisfy everyone. Interests which complain that they are not fairly treated at present might not gain a great deal under a system of competition in broadcasting. This does not mean that the present situation is incapable of improvement. Sir John Reith has stated that the only wise policy open to the B.B.C. is not to be too far behind public opinion and not too far ahead of it. Needless to say, this principle entails a high degree of judgment and discretion.

A striking illustration of the dissatisfaction arising from the unequal treatment of various economic and political interests was presented in the recent conference of the Cooperative party. Mr. A. V. Alexander, who was the First Lord of the Admiralty in the Labor Government, stated that the B.B.C.'s denial of the right to disseminate the Cooperative party's philosophy, ideals, and political outlook was "little short of a scandal." "If it is possible for the B.B.C. to give the right to a—[person] like Sir Oswald Mosley," he said— "then it is high time that our six million cooperators should have equal access to the ether as that given to Mosley." The Cooperative party has not been denied all access to the microphone, but has been refused permission to participate in particular series. In the common law, public utilities were supposed to give equal treatment to consumers desiring to use the service. Is it possible or desirable to apply this principle to the broadcasting monopoly?

The amount of controversy that has been sent over the air has increased in recent years, but as has been said, considerable dissatisfaction with the present amount still exists. In the early months of its existence the B.B.C. was forbidden to broadcast any controversial subject-matter. In January 1927 the Postmaster-General informed the Corporation that it must refrain from broadcasting any statement expressing the opinion of the Corporation on matters of public policy, and secondly, prohibited speeches or lectures containing statements on topics of political, religious, or industrial controversy. The ban on controversial broadcasts was not withdrawn until March 1928. Since that time the B.B.C.'s policies relative to the presentation of controversial subjects have developed along fairly definite lines. Discussions usually take the form of a debate, or of a question and answer conversation. Rarely is only one side of a question presented, and in such cases a speaker with opposing views is usually scheduled for a later occasion. In all of these broadcasts the platform manner is discouraged and the fireside demeanor is encouraged. If the program is broadcast from the studio the speaker is expected to submit his manuscript in advance and to adhere to it in delivery.

Criticisms of unfairness have arisen when educational talks have been used by politicians to influence opinion on current controversies, and when the opposition has not been presented with an immediate opportunity to answer political speeches. In a debate on B.B.C. policies, which occurred in the House of Commons on February 22, 1933, Sir Stafford Cripps stated that the theory of factual and non-controversial Ministerial talks had been gradually extended to cover some of the most controversial matter. There were, for instance, the four broadcasts on the Ottawa resignations; all of those who spoke took the opportunity to attack the Opposition. There was the broadcast by the Secretary of State for India, and there was the Prime Minister's broadcast on unemployment. In all of these cases, he said, the Opposition was denied any facility whatever to reply. In the same debate Mr. Churchill, who had complained several times because he had been denied the privilege of broadcasting on the India question, characterized the political talks arranged by the B.B.C. as "the copious stream of pontifical anonymous mugwumpery with which we have been dosed so long." Recognizing that the B.B.C. has had "an immensely difficult task in dealing with the question of political broadcasts, and since no one could blame them if they had committed errors of judgment or of practice (because there was no adequate machinery to assist them in carrying out the function properly)," it was suggested that an advisory committee on political broadcasts should be created. So far the proposal has not materialized satisfactorily.

Part of the B.B.C.'s difficulties appear to have been due to an unrealistic interpretation of what is comprehended by "political" and "non-political." In an effort to get away from party alignments the management has sometimes scheduled "non-political" talks on current public issues. In the average person's mind a discussion is not made non-political simply by labelling it as such, or by disclaiming any party preference. So long as modern government is concerned with almost every social issue, any discussion is bound to be political—that is, it must deal with policy. In an effort to escape from party responsibility the B.B.C. runs the risk of being accused of unfair tactics and institutional bias.

The problem of political broadcasts reaches its most acute stage at the time of general elections. Serious dissatisfaction has arisen over election broadcasts, and reform has been suggested. It has been proposed that all political broadcasting should be discontinued a week or more in advance of the general election. Herbert Morrison expressed a widely held view in these words,

"If I, personally, had had a decisive voice in the Labor party about broadcasting arrangements in connection with the 1931 general election, I should have been inclined to insist upon Labor having a bigger show or refused to have the Labor case put at all. In the latter case I would have denounced in public the proposed arrangements which gave the Coalition such superior treatment, and put the onus on the B.B.C., and/or the Government to withdraw the whole thing or to outrage public feeling by allowing the parties to the Coalition Government to put their case without the Labor case being heard. Electioneering by wireless is, however, so difficult to be fair about that there is something to be said for stopping it for a week before polling day or even altogether."

The policy in the past has been to give equal opportunity to the Government and to the Opposition. This has meant that, because of the three-party system, the Government actually received twice as much time as any other party. Now that parties have split, and that a National Government has been formed, the allotment of the opposition parties is even more unpopular. Among those who favor the continuance of election broadcasts the proposal has been originated that the parties not in power should invariably be given more broadcasting time than the party in power.

Some of the most severe criticisms of the B.B.C. have arisen because of its alleged "indiscretions." The debate on the B.B.C. which occurred in February 1933—the first one of any importance in six years—was the direct consequence of the most notable of these incidents: a broadcast on New Year's Eve which evoked a protest from the Polish Government. The difficulty arose primarily because the views expressed were not those of a responsible leader, but were an impersonal utterance. In the House of Commons it was said that the incident was not caused by the B.B.C.'s lack of independence, but solely because it was "perplexed and baffled." It might more accurately be described as a "blunder." There have been surprisingly few occurrences of this kind—far fewer, it is believed, than if broadcasting were operated as an official organ of the Government. It is human to err; and it is hard to imagine a system in which controversy is permitted which would be free from occasional indiscretions. "Censorship" is not infallible.

The encouragement of controversial broadcasts has been called "a bold experiment"; but there is rather general agreement that it has proved a successful one. There appears to be a growing conviction in Parliament that education on economic and political issues should be extended rather than diminished. For example, the Member representing the Scottish universities stated in the House of Commons that, "opinion, however dangerous, was far safer in the open air than underground." At one time the B.B.C. argued that unorthodox broadcasts should be prevented because the listener cannot protect himself, and hence must be safeguarded by rigid selectivity at Broadcasting House. This is particularly true, it has been said, in the case of subjects not suitable for broadcasting. This reasoning is not very convincing. If the listener objects he can turn off his radio, just as the reader can burn his paper. Mr. Winston Churchill said he believed he expressed the general feeling in the House in holding that there should be "a new, wider, and freer use of this great instrument, which could bring, if it was opened to the political life of the nation, enhancement of the strength of the State" and the establishment "on a more permanent basis of the great institutions which this island has evolved."

## CONCLUSION

The British broadcasting system is essentially a compromise between the commercially actuated and privately managed type of control and the political broadcasting regime operated as an instrument of the governing party. This being a realistic world, it is influenced by the social and political assumptions underlying British institutions generally. However, its underlying theories probably come as close to obtaining independence and impartiality as any form of control which could be devised. The broadcasting official is free to concentrate on his art, on public service, on programs that will increase the appreciation and the knowledge of all classes.

The B.B.C. is subject to public control in all important respects, and yet its program policies are not subject to the dictation of the party in power. Provisions in the Corporation's license which might provide this loop-hole have never been used and are not likely to be so long as present relationships continue. (However, the activity of the B.B.C. during the general strike of 1926 is held in some quarters to be undistinguishable from direct government intervention.) Hence the policies and the actions of the Corporation, in a positive sense, are the sole responsibility of the Board of Governors and of the permanent officials.

Six years of experience under the public utility trust form of organization have shown that the B.B.C.'s management is adaptable, progressive, and responsive to new opportunities and demands. This has hardly been a long enough period in which to formulate a final judgment regarding the ultimate worth of the present form, because its business has expanded so rapidly that the Corporation has not been confronted with the usual problems which arise when expansion becomes slower and the enthusiasm of youth wears off.

The framework of the B.B.C. organization affords only a partial understanding of the institution. Personality—particularly that of the Director-General—is the indispensable, the dominant consideration. The B.B.C. has "atmosphere," because the ideas and the ideals of a man have controlled its development. Everything about the organization is positive and purposeful. "I realize how important is the personal factor in an organization of the B.B.C.'s type," its Director-General has said. The object of the B.B.C. is to provide the "best" in every field of activity. But no way has yet been discovered of getting everyone to agree what is "best." This is obviously more difficult in the field of opinion than in the realm of taste. Herbert Morrison has therefore written that "it is a matter for argument as to whether the Director-General of the B.B.C. should or should not be a strong personality, if we remember the balancing of views, prejudices, and tastes which are big factors in the program-making of the B.B.C." The assertion that the B.B.C. is a "benevolent autocracy" is the only ground on which continuing differences of viewpoint are found.

The status of the B.B.C. will normally be reconsidered in 1936. At the present time there appears to be no serious question that the constitutional position of broadcasting will remain as it is. The monopolistic nature of broadcasting also seems to be unassailable. Within the framework of the organization, however, the issue is that of greater Democracy in the popular sense of the term. Judging from indications, the specific questions around which support and opposition may be expected to rally are these: greater or less accountability to Parliament; centralization or more regional autonomy; more active participation of the Board of Governors in the guidance of the Corporation; and the desirability of increasing the influence of advisory committees. These problems deserve a great deal of careful thought.

Speakers in the House of Commons frequently remind the country that the British broadcasting system is the best in the world. Imitation is undoubtedly the highest form of flattery—and the world has imitated. But it must be remembered that society not only moulds institutions; society is itself remade by institutions—particularly if they be monopolies. Broadcasting is the strategic field in which all of the country's intelligence and cooperative ability must be pooled if the stewardship granted to the B.B.C. is to be wisely used in the guidance of national development.

## CHAPTER IX

# THE FUTURE OF PUBLIC SERVICE UNDERTAKINGS

## GENERAL APPRAISAL

The growth of British public service undertakings has been characterized by opportunism and experimentation. This is to be expected, because the traditional British method is to settle problems as they arise rather than to devise a logical plan of economic organization in advance as do certain Continental nations, notably the Germans. A policy of empiricism can easily become one of "drift," and that was admittedly what had happened to public utility development in Great Britain, and to industry generally, before the war. However, post-war world economic tendencies have shaken Britain's comfortable insularity. A new outlook has begun to appear. The concept of "the public utility principle in industry" is perhaps the clearest manifestation of the fact that British leaders, rather than merely being content with private firms competing against each other, have begun to think in terms of national development to be brought about by means of controlled monopolies. The adoption of a national electricity scheme is the best evidence of this changing viewpoint. It may no longer be said that the British look with diffidence upon national plans of economic development, wherein private interests must be disciplined and the fruits of the plan cannot appear for several years. The long view, the philosophical outlook, may yet become a part of the national ideology.

Although the average Member of Parliament will stoutly insist that philosophy has not played an important part in public utility development, he would be shocked to be told that the basic principles of every new public service undertaking were not carefully considered. The first and

most important stage of private bill procedure is the attention given to underlying principles. An excellent illustration
of the importance attached to adequate consideration of
public utility principles is found in the Joint Committee
stage of the London Transport Bill.

Convincing evidence is at hand to show that the British,
even though they usually deny it, have advanced a considerable distance along the road that leads to a clear-cut
philosophy of public utility organization, management, and
control. To be sure, this philosophy is empirical, pragmatic,
relativist, and hence the champions of the "consistency of
all truth" school deny the existence of what may be properly
called philosophy. The writer believes that British public
utility development is capable of philosophical appraisal.
Moreover, due to the fact that the public utility concept
has been extended so much in recent years, and because
other important forms of enterprise are likely to be socialized
in the not distant future, it is important to take stock of the
present position, the direction, and the objectives of public
utility tendencies. This is the aim of the present chapter.

There is no reason to suppose that the existing types
of public utility enterprise will not be added to, if and when
the occasion arises. The Post Office may operate very
succesfully as a Department of State; local transport may do
very well under the statutory company form of organization;
the B.B.C. may possibly be ideally administered as a public
utility trust; but not one of these methods of organization
and control is necessarily a standard for all future development. It is quite possible that when the theory and the
possibilities of the mixed undertaking—like that represented
in the Manchester Ship Canal—are better understood,
there may be as pronounced an expansion in that direction
as has occurred on the Continent. The mutations and varieties
of public control have probably not been fully evolved.
New problems may require new forms; established methods
need not necessarily be imposed upon different situations.

For the time being, the public utility trust appears to hold out most promise of preference in the future. This form of public utility is capable of considerable variation. Moreover, it combines elements of socialization with aspects of private management, initiative, and elasticity, that should be preserved. To say that the public utility trust is the ideal form of public service undertaking, however, requires more proof than has appeared so far.

As the result of experience, it may be found that the public utility trust is too far removed from Parliament to be effectively criticized and controlled in matters relating to important financial and labor policies. This form of organization is exposed to the pressure of interest groups, with the result that log-rolling and personal influence are hard to avoid. An appointed body, with no constituency to which it is effectively responsible, will be in danger of a dulled sensitiveness to public needs unless it is honestly and carefully chosen. Salaries, fees, and overhead costs that the average person would consider too high cannot be effectively prevented. Moreover, the creation of public boards all of which possess important differences, may render the processes of popular control so complex and indirect that real responsibility will be lost. The American system of independent commissions suffers from this defect. The London Passenger Transport Board appears to be especially subject to this possible weakness. Great Britain should hesitate a long time before seriously vitiating her most valuable constitutional principle—real responsibilty for power bestowed by public authority.

The mixed undertaking, like the public utility trust, affords an opportunity for elasticity and adaptability of management, and in addition it appears to guarantee a greater degree of public control over finances and policies. In the case of the Manchester Ship Canal, for example, the municipality has invested only one-third as much in the undertaking as the private investors, but a majority of the directors must be chosen from the municipal council to represent the public's interest. The Chairman of the Manchester Ship Canal Company is chosen by the shareholders' directors, while the Deputy Chairmanship is vested in the local government. This form of cooperation, providing for day-to-day scrutiny by the representatives of both sides, possesses unquestionable advantages.

There are wide differences of opinion regarding what is most desirable in public utility development. To certain sections of the population "the public interest" is a 15 per cent return on public utility stocks; to some it is represented by cold arithmetical computations—so-called "objective efficiency"; to many the public welfare means satisfactory service at low prices: while to others the all-important consideration is "the human factor," namely the welfare of those who are responsible for doing the work and supplying the services. It is not suggested that these emphases are necessarily conflicting or that the average person would not make a certain allowance for each.

The writer will be candid about his own viewpoint. These opinions are not offered because of the weight they carry, but only because presuppositions should be revealed in order that the basis of judgment may be properly understood and weighed. In the first place, the possibility of extracting large profits needs to be eradicated from public utilities. Large profits earned on a service wherein monopoly and other forms of privilege have been granted is a clear case of anti-social exploitation. In some cases interest should be as low as three per cent. The public utility trust is a move in the right direction because it forbids profits and limits interest payments to a small percentage. If, as some economists say, money will not always be attracted unless higher interest rates are offered, the Government should supply all or part of the financial needs of the undertaking in return for complete or joint participation in the management of the service.

Claims that public service undertakings can be evaluated solely, or principally, by statistical computations and by standards of accountancy are not convincing. Figures are relative and frequently subject to the emphasis desired, and furthermore they cannot measure qualitative factors. Statistical and accounting methods are extremely useful, but their limitations need to be recognized. Efficiency is not merely a matter of figures and percentages. The attitudes and desires of consumers, the degree of improvement possible, and the best interests of those employed in the service are some of the qualitative factors which defy cold mathematical calculation. Successful public services are more fully measured by human equations, by the calibre of the men who run them, than by numerical averages. Too frequently so-called "efficiency audits" are merely another way of increasing profits irrespective of their effects in other directions. The financial yard-stick almost invariably aims at keeping down the so-called "wages bill." Failure to increase wages in consonance with the scientific improvement of industry is the principal cause of economic stagnation. However, it would undoubtedly be desirable to introduce a proper system of accounting, distinguishing on sound principles between expenditure on capital and on current account, into all public service undertakings. The system should be as uniform as possible, to facilitate comparisons.

Public utility development, if it is founded on consumers' rather than on producers' economics, should help to overcome business depression and to strengthen the economic life of the nation. By now it must be obvious that the problem of industrial reconstruction is primarily one of distribution rather than of production. Public utilities should be a means of making necessary services constantly better and cheaper. Public service undertakings should make work steady, and they should provide for profit-sharing in the form of higher wages as the consumers' demand increases. Lower prices and higher real wages are both possible if science and social organization are correlated and mastered. This is not Utopian dreaming. The alternative may be seen in the present crisis confronting national electricity development. If after science and social planning have produced cheap bulk power the problem of distribution is not effectively controlled in the public interest, profits will rise and the general benefits to the consumer, the employee, and the nation will be dissipated. Political economy is a matter of control, of the proper sort of balances; if the stockholders of an industry get too much power (large profits) the whole life of the nation will ultimately be put out of balance. This has become particularly true since the functions of finance and of management are usually found in separate hands. The problem is therefore to find the most effective form of public control.

The solution of future problems of public utility organization and control presents opportunity for a great deal of interesting speculation and necessary thought. The regulation of public service companies, like gas, tramway, and railway undertakings, does not present an example of public control that should inspire emulation in the future. The public utility trust represents a vast improvement over Victorian regulation. The necessity of finding a new legal and administrative setting for the railways is already appreciated in many quarters. Road transport and the national distribution of electricity are other problems awaiting solution.

The Department of State provides several advantages which are not offered to the same extent by other forms of public service enterprise; the principal ones being effective control, opportunity for the State to become the model employer, the existence of the best administrative traditions in the country, and greater protection from the assaults of predatory interests. On the other hand, the questions of initiative, red-tape, and commercial outlook require further improvement before the example of the Post Office is likely to be made a model for the future.

Disagreement exists relative to the monopoly or semi-monopoly services that are destined to be brought within the ambit of public service enterprises, and yet even in conservative circles further nationalization under business management is usually taken for granted. As in previous cases, a great deal depends upon the trends within the industries themselves. The effective elimination of competition, the indispensable nature of the commodities or services supplied, the necessity of the economic units in the development of the national economy, the continual earning of large dividends and the charging of exorbitant prices, and the pressure of foreign competition are tests of socialization which usually bear great weight. The conversion of the coal industry into a public utility has been considered since the extensive investigations of 1917 and 1919. In some circles discussion has centered around other basic industries as well, such as iron and steel and the chemical combine. The iron and steel industry is in the process of reorganization and unification. Then, too, for several years the joint stock banks have been the source of serious attention by the Labor party. Whether the process of accretion comes in small or in larger segments, as a result of a comprehensive plan or by empirical degrees, the problems connected with public utility control and national development deserve careful attention and immediate emphasis.

### THE SHORTCOMINGS OF REGULATION

The regulation of public service companies, as distinguished from public utility trusts, has not proved very successful in Great Britain, and there are reasons for doubting if the older forms of regulation can ever be made a desirable method of public control, at any rate for future cases. The regulation of gas undertakings, as we have seen, leaves much to be desired. Railway regulation grows increasingly less effective, and the present impasse can probably be solved only by some form of State ownership and unified administration. The fate of road transport depends largely upon the future policy relative to railways. In no case, in other words, has regulation proved a conspicuous success. Public utility regulation in the United States has proved more satisfactory in some respects, but in view of the widespread dissatisfaction of recent years it is by no means certain that commission regulation will be found universally satisfactory.[1] New departures have already begun to emerge.

In Great Britain the choice between regulation and ownership, either directly by a government unit or by a public utility trust, clearly seems to have been made in favor of the latter. In recent years Parliament has shown a marked preference for some form of non-profit making enterprise either closely or loosely within the framework of the Government, and hence free from detailed regulation, to the private company subject to restrictions and regulations which issue from government departments.

British temperament appears to have a great deal to do with the ineffectiveness of regulation. British regulation has been "timid," says a keen observer. "A regulated business," stated a Member of Parliament amidst general approval, "is worse than no business at all." This point of view is deep-rooted in the business community. The reason for this attitude is found in English temperament and tradition. Privacy in all matters, including business, is a national passion. The idea of one person's investigating another's business offends the national sensitiveness. The Englishman's skepticism regarding regulation is excellently expressed in this excerpt from an article on public utility regulation written by Sir Henry Bunbury. "The fact is," he says,

[1] Keezer and May, *The Public Control of Business*, New York, 1930; Mosher, *Electrical Utilities: The Crisis in public control*, New York, 1929; Felix Frankfurter, *The Public and its Government*, New Haven, 1930.

"that the problem is at bottom one of devising means for securing, both initially and continuously, an enlightened, efficient, and progressive management. Checks and controls can do little to secure this; they may arrest the criminal but they cannot make him good."

In the United States, public utility commissions are expected to act as umpires in the clash of interest between the producer and the consumer, and it is not uncommonly argued that regulatory officials should be special guardians of the consumers. This is the view of Governor Pinchot of Pennsylvania, and it has been prominent in New York, Oregon, Washington, and other States as well. This view is totally foreign to British conceptions. In place of vigilance there is what might be called collaboration—the "business for business' sake" attitude. Sir Cyril Hurcomb, of the Ministry of Transport, went to the heart of the matter when he wrote,

"The hand of a regulating Department should not and need not be heavy or blighting in its touch. It can and should be a supporting hand. The power should be used and, so far as my experience goes, is used only in the closest touch and after the most thorough consultation with the interests concerned, and the aim of the administration should be that the industry should regard the Department as an essential part of itself even though particular decisions may be unwelcome."

This attitude results in an interesting difference between British and American regulation: the British public is notoriously fearful of monopolies, but the Government has usually adopted the management's rather than the consumer's viewpoint; the American consumer is not particularly frightened by monopolies, but he expects the public official to "fight the utilities."

Public opinion in Great Britain does not play an appreciable part in public utility regulation, but in America it is a force of considerable magnitude. Generally speaking, when the English consumer becomes dissatisfied with the actions of a public utility concern, he merely becomes more reticent or he may possibly write a letter to the local paper; his American cousin is more likely to write to the Public Service Commission, attend a public protest meeting, or air his grievances among his friends. In most American States an informal investigation of a consumer's complaint is begun by merely posting a letter to the public utility commission, and twenty petitioners can usually start a formal investigation. In other words, it is easier and cheaper for consumers to bring about investigations of public service companies than it is in Great Britain. Moreover, the legislature may order an investigation, or the regulatory commission may act on its own initiative. The difference in the rôle played by public opinion is partly the result of temperament and tradition and partly the difference in governmental machinery. The British official who strongly insisted that "There is no public opinion regarding public utilities in this country" may have slightly exaggerated, but his next observation was very significant and true. "There is no use complaining when the charges of private companies are high," he said. "Most citizens merely seize the first opportunity to have the local authority take over and run the utility. They have confidence that it will be managed successfully." Awareness of this fact is a stimulant of very great potency. The efficiency and progressiveness of government management and the consequent confidence of the consumer in public commercial services are points at which Great Britain's superiority over the United States must be frankly admitted.

The regulation of British public utilities appears to be impaired by placing so much reliance upon the judicial method, and by the resulting failure to develop the administrative commission. Courts are useful for certain purposes, but long experience in Great Britain and in the United States indicates, in the writer's view, that other methods are preferable when public utility regulation is the objective. The judicial technique puts the judge on top, whereas public utility control requires the knowledge of the social scientist and the engineer. Judicial regulation is limited: it only solves problems when they are brought before the Tribunal; and then its attention is focussed primarily upon the parties to the dispute rather than upon the best interests of everybody concerned. The judicial method is undemocratic because access to justice is reserved only to the strong and the organized: the small trader and the consumer find the process too costly and too uncertain when counsel must be retained, work neglected, and the skill of high-paid company attorneys combated.

The selection of members of public utility courts from interest groups does not appear to be desirable in practice. The Railway Rates Tribunal is the principal case in point. The railways and the traders frequently have interests which are diametrically opposed, giving the lawyer the ultimate voice. The Tribunal is not broadly representative, because no provision is made for the unorganized traders, organized labor, agriculture, or the general public. The panels have never been used and are not likely to be, due to the fact that interests desiring their own representation rarely consider it worth-while to appear before the Tribunal; and due to the fact, it is assumed, that the litigant concludes that he would be suspected of casting aspersions upon the permanent members if he chose to supplement the membership as provided for in the Act. But of greater importance than any of these objections, the selection of members to represent interest groups does not encourage the broad view, which is frequently more "practical" than that of the person who has had experience in only one industry. Members of the Tribunal who have been nominated by special interests are never able to overcome completely their natural alignments and predilections. The reason given by the railway companies at the time of their withdrawal from the National Wages Board applies to any attempt to reconcile interest representation and judicial impartiality. "The main difficulty," said the Companies, " arises from the constitution of the board, under which representatives of the parties sit as judges, with the result that they are put in the position of having to adjudicate and sign decisions on questions in regard to which they cannot be expected to hold an impartial opinion, and on which definite views may have been expressed by them or by the parties they represent."

A new method of recruitment for regulatory tribunals is needed. The administrative tribunal, composed of members with a knowledge of public utility economics, government, and engineering, and assisted by a staff of specialists, is preferable to a court composed of members chosen from interest groups. Such a plan would give more assurance of social viewpoint and impartiality.

The British seem to have unbounded confidence in the omnipotence and omnicompetence of the judicial method of regulation. The most striking proof of this is the provision in the London Transport Act which gives the Railway Rates Tribunal power not only to fix rates but to regulate facilities and service. The Tribunal, say those who have had most to do with it, is not in a position to deal competently with facilities, because it lacks the training and the necessary staff. Yet this feature of the Act was extravagantly praised in the House of Commons, where the impartiality and the publicity of the judicial method were extolled. The psychologist would probably say that the minds of the British have been conditioned in such a way that their critical faculties cease to function whenever the symbol "judicial" is mentioned. This attitude needs to be critically explored, particularly when the judicial method is advocated for public utility regulation. We ought to realize that judges are human,[1] and that although they should be credited with efforts to

---

[1] The rational view relative to the judicial process is developing rapidly in the United States; the new approach is well illustrated in articles by Jerome Frank, "Are judges human?", (1931) 80 *Univ. of Pennsylvania Law Rev.*, 17, 233; and Karl Llewellyn, "Some realism about realism," (1931) 44 *Harvard Law Rev.*, 1222.

be impartial, they cannot escape the effect of their early education and associations, which determine their social policies and their economic alignments.

If popular control is the goal, judges are usually the last persons to whom the final authority over questions arising from public utility regulation should be entrusted. Speaking generally, most members of the judiciary appear to find it difficult to see further than property rights. "The judicial mind," which William A. Robson praises,[1] is by no means the monopoly of the legal profession, as he would undoubtedly be the first to admit; and therefore the acquisition of impartial thinking does not necessarily depend upon the use of courts of law as the medium of public utility regulation. The law is so enmeshed by assumptions, fictions, and artificial reason that sufficient attention is rarely given to the consequences and the social objectives of decisions. The American administrative tribunal has been found to be more practical than the courts to which appeals are taken.

The alleged publicity of the judicial procedure is an exaggeration. How many people outside of those vitally concerned ever hear about the decisions of the Railway Rates Tribunal? Public opinion receives as much enlightenment, and effective criticism is more practicable, when regulatory powers are entrusted to administrative officials with fixed tenures of office.

The index of British regulation is, to a large extent, the effectiveness of the Ministry of Transport.[2] In this one department are combined the control over railways, roads, harbors, electricity, and other important public utility services. Theoretically, this type of functional organization is the best form of administrative control. Under the leadership of forceful personalities such as Sir Eric Geddes, Colonel Ashley, and Hebert Morrison, the Ministry of Transport has performed its regulatory functions in a constructive

[1] *Justice and Administrative Law*, ch. v.
[2] Herbert Morrison, *Socialization and Transport*, London, 1933.

and effective manner. But during several periods in the past, when regulation has virtually lapsed, the department has been guilty of passivity and procrastination.

If regulation is to be revitalized, it appears necessary to pay special attention to the personnel, Civil Service as well as political, of the Ministry of Transport, and to stop the process of delegating so many of the Ministry's duties to ad hoc bodies. For example, in due course of time the Electricity Commission may prove to be an unnecessary spoke in the wheel of regulation. Since the Ministry of Transport was created in 1919, several attempts have been made to abolish the Ministry and to divide its powers among other departments. The feeling of living under the sword of Damocles has undoubtedly done a great deal to bring about the timid attitude which has characterized the actions of the Ministry during several periods. Members of Parliament who have resisted effective regulation by the Ministry of Transport apparently do not realize that when regulation fails government expropriation is the ultimate alternative.

In conclusion, the older methods of regulating public utilities have not proved an effective means of public control. Regulation is passive and timid, because the British are temperamentally opposed to outside interference. They rely upon limitations and regulations contained in general or special Acts of Parliament, and make little provision for enforcement. If the private company fails to satisfy, public ownership and operation are the usual methods of correcting the fault. The judicial method of public utility regulation has been adopted for rail, road, and electricity services. The judicial technique is satisfactory as a static device for protecting· and adjusting private interests, but it is inadequate as a means of safeguarding and furthering the greatest good of the greatest number. In the long run, the central department, acting through a capable minister, is likely to produce more effective control over public utilities than the ad hoc body acting judicially. It is imperative that the personnel of the Ministry of Transport should be given special attention because the department is the crux of public utility regulation and the source from which the solution of future problems must be expected.

### PROBLEMS OF PUBLIC CONTROL

One reason that public utility regulation has not received more emphasis in Great Britain is that a limited view is frequently taken of the considerations involved. To many people—perhaps to most—public control implies nothing more than the prevention of dishonesty and avarice. Due to the fact that the standard of business integrity is high in Great Britain, the average person does not appreciate the necessity of continuous control by the State over public service monopolies. This attitude fails to take into account the most important reasons for public control.

The granting of monopoly and other forms of privilege is justified only on the assumption that the national interests will be best served thereby and that the benefits to be obtained will be passed on to the consuming public. The responsibility for achieving good service, satisfactory prices, and desirable working conditions remains with the public's official agents who granted the privileges. Public control by Parliament or its representatives is a public trust, a con-structive policy rather than an onerous chore. Popular control, so conceived, involves constructive policies and effective cooperation rather than the "catch the thief" attitude. There is no room for an attitude of "do-nothingness" and complacency if effective public control is to be obtained.

The creation of a public service undertaking involves the substitution of monopoly for competition, and hence pater-nalism instead of economic "laws" must operate. It is futile to suppose that prices will be reduced and that profits will be limited unless effective guarantees are provided and enforced. It is unfair and unwise to trust natural forces for the settlement of differences arising between public service undertakings and their employees. The State should exercise control over the standards of pay and the conditions of service of employees engaged in public utility enterprises. The Industrial Court helps to fulfil this need, but adequate provision for adjusting labor relations has not been made. There are several convincing reasons for State intervention at this point. In the first place, employees engaged in monopolistic services frequently have no alternative employment to which they can turn; hence the forces of competition do not operate to increase wages. In the second place, profits may become too high or prices too low if safeguards are not provided whereby the fruits of labor will be properly rewarded. Finally, public service undertakings are not of the sort to be left to the arbitrament of the strike, although this weapon is perfectly justifiable if the State does not fulfil its duty to the workers.

If an extension of national control into additional fields of industry and commerce may be expected, a unified agency in the central government which would deal exclusively with industrial development and with resulting policies of management is to be commended. Otherwise, glaring discrepancies, lapses of effective control, and Parliamentary confusion are almost inevitable. This is particularly true if, as anticipated, a number of different forms of public utility organization will continue to coexist. A board of strategy connected to Parliament and to the Cabinet, which will plan and control national utility enterprises, is a policy which has received a great deal of attention from the Labor party. An "Economic General Staff" has also been advocated in *Britain's Industrial Future*.

Public control is the crux of national public utility development. The most effective means of assuring both capable management and public benefits must be learned by experience. This edifice is likely to be built stone by stone, but the assistance of architects will be needed. One of these, G. D. H.

Cole, has written as follows regarding a desirable method of popular control:

"A system of responsible commissioners, adapted in varying ways to the needs of different services, seems most likely to meet the need (i.e. the public control of socialized industries), and to provide for the successful socialization of industries under public control. But these separate bodies of commissioners must be really responsible, not merely in a nominal sense to Parliament which sanctions their appointment, but to some public authority capable of coordinating their several activities and defining for them the general course of policy which, as administrators, they are called upon to pursue. The system of independent commissioners is apt to work badly now, precisely because no such coordinating authority exists. They are in effect irresponsible; and the control of policy, which is not their job, as well as the control of administration, which is, rests in their hands. Parliament in setting up the commission gives it certain powers and prescribes certain functions and lines of policy. But when once the commissioners are in being they are left without any effective subsequent directions, save that spasmodic parliamentary intervention which does more harm than good. Society lacks at present a central organ for the control of economic policy. Until that is provided, no really satisfactory form can be developed for the socialization of any enterprise."[1]

The recent tendency to remove public utilities from the control of Parliament and of Ministers undermines the principle of responsibility, and if continued may lead to serious difficulties. The reason given for twice removing the control of Parliament over the London Transport Board is that "political" influences should be eradicated and commercial considerations alone should operate. This argument is not convincing. It seems to be based upon a fear that at some future time the party in power might "stack" the board with its own sympathizers, irrespective of their qualifications for the position. This nervous anxiety is not justified on the ground of past performance. It has always been a tradition for parties in power to make appointments from rival political parties. The choice of the Director-General of the B.B.C. by the Labor party provides a recent example of the deeply rooted precedent of overriding party lines in order

[1] *The Next Ten Years in British Social and Economic Policy*, 136, London, 1929.

to secure the best person for a non-political position. There appears to be no foundation for nervousness about political ramps in Great Britain, but the real danger of anti-social conspiracy is found in the powerful pressure groups representing vested interests of one sort or another, whose spokesmen in Parliament are usually the ones who talk about the dangers of political interference.

Even if there are certain drawbacks arising from Parliamentary control over public utilities, they are likely to be found less objectionable than the system of boards and commissions which has sprung up. Criticism and responsibility as ingredients in the constitutional structure are too valuable to be given up. After a period of expansion and experimentation in public utility development, the problem of the following years is likely to be one of coordination and the reestablishment of responsible public control.

Freedom of detailed administration coupled with unified responsibility for general policies—this is the desirable formula. The more effective central control becomes, the smaller and more elastic public utility organizations can remain. A former Minister of Transport, Herbert Morrison, recently uttered an important truth when he advised that "we must beware of over large units of economic management." Studies which have been made of the merger development in the United States and elsewhere support this conclusion. If operating services are to be kept small enough to be manageable, therefore, the salutary character of popular control is the paramount consideration.

### THE GENIUS OF BRITISH ADMINISTRATION

A candid appraisal of British administration, public and commercial, as compared with comparable features in foreign countries, indicates that British management has set the pace in certain respects but has lagged behind in some other ways. British leaders who have been aware of the desirability of comparative studies are alive to the necessity of improving some elements of public service administration, but others observe only the generally satisfactory character of the results produced and are inclined to be complacent. The fields of British administration in which greater attention appears to be needed are research, the more effective utilization of the services of the technician in general administration, and more emphasis upon psychology as applied to industrial management. Germany and the United States have been the pacemakers in these fields. The genius of British administration is the production of individual administrators of great capacity.

In recent years the British have made up a great deal of ground in the fields which were formerly neglected. For example, the railways, the Post Office, the Central Electricity Board, the Institute of Transport, some of the labor unions, and the national engineering institutions are constantly carrying on important researches, in which foreign methods are increasingly emphasized. These studies have done more to improve the national public service undertakings than the man in the street appreciates. For example, the national electricity scheme was largely based upon studies made in a half-dozen foreign countries. The research activities of public service enterprises may be the means of uprooting the traditional prejudice which British business leaders have held regarding academic investigations. Moreover, it is not impossible that the techniques and the results produced by the public service organizations which have been mentioned may force the universities to reexamine their research methods and emphases.

A silent revolution has been taking place in the traditional attitude toward the technician; i.e. the engineer, the scientist, the statistician. It has always been a British boast that the expert is "kept on tap, not on top." Lipservice is still paid to the alleged national suspicion of the so-called "expert." The status of the technician has improved in, and because of, the public utility developments of recent years. The new viewpoint is illustrated by the Bridgeman Committee's strong insistence that the engineer with a broad viewpoint should be given positions of responsibility in the general administration of the Post Office. The technician who has learned the art of administration is already found in high positions within the public utility services which we have been considering.

Industrial psychology has also received due recognition from public service undertakings. Here again fundamental attitudes are undergoing a change, and the life of the nation is being directed into new channels. The National Institute of Industrial Psychology is primarily responsible for the recognition accorded to industrial psychology. The Institute has conducted investigations of most of the national public utilities. When it is realized that in the past public opinion has been suspicious of, or even hostile toward, studies of human behaviour and social attitudes, the importance of the change will be appreciated. The emphasis placed upon public relations technique by the Post Office in recent years is clear proof that industrial psychology has conquered the misunderstanding and prejudice which formerly retarded its extension.

The most valuable assets of British administration are the capacity and traditions of a large number of leaders of public service undertakings. Their cultural background, broad outlook, art of management, and public service traditions are not equalled in any other country. These public utility executives, and others like them in the Civil Service and Parliament, comprise the best part of an aristocracy which has its roots in the public service traditions of the privileged classes and in the cultural opportunities of Oxford and Cambridge. British aristocracy has survived because it developed a philosophy which recognizes that privilege means responsibility. Instead of the hostility to government enterprise which business leaders in some countries manifest, the British aristocracy, and those who have been drawn into it, have made faithful public service the dominant incentive. No country can remain great without leaders who are devoted to the public service ethic. The tradition which has been established in Great Britain is the foundation of successful administration. Privilege may disappear, and the historic rôle of the older universities may tend to pass into other hands, but the aristocracy of public service must be preserved at any cost. Irrespective of possible changes in social structure, a transformation of outlook on the part of university-educated leaders is already indicated. The Oxonian should take less time to learn the art of administration after he leaves the academic cloisters—in other words, he should be more fully prepared. This seems to involve less emphasis on classics and more attention to the science of public administration, public utility economics, industrial psychology, and to labor economics.

## THE COMMERCIAL MIND

According to Lord Wolmer, all public utilities should "be administered by the Commercial Mind, the mind that can diagnose the public's requirements, and provide the service rapidly and cheaply without bureaucratic interference." In recent years Members of Parliament have talked a great deal about the merits of commercial management as compared with Civil Service administration, but almost invariably their remarks are based upon unanalyzed preconceptions and lack the reasoning contained in Lord Wolmer's utterance. It is important that the subject should be regarded dispassionately because the future conduct of public service enterprises depends in large part upon the type of individual who will manage them.

The difficulty about the issue is that public administration can be fairly accurately defined, but that speakers never explain exactly what they mean by commercial management.

x

Lord Wolmer's definition of the "commercial mind" is not what most of its proponents appear to contemplate.

Commercial management usually suggests the profit motive and competition, but these have been almost entirely removed from public service undertakings. As a rule, however, these factors are what champions of the commercial outlook seem to have in the back of their minds. Competition is a salutary incentive if it can be preserved without economic loss arising from duplication and price-cutting, but the profit motive in public utility undertakings is incompatible with the nature of the business. Moreover, education and the substitution of other incentives will supply more satisfactory propulsions than the desire to enrich the owners. Advocates of commercial management sometimes intimate that the officials of public service undertakings should have a free hand to deal with labor. We have suggested that this should not be possible, and in the present state of labor organization it cannot be so.

If, then, profit-making, competition, and freedom to deal with labor are not involved in commercial management as applied to public utilities, those who espouse the cause must mean the methods and techniques of the business community. This is really what Lord Wolmer suggests in his definition of the commercial mind; and it is the basis of possible agreement. However, a moment's reflection will indicate that the public relations technique and the public service attitude are not the monopoly of the business community. In many cases they are found in a developed state in public utilty enterprises, and there is reason to believe that they can be improved a great deal more.

Lord Wolmer is quite correct in supposing that the elimination of competition and the substitution of monopoly may result in a careless, aloof attitude toward the consumers. The "take it or leave it" attitude has been found in public service enterprises many times in the past, and it will be discovered among some today. However, the point which many fail to grasp is that the public relations technique, as the advertising experts unanimously agree, is an art that must be taught rather than one that develops automatically. The heads of large private establishments, like department stores, give their staffs instructions in the art of meeting the public and of making customers satisfied. Public service organizations can, and do, carry on the same sort of education. The public relations program of the Post Office is a good instance of what may be done.

What the proponents of commercial management usually fail to consider is that much of the so-called public relations technique is only skin deep. The veneer of amenity cannot cover up the dissatisfied interior of an employee. The finest type of public relations attitude is very rare, but it is possible to establish it in public service undertakings. In addition to teaching employees to see things through the customer's eyes, it is necessary that the employee should feel that he is treated fairly and that he should have a sincere interest in serving the public. The latter incentive, the public service ethic, is more pronounced among the higher officials of the Post Office than in any other public utility which has been encountered. It would probably be found more generally if the Post Office fulfilled its duty as a model employer. The Post Office may possibly produce the best example of the commercial mind as we have defined it, namely as a component of the public service ethic, pride of occupation, and public relations technique. The Post Office and other forms of public service monopoly should retain consulting specialists for counsel and education in public relations activities. The commercial mind is not a mystery, it is not even a monopoly of private enterprise. Public service undertakings have a better opportunity to develop a satisfactory attitude toward the public than do most private businesses.

Red-tape and delays can never be completely removed from large-scale undertakings, and this fact might as well be faced. Two factors account for this. One is the very size of the service. Improvement of speed is usually necessary and often possible. However, the other reason for delay is inevitable and desirable. Public service enterprises are subject to control and hence must follow principles relative to prices, service, and labor. Private business, on the other hand, is usually responsible only to the owner, who may have dictatorial power or if necessary arbitrary authority. Under these conditions quick action is possible, if not always obtained. But mere alacrity may be wasteful in the long run. Public control and the necessity of acting on principles are the chief causes of red-tape. They may become the excuse rather than the reason, it is true, but progressive leadership alone can cure that fault. Less speed is not necessarily a severe drawback, however, because justice and equality of treatment to both the consumers and the employees are results which are derived from enterprises based upon definite principles.

### CIVIL SERVICE AND AN INDUSTRIAL SERVICE

Those who have contemplated the future development of British public service undertakings have, almost without exception, decided that the Civil Service system is not a desirable one to be extended into industrial fields. In many cases such conclusions seem to have been based upon unanalyzed assumptions concerning the commercial mind, or upon conditions of Civil Service atmosphere as they exist outside of the Post Office. Nevertheless, it does appear that either the Civil Service should be remoulded in important respects if it is to be widely adopted for industrial uses, or else that a separate service, a State industrial corps, should be created to supplement the work performed by the Civil Service. The Civil Service would then be confined to work of departments dealing with strictly political and social functions.

The Liberal party has advocated, in *Britain's Industrial*

*Future*, an independent service for public commercial undertakings. Since "some further extension of the field of Public Concerns will probably be indicated as desirable year by year in the future, as in the past," the Liberals have proposed that:

"The method of appointing the Executive Authority of Public Boards should be reformed, business and technical efficiency being aimed at rather than the representation of interests. We need to build up an attractive career for business administration open to all talents. A regular service should be recruited for Public Boards, with a cadre and a pension scheme, with room for rapid promotion and satisfactory prizes. To cover the case of Public Boards subject to Municipal and other Local Authorities, a body might be set up similar to the Civil Service Commission."

An industrial service would clearly possess certain advantages over no system at all. In the first place, it would extend the merit system and hence encourage training for a career. The State would be better able to fulfil its duty as mediator between the officials and the employees of public service corporations. General provision could be made for superannuation, permanence of tenure, and other benefits enjoyed by the Civil Service. On the other hand, an enormous power would be entrusted to those who would administer the system, and the difficulties of maintaining a satisfactory promotion and permanent tenure scheme would arise, as they have in the Civil Service. No plan is free from difficulties, and those arising from a unified industrial service should not be minimized.

If an industrial corps, centrally administered, is desirable for local public services, the same considerations would suggest that national public service undertakings should be dealt with in the same manner. Although such a proposal may seem very desirable at first thought, all of the accompanying factors need to be weighed before concluding that another personnel system should be set up alongside of the Civil Service. In the first place, if the staff of the Post Office were placed in an industrial service and hence withdrawn from the Civil Service, the latter would be only one-third of its present size, less than 125,000. Would the two services, the industrial and the civil, then become rivals? If so, the industrial service might be given a higher level of remuneration because of its greater size and because its work would be visibly reproductive of wealth. Gradually many of the better candidates might be attracted to the industrial service and the older departments would suffer as a result. This would probably be true whether the imaginary Industrial Service Commission were controlled directly by the central government, as the Civil Service is at present, or in a looser fashion.

The machinery of the Civil Service might be broadened and altered in such a way that its present unsatisfactory features would be improved and it could then be more widely used for industrial as well as for civil employment. If this were considered desirable, the Treasury's relation to the Civil Service should be reexamined, the control of the Civil Service should be broadened to include members with an intimate knowledge of public service enterprises, the present nature of recruitment and of the entrance examination would require alteration, and a complete system of classification would be indicated.

One serious objection to enlarging the work of the Civil Service system, without alteration, would be that personnel administration in public service enterprises would be brought under the ultimate control of the Treasury, as the Civil Service is already. It seems too sanguine to suppose that the Treasury will ever be able to see beyond the point of balancing the national budget as expeditiously as possible, to the desirability of improving the status of employees engaged in public services. Wage standards and conditions of employment should be divorced from the control of the Treasury economy experts. This could be done by broadening the membership of the controlling body, by giving all industrial services a large degree of financial independence, and by withdrawing the Treasury's ultimate decision regarding personnel questions. The Civil Service might be transferred from the control of the Treasury to the Ministers responsible for industrial and commercial departments. The membership of the policy-forming council controlling the Civil Service should be drawn from the staff as well as from the official side of public services.

The present methods of recruitment and examination would obviously need to be changed if the requirements of industrial employment were to be met. The classical courses of the older universities may produce the best candidates for the present Administrative Class of the Civil Service, but public-utility management demands greater emphasis on science, engineering, political economy, administration, and psychology. Moreover, a mere broadening of the present academic examinations would not appear to suffice. Tests of ability to solve concrete problems, qualities of initiative and ingenuity, ability to direct and to get along with men would be absolutely essential—just as they need more emphasis under present Civil Service administration. Moreover, a highly diversified system of employment like the one envisaged would require a complete classification of positions and functions, in order that equal work might receive equal reward. The present Civil Service system is not thoroughly classified, and if it were taken as a model for further expansion, present injustices would be perpetuated and extended.

The general conclusion regarding the alternative of a separate industrial service as compared with a unified public service appears to be that unification of responsibility for policy is preferable, but that within the framework of a combined service as much room as possible should be made for staff cooperation and independence of management. At any rate, a unified service comparable to the one suggested in *Britain's Industrial Future* probably cannot be expected for some time. An ambitious superstructure like the one suggested should be placed upon strong foundations.

In the final analysis, the successful management of public service undertakings depends upon the calibre and the attitude of the employees, from the most important to the least important. This may sound like a platitude, but the obvious neglect of the human factor in industry proves that personnel factors are rarely given their proper weight. Many employers seem to consider personnel questions only when unavoidable problems arise, and, meanwhile, the executive officials appear to depend chiefly upon statistical computations and improvements in machinery to bring about greater efficiency. Emphasis upon the constantly growing potentialities of the machine has resulted in the comparative neglect of the human resources—the source of greater "efficiency" than machines can ever produce. "Inhuman" administration is the besetting sin of large-scale management, and yet it is in public service organizations that personal relations count for more than elsewhere.

The reputation of a public utility enterprise depends almost entirely upon the courtesy of the clerk who meets the customer when he pays his bill, or upon the attitude of the mechanic who answers service calls. In the customers' eyes the employees he meets are the embodiment of the corporation. How short-sighted it is, therefore, to pay particular attention to the higher officials of an organization, and carelessly to assume that if the rank and file of employees are not satisfactory there is always a large labor market on which to draw. The aristocratic view that ability at the top is all that matters belongs to the *limbo* of a bygone era.

The future improvement of public service enterprise depends primarily, in the writer's view, upon adequate attention to the human factor as it bears upon recruitment, training, and public relations. Public undertakings will not be really efficient until the psychologist has been given an opportunity to devote as much attention to personnel relationships as the engineer has to technical progress.

Unfortunately, the whole question is clouded by the emotional issues arising from the clash of organized labor and the management. Until a more rational view of personnel is taken, and until it is recognized that there has been misunderstanding on both sides, there is not much hope of developing a constructive labor policy for public service enterprises.

Most so-called "practical" executives would probably say that the attitudes of employees are relatively unimportant in determining the efficiency of an undertaking. They fail to grasp the truth emphasized by that great administrator, Lord Haldane, who told the Coal Commission in 1919 that "atmosphere" is everything. Efficiency cannot be expected from a dissatisfied staff, while, on the other hand, the contagion of a harmonious *esprit de corps* is immediately felt and appreciated by the public. Pride of craftsmanship and a desire to do one's best are assets which produce compound interest in any form of enterprise.

These are highly practical considerations. An individual who has been identified with railway administration for many years and whose natural sympathies are with the executives, expressed the opinion that the dogged fight of the railways to reduce wages by £5,000,000 was poor business, because the attitude of the employees would be such, if they lost, that the resulting carelessness and inefficiency would consume most of the so-called saving. He further explained that this inefficiency would not, in most cases, be purposeful and retaliatory, but merely the natural result of disappointment and lack of interest. If these factors could be measured with mathematical precision, our practical business executives would probably pay far more attention to human relationships. The loss of efficiency is significant when computed negatively, but the social loss sustained because positive policies to improve *esprit de corps* are not more widely adopted is immeasurable.

Public service enterprises present an ideal opportunity to place the emphasis on industrial progress where it belongs —on the improved status of all the employees engaged in supplying public services. Policies are usually justified on the ground that the nation, the consumer, or the stockholders will be benefited, Such views usually lose sight of the fact that real progress is impossible apart from the increased level of remuneration and conditions enjoyed by the staff. This is not a selfish view or a radical view: it is good sense. The nation and the consumers are only the sum total of workers of all classes. National strength consists of the productive power and the purchasing power of all those engaged in physical and mental labor. Steady progress depends upon maintaining effectively the right equilibrium between production and 'purchasing power. The way to increase purchasing power is to pass on to workers the increased fruits of their efforts made possible by science. If this is done generally the consumers and the nation will benefit automatically. If, on the other hand, workers are deprived of the hope of continually improving their lot, the consumers and the nation will be ultimately poorer, and the service supplied will become spiritless. Public service undertakings should therefore be model employers, i.e. they should assure their employees that increased service means increased rewards. The growth of purchasing power will stimulate business generally, so that the policy of the model employer does not create an unfair advantage, as it is sometimes claimed, but a benefit to everybody. Watered capital and high dividends are the greatest enemies of national progress because they are a millstone around the necks of employees and consumers.

We have counselled the long view and the broad view

of political economy, but the guild view is also badly needed. Industrially, a nation is the sum total of all its enterprises, but the strength of each unit in this total determines the power of the rest. The way to improve the whole is to strengthen the unit. The way to increase purchasing power is to improve the conditions of those employed in individual industries. It cannot be done all at once and it cannot be done from the top. The national economy is a spring arising in the depths of the earth, not a spring shower descending from the bountiful Gods.

The rediscovery of the guild idea is a development that may take place appropriately in public service undertakings. Those who attempt to be fair to labor often comment on the bitter, uncompromising attitude of the unions' representatives, and they deduce therefrom that industrial cooperation is illusory. Furthermore, critics of industrial Democracy often point out that a final executive authority must exist in every enterprise or else confusion would result and initiative would be stifled. Both difficulties seem to arise from a misunderstanding of the aims of industrial cooperation.

The labor unions hold that so long as executives are appointed by and are responsible to stockholders, the interests of the workers are likely to be subordinated. They would not do away with authority and leadership, but the executive heads would be made responsible to the guild instead of to the absentee stockholder. Under such circumstances each employee would feel that he was working for a corporate enterprise of which he was a direct beneficiary. Pride of craftsmanship and *esprit de corps* might then be expected to replace the complaining attitude of worlers protesting against a system which they think is wrong.

The public utility trust has eliminated the voting stockholder, so that any function of administration ordinary stockholders are usually supposed to perform does not exist in this form of public service enterprise. The guild concept may well take hold of the public utility trust, particularly in those which are clearly industrial. The Post Office is also a possible laboratory for cooperative management. As has been said, the major Post Office union has consistently advocated a guild management. Recently the Union of Post Office Workers has elaborated its proposals in greater detail. The principal features of the plan are these:

"Administration to be vested in a board composed of an equal number of State nominees and of nominees of the trade union or unions; the Postmaster-General to preside and have a casting vote. The Post-master-General to be in the Cabinet and/or a member of any other body formed to legislate for, and to control, the industrial system. The board to have power to decide and carry out 'broad issues of administration and direction involving collective deliberations and decisions.' Regional and local boards to be constituted on the lines of the Central Board, and subordinate to it, and to be responsible in their areas for administration in accordance with the Central Board's policy. On questions of pay and staff conditions, the employees' associations to negotiate with the official representatives of the Postmaster-General and the board."

In the meantime, the union will pursue a "workers' control policy" in order that the staff may gain "the administrative experience and sense of responsibility which will fit them for eventual joint control." This can be done, the union has suggested, by greater activity in the Whitley Councils; by demonstrating the interests of the staff in the problems of the service and the value of the contribution they can make; by enlarging this experience through contact with such problems; and by encroaching more and more on the spheres of work and responsibility hitherto not within the province of the Whitley Committees.

The guild principle, if practically and intelligently pursued, should do a great deal to solve the problems of public control, the relation between employers and employed, and the question of satisfactory incentives for the individual employee.

### CHECKS ON CENTRALIZATION

The extension of the public utility principle in the field of national industries would naturally raise a fear that such a concentration of power might be abused, or that the machine might become top-heavy. The British have always viewed governmental centralization with suspicion, but despite this misgiving, the tendency has made rapid headway in recent years. The increase of national powers seems inevitable and necessary. Urbanization, foreign influences, the creation of national industrial combines, and the necessity of enforcing national minimum standards are among the factors causing a growth of national powers. But the administration of economic services gives rise to far greater concentrations of power than the mere regulation of various interests, private and public, by the central departments at Whitehall. How is this power to be democratically controlled?

The development of the guild principle is one of the foremost ways of checking bureaucratic tendencies because the creation of a corporate spirit and of professional standards brings about self-regulation—the necessary basis of social responsibility. In professionalized associations like the judiciary or the Civil Service, outside control is not as necessary as in unorganized pursuits because professional standards are the most effective safeguard of the public interest. This alone is not sufficient, however, because the ingrowing tendency creates certain traits of aloofness and exclusiveness which should be overcome in services requiring a sensitive public relations policy.

The principal remaining checks on national bureaucratic tendencies within the public utility field are regionalism, representative advisory committees of users, and consumers' cooperative associations. Instances of the work performed by the first two agencies have already been provided, but a brief appraisal of all three democratizing factors is in order.

Frequent proposals have been made to regionalize Great Britain's governmental structure. There are those at the present time who suggest the creation of regional legislatures as a desirable compromise between recent centralizing tendencies and the historical freedom of local authorities. Account must be taken of the growing nationalism in Wales and Scotland, but it seems rather certain that the legislative responsibility of Parliament is likely to remain undivided and undiminished for some time at least. Administrative decentralization, on the other hand, is not only desirable in certain instances, but regional responsibility for detailed administration has already evidenced a tendency to increase.

Definite regional boundaries for public utility administration as a whole have not been established. In specific public utilities, as has been said, regional areas have been fixed. The C.E.B. has created ten areas, more than twice the number delimited by the B.B.C., while the provincial administration of the Post Office operates through more than twenty regional districts. The considerations in each case are vastly different, so that a standard division of the country for all purposes would probably not be possible. However, the wave-length requirements of broadcasting present the only example of invariability. If confusion of administrative areas is to be prevented, and if regional sentiment is to be focalized to the best advantage, it seems desirable that common regional boundaries should be established. Perhaps a British Napoleon is needed! The division established by the C.E.B. seems to take account of long-established sectional characteristics better than any other, but the number could probably be reduced in an ideal system of regional administration to seven or eight popularly recognized historical and geographical areas. If regionalism is to prove an effective element in national public service administration, considerations of geography, traditions, and local sentiment should be given due weight. Some interesting developments along these lines may be expected.

Advisory committees, representative of various interests amongst users of the service, have become a recognized part of British public utility development, with results that augur well for the expansion of the principle. The advisory committee is the best method of checking the ingrowing tendencies connected with professional and large-scale enterprises. Advisory committees are greatly to be preferred to the boards and commissions, the members of which are chosen from particular interests. The function of interest representation should be to advise, not to perform the work itself. The permanent members of the Civil Service or of an industrial service can best be trusted to perform the actual work impartially and effectively, but an advisory committee of citizens provides fresh points of view, contact with popular opinion, and an opportunity to educate the public relative to the problems of the particular service. The advisory committee of citizens, who take an interest in the work because they like it, is a desirable substitute for boards of directors, some members of which frequently do little more than collect their fees. This aspect of Democracy, the advisory committee, seems to be absolutely vital to the success of public service enterprises.

Another method of maintaining the proper equilibrium between public services and the community is by means of organizations of consumers. Speaking generally, every interest is organized except the consumers. Inasmuch as successful public control largely depends on the interest and activity of users, it is important that a consumers' psychology should be created and that organization should take place. That this want has been felt is evidenced by the remarkable success of consumers' cooperatives in Great Britain during recent years. The cooperators now number their supporters in millions and their capital investments in hundreds of millions, while the Cooperative party has described its program as "the practical and immediate alternative to the capitalist system of society." Organized consumers have taken a positive stand regarding public utility developments. They might exert a great and constructive influence on public service enterprises. However, the Cooperative party's skepticism regarding recent public utility tendencies has been expressed by its president, Alfred Barnes, as follows:

"Parliament is being used to prop up and stabilize by legal enactment a multitude of capitalist businesses, and these again are linked together in the parasitical task of exploiting the consumer. Given these conditions it is only a matter of time before the larger capitalist units will swallow the smaller ones and legal monopoly for private gain becomes the established order. What has happened in electricity and transport is being deliberately encouraged by a Tory Parliament in food production, marketing, and distribution. We stand for a cooperative service as against these State-propped private combines."

Apparently the present form of public utility control will have to be changed considerably before the largest organization of consumers will be prepared to render sympathetic criticism to Britain's national utilities!

What is the social significance of the public utility developments of recent years? The answer is not clear. A show-down may be expected within the next few years. Britain's leaders are awake to the possibilities of national public utility expansion. Electricity has been planned: London's traffic resources have been pooled in the form of a trust. Broadcasting has been placed under unified control. State-controlled monopolies are no longer distasteful, and others appear in the offing. But the older methods of regulation have not proved generally satisfactory, and exorbitant profits can still be extracted from public service enterprises. Effective public control has not been established for public service undertakings as a whole. However, British management is capable and scrupulous, and labor is ambitious to assume a larger share of responsibility. The deep trenches of vested interest do exist, but alongside are the tools and the competence to convert them into fertile fields for the nation as a whole.

# INDEX

GEORGE ALLEN & UNWIN LTD
LONDON: 40 MUSEUM STREET, W.C.1
CAPE TOWN: 73 ST. GEORGE'S STREET
SYDNEY, N.S.W.: WYNYARD SQUARE
TORONTO: 91 WELLINGTON STREET, WEST
WELLINGTON, N.Z.: 8 KINGS CRESCENT, LOWER HUTT